Mint
Condition

Mint Condition

A Christian's Guide to Complete Restoration

Connie Meisgeier

WinePressPublishing
Great Books, Defined.

WinePress Publishing (PO Box 428, Enumclaw, WA 98022) functions only as book publisher. As such, the ultimate design, content, editorial accuracy, and views expressed or implied in this work are those of the author.

Unless otherwise noted, all Scriptures are taken from the *King James Version* of the Bible.

All Scripture references marked NIV are taken from the *Holy Bible, New International Version*®, *NIV*®. Copyright ©1973, 1978, 1984 by Biblica, Inc.™ Used by permission of Zondervan. All rights reserved worldwide. www.zondervan.com

Scripture references marked NASB are taken from the *New American Standard Bible*, © 1960, 1963, 1968, 1971, 1972, 1973, 1975, 1977 by The Lockman Foundation. Used by permission.

Scripture references marked AB are taken from *The Amplified Bible, Old Testament*, © 1965 and 1987 by The Zondervan Corporation, and from *The Amplified New Testament*, © 1954, 1958, 1987 by The Lockman Foundation. Used by permission.

Scripture references marked NKJV are taken from the *New King James Version*, © 1979, 1980, 1982 by Thomas Nelson, Inc., Publishers. Used by permission.

ISBN 13: 978-1-60615-032-0
ISBN 10: 1-60615-032-4
Library of Congress Catalog Card Number: 2009941398

To my husband ...

for his generosity of spirit in sharing his ideas
and in listening to mine

Contents

Introduction

My life wasn't working. I thought I was doing better and better at applying what I was learning as a Christian, but my life seemed intolerable. I couldn't understand it. For a long time I plugged away, thinking I needed to try harder. So I did. It did not help.

One day I got on my face before God to tell Him what He already knew. With my nose in the pale green shag carpet at the foot of our king-sized bed, I told my heavenly Father that I was miserable, frustrated, and confused—even a little frightened—because I could not make Christianity work.

The answer was quick and clear. It was so simple that I was embarrassed. While I was still speaking, I realized that God would never have a plan that did not work. If what I was doing did not work, I was not working God's plan.

I agreed with God that what I was doing was not working, but I had no idea why or what to do about it. Feeling totally helpless, I told Him that He would have to send into my life what I needed. Then, after a moment, I told Him that I had no idea how to tell whether what came into my life was from Him or not, so He would have to take care of that part also.

Without realizing it, I took my life out of the hands of other people, the leaders and teachers I had been following with such zeal, and I put it into God's hands. It felt like childish helplessness. It turned out to be real, working faith in operation. Change began immediately.

What follows on these pages grew from a veritable blizzard of little, square, yellow sticky notes that had accumulated in my Bible. As God unfolded for me the breathtaking wonder of what Jesus does for us when He saves us, I just wrote and wrote. I learned that Jesus died to save us from *everything* that makes us flawed—from every single thing from which we need to be saved—and He does it thoroughly, completely, and well (Heb. 7:25). No matter how battered we are, He buffs and shines every flaw. He polishes every facet of our being in order to restore us to perfect condition—to mint condition.

Part 1

A Good Trade

Chapter One

Brand-New, Shiny, and Beautiful

Better than Factory Rebuilt

Spilt Milk! There's no point in crying over spilt milk. Did you hear that expression growing up? It is an old saying that came to mind rather often when our four children were small and a glass of milk toppled over on the dinner table. The point of the adage was that some things can't be fixed so we just learn to live with them. Once upon a time, I accepted that piece of folk wisdom. Then I opened the Bible one day and read that nothing is too hard for God. Jeremiah the prophet said it two different ways in one chapter (Jer. 32:17, 27). I guess I'd read it before, but it seemed new and surprising that day. I decided to believe it just to see what happened. I thought I could handle the possibility of a little disappointment for the sake of such an interesting experiment.

How about you? Did you ever wish that you could start over? Did you ever make a mistake so serious that the only way things could be OK again would be to back up and live that fateful day all over again? Or did you ever do a small thing that escalated into such hurt and trouble that you longed to be able to undo it? We all have those experiences, but the good news is that God is God. He is very good at being God. He can do what is impossible. If it is hard for you to accept that He can, or that He will, do impossible things for you, go find a Bible somewhere and read Luke 1:37. Then take a quick look at Matthew 17:20 and 19:26 or Mark 10:27, and then Luke 18:27. God has a plan to "fix" things that seem beyond repair—including us.

Some years ago, my husband, Charles, laid the Saturday morning paper down on his lap and made an enthusiastic announcement: "There is a car advertised that might be just right for our family. Who wants to go with me to see it?" With a jaunty sense of adventure, everyone drove off to have a look. In no time our children were climbing inside. Everyone liked it. It was a wide, roomy, navy blue Pontiac. Back then we called it a station wagon, and it was just right for our family that consisted of four children, two parents, a dainty grandmother, and a huge collie.

It was obvious that someone had taken unusual care to polish and maintain this car. Though it wasn't quite new, it looked as though it had just come off the showroom floor. It was bright and shiny inside and out. The windows sparkled, the chrome reflected the bright summer sunshine, and the radio and motor hummed along together in perfect tune.

"Clearly," the dealer pointed out, "this car is in mint condition."

It was. We drove it many happy miles.

Like our blue Pontiac, we start out in mint condition, because God's design is perfect. Unfortunately, people don't always receive the tender, loving care that is given to a new automobile. Every little abrasion is not lovingly buffed and taken care of so that the color and the sparkle do not fade. Hazards of the road soon dim our luster and dull our shine. We lose our creativity, spontaneity, and joy. Without constant tender, loving care, a sense of worth and value fades. We begin to doubt that we are unique and precious. If we come under the control of reckless or careless people, we may be seriously damaged or abused. Then what? Can we be salvaged? Can the damaged parts be repaired?

Unlike cars, people *can* be restored to mint condition, no matter how serious the damage becomes. It happens through the most amazing plan ever implemented on the earth. It is the plan of salvation.

God's Repair Shop

Growing up in a minister's home, I somehow got the idea that Jesus died to save us even though we had allowed ourselves to become badly flawed and mixed up. But I thought the stain of sin lingered somehow and we never fully could become what we might have been. In every church service there seemed to be saintly, sweet-faced old folks who had always done what was right—probably, I believed, because their parents taught them aright and they had always been compliant. But compliant was not a word that applied to me.

Without realizing it, I think I had the idea that there were lots of righteous people who hadn't sinned "enough" to really need a savior. In contrast, I saw myself as a fundamentally flawed person who was simply not capable of a stellar performance. I believed I could muddle through life, despite lots of shortcomings, because God forgives over and over but that "making up" for all of the missed opportunities to be righteous was not possible. I no longer believe that.

Factory Rebuilt Parts

I now understand salvation to be something much more wonderful than looking forward to reaching heaven safely. I see that it saves us completely and perfectly. It provides us with the resources and power to be much more than patched up and pasted together around our failures.

Now I see that I am not just a person who once had great potential that was sadly unfulfilled—and neither are you. Do you know in your heart that you "could have been a contender"? Once we receive Jesus as our Savior, we are far more than a shadow of what we might have been had we never sinned. Thank God that once we are saved we don't fall short in God's eyes anymore. Instead we are fully restored to mint condition, like that wonderful, big automobile we bought. We can be "just like new," because the plan of salvation is designed to restore everyone to mint condition—the condition of Adam and Eve in their first days of life on the earth.

Way back in the dewy, fresh days of the world when God put humanity in the Garden of Eden, the world was perfect. Adam and Eve were perfect. Everything was good. God said it was. In fact, He said it was *very* good. Just think how beautiful the world is now; then picture how beautiful that garden must have been before sin came along. It was *perfect*.

The breathtaking wonder of the gospel is that God found a way to restore our world—and to restore you and me—to the perfection for which He created us. That way is the plan of salvation. It is the way of the cross. It is the best news ever told on the earth.

Did you ever see an old collection of black-and-white photos of someone's trip to a place like Paris or Hawaii? That little piece of paper certainly could be said to be Paris, but how the reality of that city surpasses the images shown in photographs! The plan of salvation was like that for me. Other people could tell me about it and try to help me picture what it was like, but someone else's picture could not begin to convey the reality of experiencing it for myself.

Even though I grew up in the church, where everyone talked about Jesus, His salvation offers so much more than I realized. My superficial understanding from the accounts of others—from someone else's picture of salvation—was a poor substitute for the real thing. It was like a flat, gray-toned photo when compared with the vibrant color, life, and movement of the real thing.

New Light—New Understanding

When my children were small, our family enjoyed a cheery, lighthearted movie called *The Absent-Minded Professor*. In the movie, Fred MacMurray starred as a rather dithering, genius-type professor who invented "flubber." Some of his students played on the college basketball team, and he put flubber on the soles of their shoes. It enabled them to leap about the basketball court in spectacular ways and bring the glory of victory to their picturesque little college. The use of flubber on the basketball court seems nothing but wonderful as the story moves along, yet movie fans have learned to expect some kind of giant mix-up to be looming "just around the corner." Viewers watch with amusement and wonder to see what the "catch" will be. Often great ideas turn out to have hidden flaws that lead to hilarious complications. In movies, these things are funny; but in life, they are terribly disappointing.

Can it be that we view God as something like an amiable professor who clearly is more brilliant than the rest of us but nonetheless has plans that only partly work? Without realizing it, do we have the idea that God has a plan of salvation that works in theory but does not really work in life ... or only partly works ... or works only some of the time or for certain "perfect" people?

When God laid out the plan of salvation, it was a plan that *works* (Eph. 3:20–21)! That is good news for us to share. Salvation works for the kinds of people who need to be saved. People who are not sinners, people who are not failures, people who are not sick or weak or tired or foolish do not need a salvation plan. But all of us are needy somewhere along the way. Most of us are very needy. And God is God! He has a plan for you and for me that offers us salvation in every situation where it is needed (Heb. 7:25).

The plan of salvation is so perfect that, when implemented, we are made perfect without spot, stain, or blemish (Eph. 5:27). As God lovingly works in our lives, carefully tending to every little detail, we are more and more perfectly restored to what He planned for us to be. In that condition, we become able to fulfill God's wondrous plan for our lives.

Now let's be practical. Does this great plan really make a difference in the "world of reality"? Is all of this talk about perfection for when we get to heaven, or is it for now? Can it be a practical reality in the lives we live today? Yes, it can.

When you open your Bible to Corinthians, you will read: "For he says, 'In the time of my favor I heard you, and in the day of salvation I helped you.' I tell you, *now* is the time of God's favor, *now* is the day of salvation" (2 Cor. 6:2, italics mine). Salvation is for *now*!

God's will is not like "flubber." It is not so heavenly minded that it cannot be implemented in a sinful world. After all, would our brilliant and creative God design a salvation program that only patched us up well enough to limp along, or one so hard to operate that no one could really make it work? Would Jesus come down here to earth and submit to torture and then death on the cross for a salvation program that only could do a halfway job of "fixing up" whatever was wrong in our lives? Absolutely not!

Jesus has given us a perfect plan of salvation! It is one that works perfectly to make us perfect here and now (Heb. 7:25). When you read those words, what do you think? Do the faces of imperfect fellow Christians come to mind? How about incidents or situations in your church that fall short of perfection? Well, think about this: the computer program I am using to type these words works. It seems safe to say that mistakes you may pick up as you read along are mine. They are not the fault of the program. The program works when I work the program.

God's plan of salvation is perfect. It has to be. How could we be like Him, created in His image to fellowship with Him, or able to spend eternity as members of His family if that were not true? This message of the gospel is the good news that we are to share with the entire world.

A Great Adventure

We are embarking on the most exciting kind of adventure. We are going to take a brand-new look at the gospel of Jesus Christ. We are going to take a brand-new look at the plan of salvation. We are going to see that it contains great treasures of blessings that we haven't fully understood. We are going to find in the work of the cross the basis for why we can expect God to transform our lives here and now. We are going to see how it is that God restores our banged-up, battered, broken-down, or even shattered way of life to mint condition. We are going to learn how God can make us over inside and outside, *like new*!

Chapter Two

Change Your Mind

God's Will is Good, Pleasing, and Perfect

Be transformed. That is an interesting commandment to find in the Bible. It is remarkable, really! How wonderful to think of being transformed ... of being totally and absolutely transformed. Some things the Bible says are quite arresting when we pause to consider seriously what is being said. Take a moment and read the words surrounding the apostle Paul's admonition to us to be transformed (comments mine):

> Do not conform any longer to the pattern of this world [because it does not work to make you happy, and it doesn't please God], but be transformed [and here is how to do it] by the renewing of your mind. [Never underestimate the transforming power of changing your mind.] Then you will be able to test and approve what God's will is—his good, pleasing and perfect will. [You will like God's plan for your life. It is good. It will please you. In fact, you will find it is perfect.] (Rom. 12:2 NIV)

God's will for us is good. It is wonderful. It works. It offers us deep satisfaction. It can make us well and whole and give us good success (Josh. 1:8). Paul gave us this wonderful message centuries ago in Romans 12:2. The beautiful, old King James Version of the Bible renders it this way: "And be not conformed to this world: but be ye transformed by the renewing of your mind, that ye may prove what is that good, and acceptable, and perfect, will of God."

These exciting words from the Bible tell me that I do not have to live this life as I have been living it. Pressure does not have to dictate how my life will be. I can see for myself—prove for myself—that God's will for me is good. I can prove to myself that it is pleasing; that is, that I will like it. And in due time, I'll see that it is perfect.

This passage in Romans is just one example of the freedom God has given me in His Word to discard the expectations and demands of the role that I have been taught to play all of my life as a Christian. I can allow God to give me a new idea of the person He created me to be and the kind of life He wants me to live.

Think about the role life has taught *you* to play. If it is not good now—not pleasing and perfect—then the only way to make it better is to change. We have to change. We cannot continue to live the same old way and expect things to be different.

In reading this passage, my son, Steve, wryly quoted an oft-used phrase that tells us, "'Crazy' is doing the same old thing over and over and expecting a different result." If we do not like the way things are, we have to change. The question is *how?*

The answer for me became clear. My life will be transformed when I am transformed. The Bible says that the way I am transformed is by the renewing of my mind. I *can* change my mind. When I do, it will change my life. I can change my mind about what others have taught me about myself, my roles, my limitations, my goals, my purposes, and my expectations. I can be a new me.

God's Word, the Bible, says we can be made new in the attitude of our minds and put on a whole new self (Eph. 4:23 NIV). That sounds like a pretty good definition of transformation to me. A new self, operating on new ideas—on a new program—certainly means we can expect life to be different. How wonderful!

Will change be instantaneous? Some will be. But however it comes, the Holy Spirit is at work in us, bringing change in His own loving and wonderful way—change that is good. I know it will be good because the Holy Spirit will be working to accomplish God's will in my life and God's will is good and pleasing and perfect (Rom. 12:2 NIV). Philippians 1:6 says, "Being confident of this very thing, that he which hath begun a good work in you will perform it until the day of Jesus Christ."

As I look back over my life, the things that I thought needed to change for me to be entirely happy were numerous. But I have to confess that for years not one of them included the changing of my own mind or the readjusting of my own attitudes. The strange thing about it all is that when many of those things I thought I wanted so badly actually occurred, I found my feelings about my life and my reaction to it remained essentially the same. I was surprised.

My List

The most vivid example of this principle—that my life is more affected by the climate inside my heart than by my external circumstances—is the experience I had with "My List." Many years ago, in the writings of Catherine Marshall,[1] I found an idea that intrigued me. As I recall, she suggested making a list, writing down on it all the things we want and have prayed for, including those things we desire that are hidden among the secret dreams in our hearts. As I compiled my list for making my requests known to God, I was impressed in a new way by how lavish the promises in the Bible actually are and deeply touched to think of God knowing and caring about the unspoken dreams and desires of my heart (Ps. 37:4; Phil. 4:6).

As I was directed, I asked for everything I could think of. It was refreshing just to write it all out. The instructions were clear in affirming that nothing we could ask for—or imagine—was too hard for God to provide (Eph. 3:20; Matt. 19:26; Gen. 18:14; Jer. 32:17, 27). I completed the list, prayed through it in detail, tucked it in a Bible I seldom used, and promptly forgot about it.

Quite by accident, I found the list several years later and read it with no small sense of surprise. Now, you must remember as you read my list that I was a young mother busily caring for three small children (later there were four) while my husband was at the beginning of his busy and successful career. Just buying all of the basic necessities a growing family needs taxed our resources. I thought that if I only could have those "basic necessities" provided without delay or careful planning, life would change dramatically.

On my list I had asked for a new car, a full-time maid, an interesting part-time job, a new wardrobe, a house full of new furniture, regular visits to the beauty shop, lots more chances to meet interesting new people, and opportunities to go out to lunch with my husband so we could talk together more often without needing to tend to children. I was as extravagant as I could be in writing up my list (Ps. 37:4). Each of my requests seemed impossible. I had particularly asked for the opportunity to have lunch with my husband. I wanted to meet the interesting people he often met as a part of his job, and I also wanted more conversation time with him without interruption—but without having to give up family dinner with the children.

What happened? Well, I was offered a part-time job with no effort on my part. To manage it, I needed a maid and could afford to pay for a full-time one with what I earned. Of course, I needed a reliable car to get to work on an irregular part-time work schedule (and how nice it was to have a flexible one).

I still feel a sense of wonder over the way God answered my prayer about furniture. With the advent of a new baby, we really needed another bedroom. The house we found was lovely. It had been sitting empty for a year. Its owner had moved to another city to open a furniture store. To encourage us to buy his house, he agreed to sell us anything in his store at his cost in a one-time transaction and delivery. I picked out a new sofa first, then a lovely end table and lamp and a breakfast room hutch. We furnished our children's bedrooms with everything we dreamed of having for them and filled in missing pieces everywhere else. It was so exciting.

All women understand the next issue. When I joined the workforce, I needed new clothes, and interestingly, it was part of my job as a writer to meet, interview, and write about many of the same people Charles (my husband) met for business lunches. Charles and I often had lunch together with, and without, other interesting guests. A marvelous, loving nanny and housekeeper named Frankie Mae came to our home every day. We all loved her, and I thought she was an angel in disguise.

In the months that followed, I met and interviewed special advisors to the president and to the governor. I attended all kinds of meetings and interviewed the people conducting them as a member of the press. I was working only part of each week, but life was so busy and exciting that when significant things from "my list" were being added into my life, I scarcely noticed them.

Obviously, what I am describing is a drastic lifestyle change from that of full-time housewife to that of a part-time writer and editor. But the significant thing I learned was that even with all of those amazing answers to prayer—everything I had asked for—the day-to-day tone of my inner life remained just about the same. I had believed that all I dreamed of having would make my life ideal. I liked it all, but the quality of my inner feelings day in and day out was essentially unchanged. Fretting about the children or things I did not get done—all of the hectic things that bubble through our minds all of the time—continued to drain away my energy and peace.

So I have shared my experience with you. I believed that having what I dreamed of would give me inner joy and that joy would automatically obliterate any negative things that colored my day in and day out reactions to life. The joy was real, but stresses and anxieties persisted. All in all, I felt about the same most of the time. If someone had told me what I am telling you now before I experienced it for myself, I do not think I could have believed, received, or understood it. I hope you will do better than I did.

If you can hear the good news of God's plan for you, your dreams can become a reality *and* you can change on the inside as well. As for me, the overall nature of my feelings from day to day—my "felt sense" of myself, my relationships, and my world—needed to change. My "self" needed to be different as much or more than my circumstances needed to be different so that I could grow into the joy I now believe all Christians should have and share.

One of the biggest changes that occurred in my attitude was the realization that God wanted my life to be joyful. Things pertaining to God in the church of my youth were certainly beautiful and dignified and orderly, but "joyful" was not a word that described them. However, the words of Jesus in my Bible had a strong thread of joy running through them. More than a thread, really; Jesus wants our joy to be full. John 15:11 says, "These things have I spoken unto you, that my joy might remain in you, and that your joy might be full." And John 16:23–24 states, "And in that day ye shall ask me nothing. Verily, verily, I say unto you, Whatsoever ye shall ask the Father in my name, he will give it you. Hitherto have ye asked nothing in my name: ask, and ye shall receive, that your joy may be full."

When I sat down with a Bible as a young adult and began to read it, these wonderful things that Jesus said amazed me. *Could they possibly mean just what they say?* Over and over I said to myself things like *I can't believe that; that is just too good to be true; I wish I could just believe that.* For me, the greatest challenge to my early growth as a Christian was simply to believe that the Bible means just what it says.

What Should We Expect?

Often, the circumstances that surround us in life press in upon us and cause all kinds of pain. So we develop the idea that a change in those circumstances is the very thing that will ease our pain. There is a Bible story that may help us to understand this matter of the changes that we think we need in order to relieve the distress in which we live. An example of this truth is found in the gospel of Luke (Luke 24:21). Jesus' fellow Jews felt oppressed and miserable under the rule of Rome. They understood that a Messiah was coming from God, and they assumed that their Messiah would deliver them from the political, economic, and military control of a foreign power. Their idea of salvation was an external change in their circumstances.

Clearly the external circumstances of the Jews under Caesar were a source of suffering. And certainly the Jews believed that their lives would be blessed by changing those circumstances. And yet, when God sent the Messiah, He did not directly deliver them from the rule of Rome. God did not deliver the Jews by changing their circumstances for them. Rather, He provided a means of *inner* transformation. It is that inner transformation that empowers God's people with spiritual authority to contend with and be victorious over outer circumstances. Salvation comes through inner change first.

Shortly after leaving his work in public schools to return to university life, Charles established a part-time private counseling practice in partnership with a full-time Christian counselor. Often a client would telephone our home and request prayer while talking to me. I learned a lot about the nature of the problems we prayed about. In nearly every situation in which I have participated in a counseling process (with my husband or alone), the person with whom we were working came to us convinced that his or her problem resulted from the behavior of others. Husbands blame their wives for their problems. Wives blame their husbands for their pain. Parents blame their children's behavior for chaos in their families. Children of all ages blame their parents. Many people blame a supervisor or those with whom they work. Some blame people in the church. Nearly everyone wants the counseling process to be applied in their situation to persuade others to change. Or they want help in being able to present their case to other people in their lives so that those others will change and then the circumstances will change. This is the kind of help many people seek from a counselor, and it is probably the kind of help we want from God.

God's chosen people wanted a Messiah to come and deliver them from the miserable conditions in which they lived. It is clear that many, if not all, of the Jews who followed Jesus believed their Messiah would change their circumstances. They believed the abusive Romans who caused them grief would be dealt with for them. They thought they needed to be delivered from Rome as they had been delivered from Pharaoh. This attitude can be seen in the words of the two men who met and walked with the risen Savior on the road to Emmaus. Notice what they are saying as they walk along. In Luke 24:20–21 they say, "The chief priests and our rulers handed him over to be sentenced to death, and they crucified him; but we had hoped that he was the one who was going to redeem Israel. And what is more, it is the third day since all this took place" (NIV).

Perhaps no one can know for certain in this life why Judas betrayed Jesus. But I have heard teachers theorize that he was impatient to see the political change he expected. They suggest that he was trying to precipitate a crisis in which Jesus, in order to protect Himself, would be forced to act politically and perhaps accelerate what Judas hoped were Jesus' plans to liberate Israel ... and of course, Jesus would be victorious. If this scenario is anything close to correct, it would be consistent with our experience with people who are unhappy and miserable. They nearly always believe that the misery in their lives is caused by the abuse of others—that the unpleasant conditions in their lives are caused by what others have done. They are certain that it would be relieved if others were compelled to change.

As Jesus delivers us from our problems, He changes who we are way down inside—not always who others are. Change in the *outer* circumstances in a person's life is usually a part of a deep inner work that is being done at the same time on the *inside*. The men on the road to Emmaus longed to see Jesus redeem their lives. They had no understanding that He already had done the work it would require.

Our lives can be changed—*we* can be changed—by the renewing of our minds first. This great change within us empowers us to make the kinds of external changes that will bring the blessings we need and seek. I am happy to report that I have found pathways in my life both to inner healing *and* to lasting change in the concrete reality of things. Both kinds of changes came about through the same avenue of prayer and seeking God. They just did not come the way I expected.

God has given me many *things* I have asked for. All the things God has given to me are precious. I am grateful for each one, and I have enjoyed each one. I simply want to say that the greatest and most far-reaching changes have occurred in my own heart ... and not in my circumstances.

Chapter Three

Change in Lifestyle
Too Good to Be True

I sought the Lord earnestly to bring about changes in my life. He did what I asked Him to do. There were many wonderful changes—and I was grateful—but I want to say that the joy of the Lord and the effectiveness and productivity in life, spoken of in the first chapter of 2 Peter (2 Peter 1:8 NIV), are as dependent on changes in my life*style* as they are on changes in my life.

The health sciences tell us now that more than 80 percent of our illnesses are diseases caused by lifestyle. That is a staggering piece of information. Just like in our bodies, *dis*ease in our minds and hearts also grows out of lifestyle issues.

Just think! Every single aspect of your lifestyle and mine is the result of the decisions we make. Every decision I make results from what goes on in my mind. What goes on in my mind is deeply rooted in and shaped by my attitudes. So I can see why Paul would say that I should be changed in the attitude of my heart if I want to put on a new self—to be different, see change and improvement, be transformed (see Eph. 4:22 NIV). If I change my mind—if I renew my mind—my lifestyle is going to have to change along with it. So when we begin to consider the matter, the process of changing and renewing our minds has more far-reaching effects than we may think.

Exciting possibilities are opening up to those of us who want a new life, a new self, and new mental and physical health. So we ask ourselves the question: How can I renew my mind? How can I be made new in the attitude of my mind and of my heart? A little story that Charles shared comes to mind as a partial answer to that question.

Billy Can't Write!

My husband, Charles, is a professor, and everything about him seems to fit the role. More than a teacher and counselor, he is a creative and innovative researcher. Years ago, Charles was working in a prosperous suburban school district as the director of an extensive, federally funded child development project in secondary schools. One of the high school students in the project had a learning disability so severe that he was unable to write. Billy's[2] hands worked all right, it seemed, and his mind was excellent; the two just could not work together. Somewhere there was a disruption between his thoughts and his hands, so he could not form words on a page.

Charles and his team worked extensively with Billy, researching the issues thoroughly, before finally concluding that "Billy can't write." A problem somewhere in Billy's body made learning to write impossible, and none of the known creative teaching strategies seemed to help.

Once Billy's problem became clear, a new question challenged the research team: What modifications in Billy's program could be made to accommodate this disability? If Billy had had no arms at all, the need for accommodations to help him would have been obvious.[3] But since his hands appeared normal, the nature of the problem and the need for special accommodations to be made for him was not clear. The vital process of designing those special modifications required understanding and cooperation from all of his high school teachers.

What would you think if you were a teacher and someone told you, "Billy can't write"? Back then probably you would have thought something like *Billy has never been taught to write.* That is what Billy's teachers thought. In the high school this non-writing student attended, not one of them could seem to grasp the truth of the words used when the research team tried to explain. They could not understand that this perfectly normal-looking boy had a short circuit somewhere so that he was not able to write no matter how hard he tried.

In all fairness, it seems important to say that Billy did everything he could to hide the fact that he could not write. Since he was extraordinarily bright, his efforts to mask his disability were usually successful. He preferred to be seen as a belligerent teenager rather than as a student who was so far behind that he could not even write his own name legibly. He certainly succeeded in establishing a reputation as a behavior problem.

Billy's teachers heard the words "Billy can't write," and they understood what each word meant. But regardless of how it was explained to them, each teacher interpreted the meaning according to her own preconceived ideas. They thought the phrase "Billy can't write" meant "Billy will not write" or "Billy has not yet learned to write." Maybe some of them thought Charles was saying that Billy had no literary talent. Not one of them got the message that Billy was neurologically incapable of pushing a pencil across a page to create letters and words.

The teachers Charles worked with were bright and capable. They were especially selected to be involved in the research programs. Yet for quite some time they could not understand what was being said to them. Until they allowed themselves to hear what the words *really* meant, they could grasp only what they *thought* was being said, what they were in the habit of thinking those words meant.

Billy's teachers brought a lifetime habit of interpreting the phrase "can't write" to the staffing sessions where Billy was being discussed, and the habit was so strong that it was very difficult to change. Yet until it did change, little could be done to alter the boy's life and experience in school. There was no way to begin to solve the boy's problem by compensating for his disability in their various classes until the teachers understood what that disability was.

"Billy has to write," they would say. "A person has to learn to write in this world," they would insist. So there was a real struggle to communicate with those teachers until they each had that moment of revelation that allowed them to hear what was being told to them with new and broader understanding.

Wonder of wonders, one day at a staff meeting, there was a flood of understanding that allowed them to interpret three little words—"Billy can't write"—in a totally new way. After a long and frustrating meeting devoted to discussing Billy, one teacher finally said, "Oh, Dr. Meisgeier! Do you mean to tell us that Billy *can't* write? He just can't do it—physically cannot write—no matter what?"

With a sigh of relief, Charles said, "Yes! Yes, that's right. Billy can't write!"

It is this same kind of inability to hear and understand some of the plain words in the Bible that causes many of us to miss its most wonderful messages. *From this moment,* as you read these words and until we meet Jesus in heaven, it is my prayer that the words of salvation that you may have heard all of your life and read in the Bible will take on a whole wonderful new dimension of meaning.

What Jesus did for us on the cross is much more vast and wondrous than most of us are able to grasp at the beginning.

We need to allow the words in the Bible to say much more to us than we have heard them saying in the past. Just as the well-meaning teachers in Charles' research project could not grasp the full meaning of the words "can't write," we often do not understand the full wonder of what the words in the Bible say about salvation. They often seem too good to be true.

Eight Benefits of Salvation

Jesus is my Savior. He saved me. If I were to tell you that He saved me from drowning or He saved me from a fire, you would know He rescued me from something awful so I could live. Jesus did that and more. He saved me from everything. His plan of salvation saves me from everything from which I ever could need to be saved.

Let me pick out eight of the most precious benefits of what Jesus did for me ...

Benefit One: Jesus settled all claims against me.

First, Jesus settled every claim against me that anyone anywhere ever had or will have, including God—*especially* God!

Benefit Two: Jesus became guilty with my guilt.

Second, He absorbed upon and into Himself the guilt and the terrible shame for everything I ever did that was wrong. Embarrassment is the smallest part of the profound regret I feel for the abusive, offensive, selfish, foolish, cruel things that I have said and done over a lifetime. Before I opened those secret, shame-filled corners of my heart to Jesus, I did not know it was possible to be free of guilt and shame. It seemed there was always something I did or did not do that was embarrassing.

Benefit Three: Jesus removed the sin that caused my guilt.

Third, along with the guilt and shame and all of the other feelings that I have about myself because of my large and small sins of every kind, Jesus took upon Himself all of the punishment that ever could have been awaiting me as a result of another person's claim against me. He took *all* of it.

Isn't it amazing? Jesus took ownership of the sinful nature that was in me so that it became His. As He hung there on a cross, He owned my sin as though He were the one who had done it all instead of me. It became part of Him, not of me. It became who He was so that it did not have to be who I was anymore. He took away my sin itself; then He took away the shame it caused me; then He took the punishment for it; and finally, when He was tortured, executed, and consigned to hell in my place, He took upon Himself all of the destructive effects sin produces in my life. Then He worked them all together for good, for my good and for the good of the kingdom of God. As Romans 8:28a says, "And we know that all things work together for good to them that love God."

Jesus took what should have been the devastation and all of the destructive outcomes of my sin and replaced them with the good outcomes and blessings and rewards that should have been His for living a perfect life. The wonder of that still fills me with awe, even after all these years.

It is hard to realize that Jesus actually became the sinful person I was. All of my sin became His sin. That really happened. He took it away from me. He owned it as a part of who He was. It was not just a legal document, like agreeing to co-sign on a note. It was actually a fundamental change in who He was. *And* it produces a fundamental change in who I am. Because of Jesus, I am righteous through and through, on my way to being wonderful and perfect. If Jesus is your Savior too, learning to accept that fact as a working principle in your life and wrapping your mind around it marks a mighty good beginning in the transformational process that Christ Jesus brings into your life.

As Jesus was arrested, tried, tortured, and hung on the cross to die, He was treated like the nerd, the dork, the jerk, the fool, the bully, the beast, the brute, the brat, the thief, the pervert, the murderer, the liar, the selfish failure, the cheat, the criminal, and anything and everything else that has made each of us filthy sinners. He wasn't just treated like those things, He became those things and more in your place and mine. Those things became who He was so that they would not have to be who we are ever again.

Jesus became everything I was ever ashamed of so that I could become everything that makes Him absolutely glorious. Jesus has given us His glory in exchange for our shame. He has given us His very own glory. Isn't it wonderful? Read Jesus' own words for yourself: "And the glory which thou gavest me I have given them" (John 17:22a).

After He was arrested, Jesus' life immediately began to reflect the same outcomes that I experience as a selfish sinner … as a manipulator, control freak, victim, coward, wimp, criticizer, liar, bully, abuser of myself and others, etc. Though He was guilty of nothing, Jesus suffered the way that you and I suffer for all our problem behaviors and attitudes. These attitudes may include being arrogant, scornful, compulsive, addicted, anxious, negative, driven, self-centered, perfectionistic, angry, and ungrateful. They also may include many others. Jesus experienced life as one flawed with the shortcomings of every person who ever lived when He took our sin.

In 2 Corinthians 5:21, Paul describes this core truth about salvation by saying, "God made him who had no sin to *be* sin for us, so that in him we might become the righteousness of God" (italics mine). Jesus became like me. He fully experienced the shame and pain of *being* all kinds of negative things, along with being punished for them. All of the weaknesses that prevent me from overcoming the negative qualities in my life made Jesus weak and vulnerable because He made a covenant with us to take on Himself all of our weaknesses and flaws. Jesus removed everything bad (sinful) from me and took it upon Himself. Then—though I didn't deserve it and cannot buy it or earn it—He took everything good (everything right, lovely, righteous, and good) about Himself and gave it to me. He made it part of me. He gave it to me as a *free gift*.

When a person receives Jesus as his or her Savior, that person receives all of who Jesus is so that he or she is restored to being like Jesus, made in the image of God, the way Adam was before he sinned. Through the plan of salvation, anyone who accepts Jesus is re-created in the image and likeness of God (Gen. 1:27; Heb. 7:25), because the perfection of Jesus is built into that person ... like being remade and reborn or completely factory rebuilt and restored to mint condition.

It is important to say here that in God's eyes we walk in the lovely righteousness and perfection that we receive from Jesus. In the practical arena of everyday life in this world, this transformation is a process. What is actually happening is that we are re-creating our lives and reshaping the kind of people we'll become. We are privileged to participate in that process, cooperating with the Holy Spirit and making decisions and choices that set the direction for the change process. This opportunity to determine something of the person we'll become is really a wonderful privilege and gift from God.

In Jeremiah 29:11, God tells us about the plans that He has for us: "For I know the plans I have for you," declares the LORD, "plans to prosper you and not to harm you, plans to give you hope and a future" (NIV). Then in Psalm 37:4, He promises to give us the desires of our hearts when we delight in Him: "Delight yourself in the LORD and he will give you the desires of your heart" (NIV). Psalm 20:4 says, "May he give you the desire of your heart and make all your plans succeed" (NIV). So God has some things in mind for us. He has a plan for our lives. But He has made provision for the things we would like to do and be as well. Isn't that a wonderful and loving combination of blessing and freedom (John 14:14)?

This dynamic process of change is accomplished by faith. It occurs day by day as we apply faith to the exceedingly great promises God has given us in the Bible (2 Peter 1:2–4). If God were to do the whole thing in one sweeping action, we really would have no opportunity to be a part of the process and make some of our own choices. By the way, these exciting changes that unfold in our lives have a rather weighty theological name—sanctification.

Even after all of this was done for me, Jesus was not through. There was more, much more.

Benefit Four: Jesus took my failure and its consequences.

Did you ever have a dear old Sunday school teacher who taught you that the word *sin* means "missing the mark"? I did. I am so grateful for that understanding of what Jesus did when He saved me from my sins. I learned that He excused me for every time I do not hit the bull's eye perfectly ... for every time I fall short. That was the fourth thing that Jesus did for me; He reviewed my whole life and how it was working, and He took away everything in me that was failing ... that was missing the mark ... that was unproductive or ineffective ... that was grating and grinding like gears that do not mesh properly ... that was *sin* (2 Peter 1:3–8 NIV).

Benefit Five: Jesus took my feelings of inadequacy.

Next, in addition to all of that, wonder of wonders, Jesus took upon Himself all of the terrible negative impact that sin and failure have had on me. He took away all the sad, gut-wrenching feelings of disgrace that sin and failure left me with. He took away the horror and dismay I felt over being the kind of person I was not proud to be. Whether I came to realize that I had been sneaky all of my life or a rat, a nerd, a fool, a brute, a nag, a bully, a whiner, a cheat, an abuser, a liar, a thief, or even a murderer, Jesus not only took all of the guilt and punishment, but also He took upon Himself all of the terrible shame that came with it.[4] I hated realizing that I was any or all of those things, but Jesus did make it possible for me to stop being any of them when I got my faith in gear. He made it possible for me to become a different kind of person (John 1:12; Rom. 6:4; Eph. 4:24; Heb. 7:25).

In place of shame and dismay, Jesus gave me His marvelous peace and joy and goodness—even His own godliness (2 Peter 1:3). I became a fine person, a good person, an honorable person, a respectable person, a beloved and cherished person to God. The core of my being has been changed forever because of God's salvation plan.

There is so much more to this fifth aspect of salvation that I have to resist beginning to tell you about it all right here. Keep reading, and we shall explore this wonderful salvation in greater detail. Meanwhile, as wonderful as all these things are that we have already discussed, there is still more that Jesus has done for us.

Benefit Six: Jesus saved me from other people's sin.

Jesus saved me from my own sin, but it is not the only sin that tears at my heart and wreaks havoc in my life. The sins of others affect me too. This is the sixth thing that Jesus did for me: He delivered and saved me not only from my sins but also from everyone else's sins. Others no longer have the power to devastate me through their choices and behaviors. I have help in overcoming the effects of the sin or failures of others. I have a wonderful antidote for the poison of other people's spite or viciousness, and even their violence. My life operates on a plan under which *all* things work together for good (Rom. 8:28).

Benefit Seven: Jesus transformed my drab world into living color.

Seventh, in addition to all of that, Jesus, my Savior, delivered me from death *now*. He took from me, and wants to take from you, a state of inner drabness that colors the outer world with awful grayness. He teaches me to choose life, not death, every day. All of us have to cope with a zombie-like lack of vitality and aliveness, at least some of the time. But the drabness I am talking about comes from inner deadness. Thank God there is a way to choose life (Deut. 30:15–20). The Bible tells us that death came into our lives—into humankind—when Adam and Eve sinned. Death did not just terminate them immediately. It settled over them as darkness while they were still alive, and they walked about in the shadow of looming death until their bodies died (Luke 1:79; Ps. 23:4).

Death is all over sinful humanity like an oppressive fog. Our experience of daily existence is as radically unlike what God wants us to have as death is unlike life. On the cross, Jesus arranged to reprogram us so He could replace all of that with a vibrant capacity for life … for living … for being *alive*! (See John 10:10.)

Benefit Eight: Jesus freed me to be the person God had in mind.

The last part of what Jesus did for me through His salvation is He made me a new person who is living a new life. I don't have to be like Adam and Eve, who were guilty and hid themselves in the bushes because they could not face God. I am no longer someone shaped by guilt and shame who needs to hide my inner self from others (Gen. 3:8). That type of behavior, where I hide myself, is a terrible bondage to hypocrisy—to playing a role ... endlessly playing a role as tough or strong or good or competent or whatever my life seems to demand ... in order to appear good and righteous and worth something. I'm not projecting an image that is not the real me, not how I really feel about myself. People who feel they have to hide who they really are spend life hiding behind a wall of lies that becomes a prison of their own making. Because of Jesus, hypocrisy has to release its death grip on me now.

Jesus Himself told us in Luke 4:18 that He was sent by the Spirit of the Lord to heal the brokenhearted and preach deliverance to the captives. He goes on to say that He is to set at liberty all who are bruised. Why do bruised people need to be liberated? When we are hurt and bruised, we put walls up to protect ourselves from being hurt again. Those walls by which we try to defend ourselves become prison walls behind which many hide. No one needs to remain in a prison created by his or her own thoughts or the teachings or actions of others. Jesus came to set us free.

Getting Real

As a Christian, I no longer have to labor to project an image of myself that I hope others will like and accept. I don't have to appear strong or competent when I'm not. I do not have to try to pretend I am something wonderful when I feel like I am not wonderful at all. I do not have to pretend that I don't care when I care very much. I can relax and be real and accept the person I really am, the person God made me to be and loves, a person who is growing and changing and becoming more and more like Jesus. How does this happen? It happens as a result of my faith in operation (1 John 5:4). What is operational faith?

It is my decision to believe what the Bible says and conduct my life based on what it says, on those marvelous, extravagant promises of His care and blessing (Phil. 4:19).

I receive the ability to be like Jesus because He removes from me and takes upon Himself the qualities and characteristics that make me a sinner and bestows upon me instead everything about Himself that makes Him the beloved Son of God. He restores me to mint condition, the way He created Adam at the dewy fresh dawn of time. May the Lord give us grace to understand what we really receive when we receive Jesus.

My Salvation Is in Good Working Order

All eight of these wonderful things that Jesus did for me are benefits included in the phrase "Jesus saved me." Of course they do not cover everything. There is so much to salvation that I just did not see growing up and that I did not have in good working order in my life as a Christian for so long. It was like having a computer and not knowing that there are programs on it that I have never opened or used.

A computer is a very good example of something we can have without enjoying all of its benefits. I love my computer. I understand very well the one little job my computer does for me: word processing. But I used it for years without knowing the slightest thing about its capacity for bookkeeping; sophisticated mathematical calculation; complex games; or communication on the Internet, modem, or fax—or even its usefulness in the management of my daily business affairs, bill-paying, and calendar. I daresay that there are many other things it can do that I do not even know enough about to list here.

How could I use a computer for more than twenty years without knowing all of the good things it can do for me? It's easy. I never read the book that explains it all to me. I never really got into reading it so I could understand the whole picture of what it is designed to provide. I only consult it frantically when I am in trouble. And then I only look up the word or phrase that describes my current problem. Otherwise I leave it alone, because to a novice like me, it is hard to understand. At some level, I do know that my computer has wondrous capacities I have not explored, but I do not get into the manual and study it. Think of the new worlds that will open up for me when I do!

For years after I became a Christian, I treated the Bible the same way that I treat my computer manual. I consulted it in a panic when I had a problem, but I never explored the potential that I know it contains.

We can all think of the Bible as the *User's Guide* for the plan of salvation. There are many wonderful promises that we hear about vaguely when other people talk about them. Why don't we pursue the idea that they could be real and useful and wonderful in our own lives? I do not know. Why do I own a computer that can do marvelous things that I do not try to understand and use?

God Is Not a Disappointment

I believe that many of God's promises to us are stated in the Bible in phrases that seem too good to be true. We have difficulty grasping the full meaning. Maybe it is because others withheld love or nurture, approval or support when we were young and we got used to having unmet needs. Maybe we were disappointed many times in childhood by things that offered exciting possibilities that never materialized. Perhaps we are careful to protect ourselves from further disappointments in life by refusing to hope that good things dangled before us could actually happen.

Please know this: God is not a disappointment. The plan of salvation is more and not less than we hoped. The byword of heaven is not "ever less and less"; it is "ever more."

Chapter Four

Don't Make My Mistakes
Truth or Dare?

I loved Easter when I was growing up. It marked the coming of spring in Philadelphia, where I lived, and we were well rid of the ugly slush of dirty, melting snow along the curbs and the dreary, overcast days of early March. With the change of seasons, we gals often got new clothes, and Easter Sunday usually meant a new outfit for church. Then there were the grand chocolate bunnies and baskets of treats to be enjoyed. Easter was a wonderful time—except for its awful message.

I hated the Easter story. I was appalled and, to tell the truth, frightened by the whole story of the crucifixion. Every year its repetition confirmed for me again that I did not feel quite safe trying to have a cozy, loving relationship with a God who would do a thing like that to His own Son. How could such a God love me or anyone else? And how could I possibly love Him? I was very grateful that my new Kelly green suit and chocolate eggs distracted my mind from the point of it all.

Remember my earlier comments about not having things right in my Christian life? Well, I lived for many unhappy years with some pretty big misunderstandings about the gospel message and the Christian life. I hope you can profit from my mistakes.

The Truth Will Set You Free

Before we get into the specific inner workings of how the plan of salvation began to work in practical ways in my life, let's take a brief look at the worst of my mistakes in the hope that you won't have to make them too. Let's consider my old list of things that I thought Jesus did as my Savior—the way I used to think salvation worked—and contrast my errors with the truth as I now understand it:

1. **The truth:** *Jesus saves me in practical ways in this life.*
   My error: For years, my whole understanding of the words "Jesus saves" was that He saved me from having to go to hell for the sins that made God mad at me. It was a message with impact in the future only, not with very much impact in the present. I did not see how salvation made much of a difference "right now." I had no practical understanding of the fact that He could rescue me from problems I would face at work tomorrow or anywhere else. I had no idea He could do that.

2. **The truth:** *Jesus saves me by what He did and does, not by what I try to do.*
   My error: I believed that I was supposed to think about the terrible suffering that my failures and offenses caused Jesus on the cross and feel so guilty that I would finally try harder and harder until I stopped messing up. Never mind that it never worked. I thought that the practical outworking of my Christianity consisted of constantly opening my heart to rebuke because my sin made Jesus suffer until I finally managed to get one sin after another out of my life. I had no idea that Jesus came to help

me. He didn't come just to give me so much guilt that I would finally get my act together by myself. He knows very well that I will never be able to do that. I may not know it. I may go years thinking that I should be able to win in a war against my own sin, but I never will. Sinning is a fundamental part of my natural makeup, and I'll never be able to stop doing it until Jesus gives me a new nature.

3. **The truth:** *Jesus saves me by giving me the power to do what pleases God.*

   My error: I believed that obedience to all of God's rules and commandments would make my life work. The trouble was that I never seemed to be able to "get it all together." I felt so defeated. I thought it was my responsibility to make it all work right, but I couldn't. I believed that I was woefully lacking in the self-discipline required for an exemplary Christian performance. In between periods of giving up and just going on about my life, I worked harder doing what did not work. Now I receive God's help and power by faith as a free gift from the cross to me. Such unconditional love and acceptance and generosity still seems beyond wondrous to me.

4. **The truth:** *Jesus saved me by taking away my guilty feelings and my shame.*

   My error: If you had asked me, I probably would have told you that the presence of the Holy Spirit was essentially expressed through the working of my guilty conscience day by day. I thought my shame served me well as a constant deterrent. I believed Jesus worked through the Holy Spirit to point out my inadequacies day after day, shaming me onto the path of righteousness. Those ideas made me think shame was a good thing and I needed more of it. After all, didn't people say, "You ought to be ashamed!" I had no idea that He died to take away my shame. That was an astonishing idea.

5. **The truth:** *Jesus saves me from what I have failed to be.*

   My error: I did not know that Jesus would help me to overcome my sins of *commission*, let alone my sins of *omission*. I did not know that He could help me to do better, to get better, to be a better person, to accomplish something. I thought He was always on the verge of writing me off because I could not seem to do better by myself. I did not realize that He knew going in that I could not do it on my own (John 15:5).

6. **The truth:** *Jesus saves me completely from heartbreak and disappointment.*

   My error: I did not know that Jesus could save me from feeling crushed and heartbroken as I cope with large and small disappointments, large and small failures, and large and small rejections (Isa. 61:1). I didn't understand that everyone else needed Him as much as I did to cope with daily feelings of hurt, dismay, and disappointment, no matter what the cause.

I hope that what I am going to tell you now is not what I looked like to other people. I hope I managed to hide some of what was going on in me from the world—even though I know that hope indicates that hypocrisy is still driving some of my responses. But I am going to share with you what was happening in the deepest places in my heart as a young Christian. Looking back, I can see that I felt both God and people found that virtually nothing in me was working quite the way it should be. I never felt I measured up.

True Confessions

My particular personality type profile suggests that I am rather sensitive to criticism. I thrive with a whole lot of affirmation and not very much rebuke. Since that kind of treatment does not come to us very often in the adult work world, I worried all the time that I did not measure up. I guess some silly childhood idea made me think that if I did not do something that was "wonderful," I had failed. It's called perfectionism. It also is called grandiosity—and it is not functional.

I suppose there were a few things that I thought I had practiced over and over to the point that they were working well enough to satisfy the world's demands, and that was good. But it was not enough. I knew there were vital pieces missing in my life so that those seemingly functional parts did not add up to my ideal of success.

With the new understanding I now have, I am more convinced than ever of my own faults and failings, but it doesn't hurt so much anymore. I now believe that God looked things over in my life back then and rejoiced with me in the things I had learned to understand and do well. Nonetheless, He found me just about completely dysfunctional. After all, one major system out of whack can keep a whole car from running, even if other parts are operating perfectly. I certainly had more than one "system" out of order. More than one aspect of my life was dysfunctional. Dysfunctional behavior misses the mark. I had lots of systems missing or malfunctioning. God summed all this up in just one word: *sin*.

My situation was pretty desperate. When I wanted to do and be good, I did evil. What I wanted to do, I could not seem to do, even though I tried. And what I did not want to do, I seemed to be doing over and over. My struggles with weight control and dieting alone demonstrated over and over how true these words were. So did my resolutions to read the

Bible every day, to exercise, to be patient with my children, to organize my meal planning, to maintain an orderly household, to keep better financial records, to be on time, to buy gifts and plan activities before a deadline arrived ... and so on and so on. Even telling the truth challenged me, and lying seemed an easy way to stay out of trouble and avoid embarrassment. How could I ever hope to escape the cycle of falling short?

The only possible reason why everyone would not admit to being in the same situation I was in is because people are in denial. We cannot really believe that we do the stupid things we do over and over. It is hard to face the truth about ourselves. The biggest reason why we have to resort to denial is that we can't make any sense out of our own failure to do what we know to be the best thing.

There Is a Way Out

Jesus alone had a solution for me that would finally work. He is like a brilliant computer programmer who can reprogram my brain to run my whole life differently. He installs a whole new operating system that is designed to be crash proof. *It will not fail.* How grateful I am that while He installs His new program in me, He does not condemn me for all of my faults and failures. It is so comforting to read the words of Paul the great apostle that are found in Romans 7:15 through Romans 8:2 and see how accurately the Bible describes how we all feel. It says:

> I do not understand what I do. For what I want to do I do not do, but what I hate I do. And if I do what I do not want to do, I agree that the law is good. As it is, it is no longer I myself who do it, but it is sin living in me. I know that nothing good lives in me, that is, in my sinful nature. For I have the desire to do what is good, but I cannot carry it

out. For what I do is not the good I want to do; no, the evil I do not want to do—this I keep on doing. Now if I do what I do not want to do, it is no longer I who do it, but it is sin living in me that does it.

So I find this law at work: When I want to do good, evil is right there with me. For in my inner being I delight in God's law; but I see another law at work in the members of my body, waging war against the law of my mind and making me a prisoner of the law of sin at work within my members. What a wretched man I am! Who will rescue me from this body of death? Thanks be to God—through Jesus Christ our Lord!

So then, I myself in my mind am a slave to God's law, but in the sinful nature a slave to the law of sin. Therefore, there is now no condemnation for those who are in Christ Jesus, because through Christ Jesus the law of the Spirit of life set me free from the law of sin and death. (Rom. 7:15—8:2 NIV)

I never grow tired of the reassuring words in Romans 8:1 that tell me that God is not condemning me for my natural tendencies to constant sin—not one bit! Instead of scolding and rebuking me, He loves me and managed to think of a perfect way to "fix" me. On the cross He provided a way for me to get rid of my sin.

The Gospel Is Good News

Jesus took all of my sin to the cross. These are familiar words that many of us have heard over and over all our lives. The message they conveyed to me as a child was wonderful, but they can be like the words "this student can't write." They contain much more meaning than I was able to grasp. They were so familiar that I did not mull them over to see what deeper meaning might be there. When I finally gave them the kind of attention they deserved, I found that all the good, solid teachings of my childhood remained and that vast new insights were added to them.

I need to get rid of my sin, but sin is not just something I do. Sin has become who I am. So how can I get rid of it? Jesus does that for me. He does not just take away the guilt. He does not just take away the punishment. He takes away the sin itself. He absorbs it into Himself (2 Cor. 5:21; Isa. 53:4–5). He takes it away from me by making it a part of Himself. He owns it. He becomes responsible for it and all it has caused.

Long ago, after God created the world, He created Adam to live in it. He created Adam in two steps: First, He formed him from the dust of the earth; second, He breathed life into him. Adam was a living soul until he sinned. When sin came, life left and death came. Then it was the "dust of the earth" part of him that remained while he toiled away in the fields, far from God's beautiful garden.

So, the Lord God formed man of the dust of the ground (Gen. 2:7). He formed you and He formed me of the dust of the earth. That "dust of the earth" part was the part that remained for Adam, and it was the part that remained for you, for me, for us all. Oh! But then … the blood of Jesus fell drop by drop on the dusty earth beneath that cross.

The Bible teaches that the life in a person or an animal is in the blood (Lev. 17:11). Jesus' life is in His blood. In His blood is His whole life, everything that makes Him the glorious and perfect Son of God, who is like God and who *is* God. As Jesus shed His blood on the cross, drop by drop, His perfect life was poured out on the ground beneath the cross. His blood was poured out on the dust of the earth—His life was poured out on the dust of the earth. In the same way, Jesus' blood is poured out on us when we receive Him. Just as the breath of God breathed life into Adam, so the blood of Jesus suffuses every part of who we are with the life of God's own Son—with the life of God, the Son. The dusty, lifeless ground that received Jesus' blood perfectly symbolizes who we are as descendents of Adam after sin took away the life God created us to have and before the blood of Jesus gives us new life.

The home our family lived in for many years in Houston, the home in which most of this book was written, had a front door that was set in the front wall of the house with no porch or roof over it at all. Instead, there was a dense canopy of trees covering the sidewalk just in front of the house. Many times after a heavy Houston rain shower, I stood under those tall trees long after the shower was over with my front door key in my hand, feeling raindrops falling, one by one, from the wet branches onto my head.

One day I happened to kneel at the sofa in our living room to pray when I had an unusual experience. I distinctly felt drops falling, one by one, on my head. It was a sensation so real that I reached up quickly to feel the top of my head. In something of a panic, I got up to see whether a pipe had broken in a bathroom on the second floor above me, causing a leak through the ceiling. There was nothing anywhere to account for the gentle feeling of drops on my head.

In my walk with the Lord, I have come to believe that even when clearly supernatural things happen, I must accept them by faith. Faith is part of the process. The sensation of those drops on my head was intensely real. Nevertheless, believing that what happened to me was from God required faith. I had to believe in its significance in order to think and pray about it long enough to find its meaning.

God brought to my mind the verses in the Old Testament that tell us that the life is in the blood. Then came the scripture about Adam being a lifeless form made of dust in the first step of his creation (Lev. 17:11; Gen. 2:7). Next I understood that when I knelt in prayer, imagining myself kneeling at the foot of the cross, the blood of Jesus falls on me in a very real way. As I kneel there presenting my need and giving Him my sorrows, my grief, or whatever else draws me to Him in prayer, the blood is always there for me. It ever flows over me. And a wondrous exchange takes place: Jesus takes away the sorrow that fills my heart and suffuses my whole being with His very life—all of who He is. In exchange for the thing that is not right in my life (not righteous), Jesus gives me His life, the life He laid down for me.

A part of the life of Christ that you will receive at the foot of the cross will be His joy and His peace (Isa. 53:4–5; John 10:10; 14:27; 15:11). He exchanges His very own peace and joy for your sorrow and grief. We'll explore this marvelous trade in depth in the second section of this book.

In just the same way that His blood soaked into the dry, dusty ground under the cross, Jesus' blood soaks into me and becomes a part of who I am. It becomes my new DNA. As I kneel below that cross and make Him Lord, His blood is all over me and all through me. At the very moment I bow before Him and receive Him as my Savior, His goodness and perfection and righteousness are poured all over me, while my sin and shame and guilt all become His and cover Him as He hangs there.

Have you ever done that? Have you ever received Jesus as your Savior? Do it now. Speak aloud so your own ears can hear you, just as all the hosts of heaven, who are joyfully listening to you, hear you as well. Tell Jesus you believe that He is God's Son and the Savior of the world, He suffered on the cross, and He died and was resurrected from the dead. Tell Him that you receive Him as your Lord. Tell Him that you are sorry for your sins, your failures, and your shortcomings, and that you believe He is taking away all your sin and replacing it with His perfect righteousness. Tell Him that you believe what the apostle Paul said in 2 Corinthians 5:21, when he wrote, "God made him who had no sin to be sin for us, so that in him we might become the righteousness of God." Tell Him that you believe that God Almighty now sees you and receives you as a person who is as righteous and sin free as Jesus Christ. Then tell someone you trust about your decision, and make the Bible the basis for your new life plan.

What Have I Done? What Has Happened to Me?

It means much more to say, "Jesus took away my sin," than to say, "Jesus expunged all the court records against me to save me from going to prison (hell)." It means that Jesus reached into my mind and body and removed all of the defective circuitry in the whole system (my sin) and replaced it with perfect new circuitry so that I work properly. Here is the heart of what this book is all about. The circuitry that He replaced my circuitry with was not just any old circuitry; it was His own—His very own—that He took out of His being and put into mine.

When perfect circuitry was taken out of Jesus and given to me, the defective circuitry that had been mine was installed in Jesus. That meant that He had to go to the cross and cope with everything that happened to Him there with my defective parts installed (with my sin nature operating) instead of His own perfect ones. That is how Jesus took my sin to the cross. That is how Jesus became sin. That is how Jesus overcame my sin. He overcame all of the temptations to commit sin and to become sinful in His attitudes and behavior with nothing better to help Him than my defective "circuitry."

When He was born, while He lived on the earth, and when He died, Jesus was fully God and fully man. I certainly cannot explain the mystery of it. He never stopped being God, yet I believe that as He functioned on the earth as a human being, He ceased to be sinless and perfect when He entered into covenant with you and with me. I believe that because He told us that He is *in us* and we are *in Him* (John 14:20; 15:5; 17:21). With great love for us, Jesus joined Himself with us in that covenant

43

and became flawed with our sin (2 Cor. 5:21). The introduction of sin into His nature weakened and corrupted Him the way it weakens and corrupts all of us. Yet weakened as He was, He never yielded to sin. It was a mighty victory! It was a victory that was won not with the power and authority of God's Son, but in all the weakness of human flesh.

The wonder of what is written above has so transformed my life that I am at a loss to know how to convey to you the power it contains. It is the power of the gospel. Paul describes the gospel in the first chapter of Romans as "the power of God for the salvation of everyone who believes." When I receive Jesus, I receive *in a very literal way* blessings that have concrete, practical value in every area of my life. They have practical and real functions today as well as spiritual and eternal ones.

The expanded understanding I now have of what happened to Jesus on the cross has helped me to understand how He overcame Satan's claim on all of us. He did not triumphantly get through the whole ordeal without sinning in the tiniest little way because He had Godlike strength to draw upon. Not at all. He did it after He had taken all of His own strength, perfection, and personal resources out of Himself and put them into each one of us.

Jesus traded out the parts and installed the defective ones He got from me in place of His own perfect ones. He did it when He picked up the cup in the upper room just before His arrest and made a covenant with you and me. He told His disciples that the cup was the new covenant in His blood (Matt. 26:27–28). Under that covenant, Jesus took all of your sin and mine and gave us all His righteousness (2 Cor. 5:21). So when He endured all of the world's cruelty and overcame all of Satan's temptations, He was equipped only with your inadequacies—and mine.

The wonder is that even with all of my defects—and your defects—replacing His perfection and weakening Him during

His struggle, *Jesus did not sin*. What a victory! He won my victory—the one I should have won, the victory that *had* to be won to free me from Satan's hold. He won that victory not with His heavenly perfection, but with the imperfections and failings of sinful humanity (2 Cor. 5:21).

For me, the dawning of that revelation was so full of wonder that the whole of the universe seemed to pause in infinite awe and stillness and worship while I tried to absorb its full meaning. I was sitting at my computer beside a second floor window in our Houston home when God granted me a revelation and understanding of what Jesus really did for us. Flowers were blooming in the front yards up and down our street. The trees were waving gracefully in the breeze, squirrels were chasing one another up and down the tree trunks in our yard right outside my window, and birds were flitting around. Yet a great stillness fell over it all.

I could never describe the beauty of the world around me in those types of moments or the vast stillness that seems filled with the presence and holiness of the Lord Himself. Even years later, as I review this passage for final editorial changes, the tears flow down my cheeks in wonder and gratitude at what Jesus experienced for me, at what He did for me.

The Meaning of the Cross

When Jesus made a new covenant with His disciples in the upper room on the night He was betrayed, that covenant contained all that He was and all that He had. He gave us no less. Jesus gave us His life. That is what we receive when we receive Him. He offers everyone the privilege of "receiving Him." In return, He asks us to give Him our lives. What a trade. He took all our sorrow and grief and pain and sickness and inadequacy. He took everything in us that is hateful, vile, and reprehensible. In its place He gave us His love, His ability to love, and His perfection. Thus He restored us to "mint condition," just like Adam and Eve on the first day of the world when they were perfectly made in God's image and likeness, and just like Jesus, who perfectly reflects God's glory, image, and likeness (Gen. 1:26; Heb. 1:3; John 17:20–23).

Jesus put His righteousness—His very own perfect functionality or "circuitry"—into me so that I am now righteous with Jesus' own righteousness. Jesus takes out of me everything— every part of me—that does not work the way that God created it to work and gives me, piece by piece, parts of Himself, like perfect spare parts from the manufacturer. Jesus ends up having to replace quite a lot.

Let's take time to look again at the marvelous way that the apostle Paul describes the whole process in one amazing sentence. In 2 Corinthians 5:21 (NIV), he says, "God made him [Jesus] who had no sin to be sin for us, so that in him we might become the righteousness of God."

In Romans, Paul tells us, "This righteousness from God comes through faith in Jesus Christ to all who believe. There is no difference, for all have sinned and fall short of the glory of God, and are justified freely by his grace through the redemption that came by Christ Jesus" (Rom. 3:22–24 NIV). The righteousness of God is a free gift to everyone, and it comes to us just by our believing and accepting it.

Often in the book of Psalms, there is a term used that I want to put here. It is "Selah." It means to "pause" or to suspend the music. Stop the music and let that idea sink deeply into our understanding. Jesus became sin with our sin so that we can become righteous with His righteousness.

Other translations of the Bible render 2 Corinthians 5:21 this way:

- The King James Version: "For he hath made him to be sin for us, who knew no sin; that we might be made the righteousness of God in him."
- The New American Standard Bible: "He made Him who knew no sin to be sin on our behalf, that we might become the righteousness of God in Him."
- The Amplified Bible: "For our sake He made Christ [virtually] to be sin Who knew no sin, so that in *and* through Him we might become [endued with, viewed as being in, and examples of] the righteousness of God [what we ought to be, approved and acceptable and in right relationship with Him, by His goodness]."

No single sentence in the entire world ever contained more transforming power than these amazing words. In them is found the way to change everything we ever did so that it works for good and not bad no matter what it was. In them is found the way to wipe away every spot on your record and every blemish in your character. In them is laid out the way to go from losing to winning—from death to life. (Read Romans 8:28; Ephesians 5:27; Hebrews 7:25; 1 John 5:4.)

In the gospel message that Jesus took away our sins lies the truth that God wants to give all of us a chance to start over. He wants us to feel and to be brand-new. He wants to give us the opportunity to have a new life. He wants to restore us to mint condition.

Chapter Five

The Repair Shop
God's Mechanic Is the Holy Spirit

At this point, one may well ask: If I am saved and Jesus did all of this for me, why am I still the way I am? I know I have been changed, but there is still so much that doesn't seem to reflect the perfection I should have. Why?

The Process of Sanctification

The Bible describes the way the plan of salvation deals with my sin in a clear way in the passage we are studying from 2 Corinthians 5:21. Read it again. "God made him who had no sin to be sin for us, so that in him we might *become* the righteousness of God" (emphasis added). Note the use of the word *become* as opposed to the use of a word such as *be*. It suggests a process as well as an event.

The sin part describes what Jesus has already done as perfect and complete, while the part about my *becoming* the righteousness of God seems to be a *process*. This process is underway in me. It is not complete. This verse makes it clear that there is an aspect of salvation that is not like excising (cutting out) a corrupt piece of us. It is not the same as pruning us in such a way that certain branches are removed.

My understanding is that we *do* undergo a process that Jesus described as pruning. It is a process that removes such things as addictions and alcoholism. We do need to be pruned, and we *are* pruned as we grow in the Lord, but I do not think pruning is what is being described by Paul in this verse in 2 Corinthians. The sin that Jesus removes is not a chunk of us or a "branch." It is a quality that permeates every part of us. Like DNA, it is in every cell. Before Jesus takes it away, it is one of the identifying markers for humankind. It is the genetic marker that is the precursor for death. It works dysfunctionality into every area of life, with the aim of keeping the death process constantly at work in us.

Researchers have found genetic markers that seem to predict specific future health problems like Alzheimer's or Huntington's or certain kinds of cancers. Many more will surely be found in the years ahead. Similarly, we all have an identifying marker inherited from Adam and Eve. It is sin, and without a Savior, it predicts inevitable death for us all, even though that is not what God wants for us. Salvation, on the other hand, provides the greatest genetic therapy the world has ever seen.

Death Has to Work Hard

The other day I noticed a green leaf pushing its way up between the cement of our driveway and the foundation of the brick wall of our garage. A day or two later, I was amazed to see that several leaves and a flower had grown. How could it be? That hardy weed looked healthy and strong. I was impressed anew at the power of a seed to spring to life.

It would be easy to see our lives here on earth as full of death and defeat and disappointment all of the time. History shows humanity has suffered continual conflict with war, famine, disease, and human depravity. But I've come to believe that it is not easy to succeed in bringing about so constant an experience of misery in God's wonderful and beautiful creation. I am convinced that it requires relentless effort on the part of Satan and those in his domain to maintain steady pressure toward death in a world created by the God of life. Every evil force has to be on the job continually to keep life from springing up all the time ... from every crack in the sidewalk. Every human social system and organization has to be hovered over and negatively anointed with depravity and stupidity by the forces of evil to keep death at work. We call that negative anointing "corruption."

It is important to realize that corruption is everywhere, all around us, and our enemy is always on duty. So we have to be alert and sober also. As the mighty apostle Peter tells us, "Be self-controlled and alert. Your enemy the devil prowls around like a roaring lion looking for someone to devour. Resist him, standing firm in the faith, because you know that your brothers throughout the world are undergoing the same kind of sufferings" (1 Peter 5:8–9 NIV).

You know that there are lions in the world. So do I. There are things that can and must be done to manage lions, but it is possible for most of us to live most of our lives without having to focus on the literal threat of a lion. Perhaps a helpful modern illustration of what Peter meant us to comprehend would involve our understanding of germs.

We know that germs are a constant threat. We have to address that threat all of the time. We wash our hands. We are careful not to eat contaminated foods. We keep our clothes and houses and bodies clean. We do not eat from utensils used by others. We take vitamins, and we need to be properly rested. We vaccinate our children. We disinfect things that are used by sick people. Once we do all these things, we can set aside our constant battle against germs to focus on other things in life. As a matter of fact, most of the time we really do not permit our constant battle against germs to divert us from the business of living.

The power of evil is real. We do have to take it into account. We have to do the work necessary to handle the constant and real threat of an evil enemy in life. In truth, we can never let up in our efforts to keep him controlled. But after we have done the basic things required to handle him, the way we do the basic things we do to handle germs, the devil's efforts and threats need not occupy a central place in our lives. The power of God to give us salvation and new life in Christ is also continually at work, and nothing on this earth can withstand the power and wonder of the plan of salvation.

Believe it or not, what I am really trying to say is that it is hard work for the devil to get us sick in God's healthy world. It is hard for the devil to make us poor in the midst of God's abundance. It is hard for the devil to make us lonely in the presence of God's people and of His Holy Spirit. It is hard for the devil to defeat us and make us fail when God has created us to be so full of talent, energy, and zest for life—and when the Holy Spirit Himself stands ready to help us. The devil has to work, and work hard, to cause us problems.

Making Salvation Work

Salvation is a practical plan. Jesus takes away my sin in such a way that it becomes a part of who He is, just as it used to be a part of who I was. Then He infuses me with the righteousness that was His before the foundation of the world. It is not put into or on or around me. It becomes me. It is who I am. I *become* the righteousness of God. It's amazing! Once I am changed—that is, once the very substance of who I am is changed—the process of changing my life can begin.

Let me share one of the entertaining ways God chose to help me understand this vital principle of change. God has a wonderful, delightful sense of humor.

Years ago, when I was a young mother with four little ones of my own, my mother and I used to pull my great-grandfather's old *Precious Promises* Bible down off the shelf in my father's study and use it in our prayer times together. All of the promises in the Bible were underlined in red. What a grand edition of the Bible it was. I hope someone reprints it.

Once Mother had the big, old Bible on her lap, she and I would pray together most earnestly about whatever happened to be on our minds at the moment. Then we would ask God to guide us in allowing the Bible to fall open to whatever underlined promise He wanted us to apply. Since all of them are wonderful, it seemed hard to go wrong.

Perhaps I should mention here that my father, a Presbyterian minister, was disturbed by our practice of "Bible poking," or letting the Bible fall open, and believing that God controlled the page to which it opened. I believe he considered it presumptuous or perhaps a little superstitious. Maybe he thought it was like playing games of chance with God, so I do not endorse the practice or recommend it to you—though I do say that we often were blessed. I simply tell you what happened.

(I will mention here also that I have attempted "Bible poking" on my own with much less special blessing and anointing on the outcome. The power of two or more people coming together in fervent, agreeing prayer may be the reason for this difference since the Bible tells us that Jesus is present then in a different way [Matthew 18:19]. Perhaps we constitute a heavenly quorum with another believer or two. Or maybe my mother's childlike faith in the matter pleased the Lord in a special way. God may choose not to reward a shortcut to an answer from Him that does not involve thoughtful study or time spent focusing our attention upon Him.)

On this particular morning, I prayed a long time about something or other that was on my mind. Actually, I just got downright wordy. I guess it was because I really wanted an answer and my faith was wavering. Perhaps I did not have perfect assurance that God would provide one. I was more focused on the problem than on God's promises.

Finally, I finished my long, repetitious prayer. Mother prayed quietly a little while and then opened the Bible. Looking over her shoulder, I found the passage marked by her thumb. It was Job 11:1–2, which says, "Then answered Zophar the Naamathite and said 'should not the multitude of words be answered?'" I giggled with embarrassment, because I knew I had repeated my prayer in several different ways and God seemed to respond in such a personal way, almost teasing me a little. It felt very warm and personal.

Then I read on in some puzzlement, looking for something that seemed to provide insight. God is so loving and gentle. I knew that we are not to accept the words of Job's three friends as God's truth, so I did not know what to think. On that day, I kept reading down the page, looking for the wonderful comfort that always came when we found the right verse, the one on which we were to set our faith. Then something remarkable happened. Verse 12 caught my eye: "For vain man would be wise, though man be born like a wild ass's colt." I stopped in surprise, for a vivid picture formed itself in my mind.

Donkeys, Mules, and Stallions

I saw a number of paddocks with many beautiful white horses in them. Some of them looked like elegantly trained and groomed Austrian Lipizzaner stallions, and others were mares. As I watched, something happened.

Before I tell you what it was, I feel compelled to explain something about horses and mules. One time when I shared this story, a very well-educated person who was listening confessed that he grew up as a "city boy" and had no idea that mules were produced by breeding a donkey—sometimes called a jackass—with a mare (female horse). Neither did he know that because mules are produced by crossbreeding between two species, the resulting offspring are sterile and not able to reproduce. It is interesting to note that the Bible tells us not to breed two animals that are not of the same species (Lev. 19:19).

Now, back to my story. As the picture formed itself in my mind, a scruffy-looking, unkempt donkey came into view, moving through underbrush that grew close to the paddocks. He seemed sneaky. Unnoticed by anyone caring for the horses, the donkey jumped the fence and impregnated one of a group of beautiful mares. So a coarse mule was born to an elegant thoroughbred mare. Then these words went through my mind: "Sanctification is the process by which the jackass is taken out of the mule without killing the horse." I laughed. It was a light and amusing way to describe something that is very serious. It brought a revelation that was designed to help me understand salvation.

The sin within us is very much like a genetic marker. It is like DNA. The righteousness of God that changes us at salvation is so fundamental that it affects every part of our being the way the life of the donkey affects every cell in its offspring ... in this case, making it a mule and not a horse.

Jesus told the people He was preaching to in John 8:44 (NIV): "You belong to your father, the devil." These are surprising words to hear from our Savior. They came immediately into my mind with the picture of the outlaw donkey fresh in my mind. Contrary to general opinion, the Bible does not teach that we are all children of God. Rather, it teaches that we are children of the devil. It also teaches that God freely provides everyone with the opportunity to *become* a child of God by receiving Jesus Christ as his or her Savior. John 1:12 says, "But as many as received him, to them gave he power to become the sons of God." Until we receive Jesus as Lord and Savior, we are genetically linked to the prince of this world. And we all do tend to have qualities and characteristics that resemble him.

Having a fundamentally sinful nature removed from us—without killing us—is very like the kind of process it would take to remove the genetic material provided to a mule by the donkey that sired it. What would have to be taken out is very much a part of the mule's being. Removing it all at once would have to involve every part of the animal.

One more thought about the contrast between a mule and a thoroughbred horse. A mule can never be trained or taught enough to become a horse. And even if the mule were transformed into the strongest, smartest, most perfect specimen of a horse ever seen on the earth, it would still have to go through the training process common to all horses. The difference is that for a mule, all the training in the world could never provide the breeding and beauty he lacked. But for the thoroughbred horse, the potential for glory is there, and the height of his achievement is largely determined by his cooperation in the training process.

Once you and I undergo the miraculous process of salvation, our sinful nature is changed. We are mules who are changed into horses because the jackass is removed. We are completely and genetically changed. Before the change process took place, no amount of training ever could have made us elegant and beautiful horses. After the change occurs, we still need to undergo the intensive training necessary to become one of the lovely performing dressage horses, but we can do it.

Becoming Beautiful and Perfect

The project we are undertaking together throughout this book is actually the theological process known as sanctification.

I had heard the term *sanctification* all through my life growing up in a minister's home; however, it did not have much concrete meaning for me. I understood its meaning theoretically, to some degree, but it had little impact on my daily life.

Thank God, I have come to understand sanctification as the hand of God helping me to reconstruct what is not working right for me in each area of living. I realize that He is at work in me and in you in many practical ways to make of us something beautiful and elegant and powerful. We learn to respond to His gentle guidance with graceful obedience. God has always loved us. Now He loves and sees in us the same beauty and perfection He sees in Jesus. As sanctification progresses, we find joy in the person we are becoming as we move in harmony with God.

More Help from Horses

Many years ago, on a pretty Texas morning, I hurried to pick up my ringing phone and was greeted by the sound of my mother's cheerful voice. We shared special insights and blessings we received from the Lord as often as we could. When she telephoned, I was eager to hear what was on her mind. On this particular morning, she read to me from Isaiah 30:18–21. The beautiful phrases flowed over my ears: "that he may be gracious unto you ..."; "that he may have mercy upon you ..."; "he will answer thee ..."; "he will be very gracious unto thee at the voice of thy cry ..." It was refreshing and beautiful just to listen. Then two verses came into sharp focus, especially verse 20. Isaiah 30:20–21 says, "And though the Lord give you the bread of adversity, and the water of affliction, yet shall not thy teachers be removed into a corner any more, but thine eyes shall see thy teachers: And thine ears shall hear a word behind thee, saying, This is the way, walk ye in it, when ye turn to the right hand, and when ye turn to the left."

My mother loved horses. She loved them all of her life. Before she could walk, her father set her up on a horse whose name, I think, was Ebenezer; and she believed at once that the horse was hers. Above all, she loved to watch an elegant white Lipizzaner stallion perform.

"Do you see it, Connie?" Mother's voice was happy and intense. "The Holy Spirit is like the rider on the stallion's back. Together they move as one. No one can see the subtle signals the rider gives the horse. They are so attuned to one another that the slightest movement by the rider is enough to give the horse the guidance he needs. The rider is like the voice of one behind the horse's ears, communicating to the horse alone. When we stay closely attuned to the Holy Spirit, we'll always know what to do!"

And the outcome will be beautiful, I thought with a smile.

It was thrilling to Mother to think that the Lord wants us all to perform in life with the power and grace of those marvelous horses rising up on their hind legs. What a victorious stance it is. It delighted her to realize that it was possible to cooperate with God closely and successfully, as a team, like the horse and rider. God speaks to each one of us in the language of our own experiences. How precious are the things we hear when we keep our ears attuned to the "voice of one behind us."

A New Life

Christianity gives every person who will receive it a new life. It is a complete reconstruction process. It is a daily unfolding of change and renewal that is new every morning. Lamentations 3:22–23 says, "The LORD's lovingkindnesses indeed never cease, For His compassions never fail. They are new every morning: Great is Your faithfulness" (NASB).

A lovely acquaintance of ours, Edie McNeil wrote a very refreshing gospel chorus based on this verse.[5] The words go like this:

> The steadfast love of the Lord never ceases.
> His mercies, they never come to an end.
> They are new every morning ...
> New every morning ...
> Great is thy faithfulness, O Lord,
> Great is thy faithfulness.

Yes, Lord. Great is Your faithfulness to love us and work with us all the days of our lives so that we may be truly alive in a dead world!

Through the redemptive work of Jesus on the cross, God's love opens to us a transforming power that is absolute and perfect. It is a wonderful process. At this time in my life, several significant principles concerning it have emerged. The reconstruction of my life has turned out to be:

1. A process and not an event.
2. A part of a relationship with God in which I am treated with respect and constant kindness.
3. A way of life that does not violate my will, but does require my steady cooperation.
4. Energized by my joyful expectation of good things (which is a wonderful way to describe faith).
5. Fully dependent on the work of Jesus on the cross.

The true wonder of this transaction of repair and renewal is that even though the replacement parts and pieces are perfect gifts from Jesus, when they are all put together, they still form me. I am still the free, sovereign individual that God created me to be in the first place. It is my capacity for wondrous new life that has changed. God has given me a new life without compromising my free will or my identity as a unique, separate, whole person. Though I am made in His perfect image, I still possess all of the privileges of choosing my own life. "But as many as received him, to them gave he power to become the sons of God" (John 1:12). The choice that Adam and Eve had is restored to me, along with the sinless perfection they enjoyed.

Every day of my life, I can choose whether or not I will obey God. I decide whether or not I trust His goodness enough to believe that I will like His will for me and be glad I chose it. Sometimes I do not choose it. The blessed difference between us and Adam is that when I make a wrong choice, I have the privilege of repentance.

Just as Adam and Eve had to decide what they were going to do in this world, we have to decide. Salvation gives us the "*power* to become," but it does not *compel* us to become anything. God does not force us or violate your will or mine. It seems to me that Adam and Eve sinned before they had enough time to begin to wonder why God created them and what He wanted them to do. I hope we can do better.

God provided everything Adam and Eve needed in the Garden of Eden. He is the perfect nurturer and provider for all of us. He knows what we need before we ask Him (Isa. 65:24). While He knows what is best for us, God never forces anything on us. He maintains perfect respect for our sovereignty and autonomy. Sovereignty and autonomy are two vital qualities that we have to have if we are to be made in the image and likeness of God (Gen. 1:27). God gave us both, and He never takes them back (Rom. 11:29).

If you want God to change your life, and if you can thoughtfully and deliberately decide to believe that His will for you will be good and pleasant and desirable (Rom. 12:2), then the ball is in your court. The work of the cross is done. Now it is in your hands. You must ask Him to work with you and in you.

Until you ask, He will be most courteous toward you. He will honor the gift of sovereignty that He gave you. He will respect your personal boundaries and your freedom of choice.

Years of praying have persuaded me that God intrudes very little in your life, even if someone is praying for you, unless you invite Jesus to be Lord and Teacher as well as your Savior. When you are being prayed for, things about God seem to crop up everywhere you turn. All kinds of situations occur that present you with the love of Jesus and the power of the gospel. Events direct your attention to issues of life and death. Opportunities to choose may be put before you day and night, but I do not believe that God forces a choice upon any of us. Even to the point of allowing us to choose death and hell, God will honor our freedom to choose our own destiny—short term or long term.

For an interesting example of the graciousness of God, read the nineteenth chapter of Exodus. In it, God speaks to Moses from the mountain. He points out to Moses that He has delivered the people from slavery and bondage to Pharaoh (without one single person having to fight and without a drop of blood being shed), and He respectfully instructs Moses to ask the people if they are willing to accept Him as their God and to obey His voice. It was not until the people agreed to accept Him and honor Him as God by listening to Him and obeying Him that He laid out for them His commandments (Ex. 19:8). Doesn't God have the most beautiful manners?

If you want God to change your life, it is your privilege and responsibility to ask Him to do it. Reading a book, even a book about God, may change you very little. Only when it is a tool in the hands of the Holy Spirit can any book bring real transformation in a person's life. So if you want God to be *your* God and Jesus to implement His wonderful plan of redemption—of change—in your life, pause now and ask Him to do it for you. You can trust Him completely.

Sharing the Blessing

It is so exciting for me to be sharing all of this with you that I want to get right into the specifics of the "good news." Until God really began the transforming process in my life, it was hard to realize that sharing the gospel really *was* sharing good news. I guess I thought that sharing the message of salvation was more like giving a vital but gloomy condemnation of sin and threat of hell than the offering of great blessing. But not now. The gospel message is the most wonderful message ever received. There is so much good news I want to tell you about that I am eager to get started. We are about to enter consciously and deliberately into the process of change that Jesus died to make possible for us. I believe that the Holy Spirit has been working to bring about these wonderful changes in us all along. It works so much better and faster when we understand our role and consciously cooperate.

Chapter Six

Let Change Begin

With Isaiah Chapter 53

God's way of loving us is full of respect, gentleness, courtesy, and graciousness. With ultimate kindness He helps us to change the way we are, the way we think, the way we feel, and the way we act without tearing us down or wounding us.

In contrast, most groups or situations in the world teach us through the school of hard knocks. We attend that school every day. God certainly does permit us to learn that way, even though what we learn often is not God's truth or His will. Nonetheless, He relinquishes our education to the world if that is our choice. But He always holds open His offer to teach us His ways when we are ready.

The psalmist tells us that the Lord is good and His mercy is everlasting (Ps. 100:5). No one else who ever tried to help us was so deserving of our wholehearted trust. His program for transforming us and giving us a new life is absolutely brilliant. Everything we need is right there for us in Jesus Christ. So let's dare to believe God and wholeheartedly put our lives in His hands. Let's see what will happen when we choose to trust that God's will for us will be good, that it will please us; indeed, that it will be perfect. The Bible tells us that we'll be able to put God's will for us to the test. When we do, we shall approve of His plan. We shall find it good and pleasing and perfect. Romans 12:2 says, "Do not conform any longer to the pattern of this world, but be transformed by the renewing of your mind. Then you will be able to test and approve what God's will is—his good, pleasing and perfect will" (NIV).

Can it be that people shrink back from total trust in God because they secretly expect Him to declare everything they like to do sinful? Maybe so. But God may be a stronger advocate for freedom than most of us realize. There is an interesting passage in Romans 14 that encourages us not let ourselves become bound up in legalistic rules and the all-too-human tendency to judge one another or burden others with rules and restrictions (Matt. 7:1). People may be the source of the constricted lifestyle some attribute to Christianity. We are free in Christ. Living in that freedom, loving God and one another, helps us trust God to establish in each one of us the attitudes that govern our lives "because anyone who serves Christ in this way is pleasing to God and approved by men" (Rom. 14:18 NIV).

So now our study can begin. The wonderful exploration of what is really available to us in Christ can get underway. We may not be able to understand it all until we get to heaven, but what we *can* understand is enough to change our lives.

A Search for Buried Treasure

I am saved by exchanging my sin for Jesus' righteousness. When I decide to do that, my choice is recorded in heaven, like a legal deed is recorded at city hall when I buy a new home. I may not have moved into my new house to begin my new life there when the deed is officially recorded, but the whole house is mine nonetheless. The very next day, I may begin moving in pieces of my old furniture, but over time, I probably expect to exchange the old for new. As I do, the old furniture that is all around me still forms the stage upon which I live out the process for a while.

When I receive Jesus, my legal status is recorded in heaven and established forever. But my residence here on earth is just beginning a long process of change. By setting out to exchange my sin for His righteousness on the cross, I take the first step in learning what took place for me on that hill outside of Jerusalem. I begin rearranging my understanding of who I am, what I have, and what I can do.

Jesus faced a death that should have been mine so that I can live a life that should have been His. That is the principle of the exchange that transforms my life. It is my privilege to live my life today as Jesus lived. The works that He did, I shall expect to do (John 14:12). The love that Jesus expressed everywhere He went will radiate from my life (Rom. 5:5). The resources and wealth that we expect to belong to the Prince of Heaven, God's Son, become available to me because Jesus hung on the cross in hunger, thirst, nakedness, and want of all things—an absolute picture of total poverty and lack (2 Cor. 8:9; Phil. 2:7). Lest you think this is so marvelous that it is impossible, look at an example of the things in the Bible that appear too good to be true. Read 2 Corinthians 8:9 from the Amplified Bible: "For you are becoming progressively acquainted with *and* recognizing more strongly *and* clearly the grace of our Lord Jesus Christ (His kindness, His gracious generosity, His undeserved favor and spiritual blessing), [in] that though He was [so very] rich, yet for your sakes He became [so very] poor, in order that by His poverty you might become enriched (abundantly supplied)."

I believe that some of you will go get your Bibles to see if that verse is really in there. I know it was amazing to me to find it. Again, let it be said that the real challenge in this study is to believe that these wonderful words and promises in the Bible are true—and not "too good to be true."

Jesus Bore My Sorrow and Grief

One of the more surprising insights for me in all that is shared here is that before the first nail was driven through His body into the wood of the cross, Jesus had already done a huge part of the work needed to transform my life, to give me a new life. Jesus experienced the painful, gut-wrenching, and tragic experiences of your life and mine so that we could experience the triumph and glory that should have been His.

Jesus was humiliated, spat upon, tortured, tormented, whipped, deprived, and denied the justice He deserved before the first nail pierced His body so that He could save me from the harsh justice I deserve and heal my heart from the pain of having any of those things happen to me.

Jesus—who was perfect—was rejected, ignored by passersby, looked down upon, scorned, mocked, ridiculed, and made fun of during His trial and torture so that I, who have so little to recommend me, might receive the respect and honor due a child of God.

Jesus—who possessed all power—suffered intensely, and yet He allowed Himself to remain powerless to make the suffering stop. He freely chose to be helpless and powerless because He had a covenant with you and with me in which He gave away all His power and everything else in His life that made Him God's glorious Son (Matt. 26:53; 28:18; Luke 10:19; Acts 1:8).

Jesus—who was flawless in His perfection—suffered the ignominious death of a gross offender outside the city walls so He could bestow His flawless perfection upon all of us (Heb. 4:15).

During His trial and various legal hearings and during His abuse at the hands of the soldiers, Jesus was lonely, isolated, betrayed, and without support or encouragement of any kind from God or man (Matt. 26:56). Though everything He did throughout His whole life was right and good, God did not grant His plea for deliverance and did not intervene to help

Him in any way throughout His Passion (Matt. 26:39). I believe that happened to Jesus so that you and I may turn to God all the days of our lives and expect to receive the help we ask for, regardless of whether or not we are worthy of it (Ps. 91:15–16; Isa. 41:10). Now you may ask for anything in His name and He will do it for you (Matt. 26:39; Mark 11:24). Let your faith just grow and grow to believe the wonderful promise Jesus gives directly and personally to you in John 14:14.

Though Jesus never denied Him or turned away or turned back, in the end, the Father abandoned Jesus, utterly forsaking Him and leaving Him alone on the cross in filth, shame, helplessness, and pain—struggling for every breath—until He died without God, hanging there where I should have been (Matt. 26:46). He did it so that no matter what we have done, you and I never need to die without God. He did it so that we will never have to live for one moment without Him, without His love and care.

As we read in the Bible about the events surrounding His crucifixion, we can begin to understand what Jesus absorbed and felt in your place and mine. He took it all upon Himself so that He could take away our pain and free us from the crippling effect of each traumatic experience. Hell after death was not all of Satan's torment that Jesus experienced on your behalf and mine.

When I understand what it is that Jesus took out of my life by experiencing it for me, I begin to understand the good news of what He has given me in its place. And since what He has given me is mine to receive freely by faith, it is important for me to understand what is there for me, so I can exercise my faith to receive it.

Jesus—Perfect Everything

Jesus is perfect everything. Great Christian writers of the past have gloriously shown us His perfection and stirred our hearts to give Him praise and worship for the greatness of that perfection. Nevertheless, early one morning, I was deeply moved during my prayer time when I heard the loving and wonderful inner voice of the Lord asking me whether or not I truly believed that. Did I believe that Jesus was perfect everything? Of course I did. It was easy to say, "Yes, Jesus is everything perfect!"

Then came the question that changed so much in my life: *Do you believe that Jesus was the perfect pattern of evil?* I was aghast. Again, that vast stillness filled the room around me with an infinite sense of waiting. But this time I was shocked and troubled. Why would He ask me that? Where would such a question come from? "No," I wanted to protest. Of course I didn't believe that, but I couldn't say a word. It was obvious that if Jesus was perfect everything, then He was the perfect pattern of evil also. It was part of everything. *But how could He be that?* I was shocked. I was confused ... almost frightened. Where did that voice come from? *How could anything about Jesus be the perfect pattern of evil?*

The Perfect Pattern of Evil

How was Jesus the perfect pattern of evil? Why would the Lord ask me that question? Why was He that pattern and why is it important to us?

All His life on this earth, no one could ever say "Gotcha!" to Jesus. No one ever ensnared Him. No one ever "roped Him in." No one ever "conned" Him or fooled Him. Throughout His ministry of teaching and healing, Jesus did not allow Himself to be drawn in or controlled by any political, social, economic, or ecclesiastical system in this world. Nothing ever "got" to Him. No group ever enmeshed Him (John 14:30). He was absolutely free to move about and obey God and do exactly as He felt led and called to do—until the moment He was betrayed, arrested, bound, and taken into captivity.

Jesus never sinned or fell short in any way. All of His life, everything He did was good. But from the moment the authorities in this world captured Him, goodness vanished. As soon as the "prince of this world" had God's Son in his clutches, he (Satan) set in motion his evil plan for Jesus' life (John 12:31).

God's will and plan for us is to be whole and blessed and free. Jesus demonstrated that freedom until the time of His arrest. He had been living a life free of sin and free of bondage. All that changed from the moment He was betrayed by Judas' kiss. Jesus was taken captive, and immediately His life began to be controlled by Satan's plan. It is the same plan Satan has for your life, my life, and every life. There is a lot of valuable, practical information for us in understanding what God's plan and Satan's plan look like when they are held up side by side. For that reason, it is helpful to see what happened to Jesus as a pattern for the kinds of destructive things the devil is working to accomplish in your life.

Exposing Enemy Plans

Jesus taught us that we all have an enemy whose name is Satan (Luke 10:17–21; John 8:44). From Genesis 3:15 to Revelation 12:7–12, our struggle with the devil is clearly described. Satan has a plan for our lives, just as God has a plan. He has the same plan today for your life and for my life that he had two thousand years ago for Jesus' life. His plan for Jesus was fully carried out, beginning with the moment he managed to have Him arrested and continuing until He died and "descended into hell." By studying what happened to Jesus, we get a better idea of what we are up against every day.

God's Plan and Satan's Plan

Jesus contrasted God's plan and Satan's plan quite dramatically in John 10:10 (NIV). He tells us, "The thief comes only to steal and kill and destroy; I have come that they may have life and have it to the full." The beautiful King James translation of this Bible passage tells us that Jesus came that His people "might have life, and that they might have it more abundantly."

In plain words Jesus told His disciples that the evil systems of this world would be free to do everything to Him that they wanted to do once they got Him under their control. He said this following the dramatic events surrounding the transfiguration of Jesus that is described in Matthew 17:1–11.

Jesus explained to His disciples that John the Baptist had come to the world speaking with the same power and anointing that the prophet Elijah had. "Elijah has come," He told Peter, James, and John, and "… they did not recognize him [John], but have done to him everything they wished." We know that John was beheaded at the request of a dancing girl (Matt. 14:1–11). Then, in the clearest way, Jesus went on to say in Matthew 17:12 that He was about to suffer at their hands as well.

Satan did to Jesus everything he wished. He tried to do to Jesus every dreadful thing he had ever thought to do to humankind in all of history before or since … and he did it all during the three days and three nights he had the Lord under his arrest and control. Every cruel idea Satan ever had was included in his plan for killing Jesus. He tortured, humiliated, isolated, ridiculed, and belittled Him. He attacked and dismissed His work as without any merit whatsoever before the Sanhedrin. Using the high priest and Pharisees as instruments, the devil publically labeled Jesus' healing ministry of compassion "evil" because He did it on the Sabbath. He disdained Jesus' life as utterly without value, declaring Him unworthy even to be alive. He completely rejected Him through the voices of mobs of people, who cried (paraphrased), "Give us Barabbas, and crucify Jesus."

Often we experience rejection or failure or humiliation, the kinds of things that happened to Jesus. Sometimes we think we are rejected because people do not like us, because we are not attractive, interesting, brilliant, or lovable. It is comforting to realize that these things happened to Jesus despite the fact that He was perfect. They happen to us because we have an enemy who is a liar—he lies to us and about us. We have an enemy who strives at all times to promote the dark side of who we are and every unlovely aspect of our lives.

Satan's whole plan was carried out against our Lord in the three days between His arrest and His resurrection. That horrible period of time is the three days and three nights Jesus spent in "the heart of the earth" (Matt. 12:40). The "heart of the earth" is the spiritual core of a fallen world. For the whole of His previous life on earth, Jesus avoided being ensnared or enmeshed there. You and I live out our whole lives in that place.

How It Happened

When I was a child, no one was allowed to become too bossy in the group. Anyone attempting to control things in any group I belonged to was usually challenged. None too kindly, they might be asked something like, "Who died and made you king?" We might ask the same question about the devil. How did Satan ever get the power to do awful things in God's beautiful world? What is the answer to that question? It's this: Adam and Eve sinned and gave it to him. They obeyed the serpent, and that automatically put him in charge.

God gave Adam and Eve dominion over the earth and commanded them to use it to subdue the earth (Gen. 1:28). Instead of using the authority given them, they submitted themselves to Satan's plan and directions. By doing that, they gave away their dominion to Satan, and Satan used it to subdue the world to himself.

Both Adam and Eve ate fruit from the tree of the knowledge of good and evil. Satan persuaded them to do it, even though it was the only thing that God had told them not to do. So in a sense they got their information about the important subjects of good and evil by doing the devil's will and not God's. Obeying Satan and doing his will is not the best way to learn anything. Certainly it is not the best way to learn about good and evil.

Because God's enemy deceived someone into obeying him, all of the dominion over this lovely planet that God had given to Adam and Eve passed into Satan's hands. Romans 6:16 says, "Know ye not, that to whom ye yield yourselves servants to obey, his servants ye are to whom ye obey; whether of sin unto death, or of obedience unto righteousness?" Ever since they obeyed the tempter's voice and did his will by eating the forbidden fruit, Satan has been shaping human lives in harshness, sorrow, and neediness.

This short verse (6:16) from Paul's letter to the Romans gives us a wealth of understanding about the world. When we give the devil influence, power, control, or authority, he takes ownership. Perhaps The Amplified Bible's version of the verse will be helpful: "Don't you know that when you offer yourselves to someone to obey him as slaves, you are slaves to the one whom you obey ..."

To accomplish his purposes—purposes born out of his enmity towards God—Satan has been at work throughout history to bring endless suffering. God's will for people is blessing. When He put Adam and Eve in the Garden of Eden, He blessed them (Gen. 1:28). Satan is diametrically opposed to anything that blesses us. The name for the devil's program— that is, the name for whatever is the opposite of the Lord's blessing—is "the curse." Remember, Paul wrote in his epistle that everyone who hangs on a tree is cursed (Gal. 3:13–14).

To understand the devil's program for your life in detail, you need only to look at what happened to Jesus after His arrest. Event by event, it is all laid out for us there. As it unfolds, we see in Jesus' experiences the perfect pattern of evil. We see everything our Savior died to save us from.

I believe that the negative, hurtful things that happen to us are not the work of God. They are the work of Satan. It is important to sort this out. How can we love a God we think puts us into terrible difficulties all of the time? As long as we think our suffering and problems come from God, can we find it easy to love or trust Him?

The world's "truth," the world's "ungospel," grows out of seeds sown in our hearts and lives by Satan. He is a liar and the father of lies (John 8:44). As long as we are unaware of Satan's work in our lives, we are deceived. We cannot break free of his program for us until we grasp God's power and get His plan of salvation up and running. If we do not trust God, we will not do the work necessary to seek Him and come to an understanding of His plan (His will) and His power to help us.

Chapter Seven

Every Day I Choose

Blessing or Cursing?

Choose Life

Everything in this life and in eternity rests on whether or not we decide to make God's choice. He sets the choice before us every day. Do I take charge of my life and make a choice, or does life choose for me by default because I have not made a decision? If I do address the choice squarely, do I choose God?

Everything that happens in our lives is determined by whether we choose God's plan or Satan's plan. God's plan is one of blessing; Satan's plan is a curse. We must choose whether it will be God's good and loving will that we'll experience or Satan's very unpleasant program that we actually live out day by day. In Deuteronomy 30:15–16, God tells the Israelites (and us): "See, I have set before thee this day life and good, and death and evil: in that I command thee this day to love the LORD thy God, to walk in his ways, and to keep his commandments and his statutes and his judgments, that thou mayest live and multiply: and the LORD thy God shall bless thee in the land whither thou goest to possess it."

This old world that you and I live in is a mine field. Disaster, pain, and fear are buried everywhere, ready to explode in our faces if we take a wrong step. Understanding God's ways and keeping His commandments gives us the only safe map through the hazardous terrain. If we pay close attention to God's directions, we can move about freely without fear. On the other hand, we tend to walk into conflicts, confusion, and disaster if we do not have the guidance we need to avoid them. Where is freedom really to be found?

Facing the Truth

Now take a moment to look at the truth about what is in your own heart. Do you believe that you will miss something in life if you obey God? Adam and Eve were deceived into believing that God's commandments would deny them something desirable instead of protecting them from something *very* undesirable. They were terribly wrong.

God puts the same choice before you that Adam and Eve faced. Make a decision now as you read. Do you believe that God's will for you is good? Your whole future rests on your "leap of faith" to trust that God's idea of what should happen in your life is the best idea. Hidden in the corner of your heart, is there a fear that it is risky to choose God wholeheartedly and believe that He will bring you joy? Do the things you see in the lives of other Christians make you shrink back in dismay from unconditional trust in God's will for your life as good and satisfying and right?

Throughout history I believe that many rigid church teachings have indeed tried to deny us blessings that God intended us to have. But you know as well as I do that no one is perfect. Even with the best intentions, not every church and not every preacher has had the pure truth in all of their teachings. Certainly the Pharisees, who were the great religious teachers of Jesus' day, did not understand the Scriptures perfectly. Jesus Himself told us to be wary of their teachings. He described them as willing to lay heavy burdens on others:

> Then spake Jesus to the multitude, and to his disciples, Saying, The scribes and the Pharisees sit in Moses' seat: All therefore whatsoever they bid you observe, that observe and do; but do not ye after their works: for they say, and do not. For they bind heavy burdens and grievous to be borne, and lay them on men's shoulders; but they themselves will not move them with one of their fingers. (Matt. 23:1–4)

Jesus acknowledged that there were hypocrites in high places in the temple, but let's view them with grace (1 Peter 4:8). None of us has the right to judge imperfections in another person (Matt. 7:1). We do, however, have both the privilege and the responsibility to sort through teachings that seem heavy and oppressive to search out the truth that will govern our own lives. And we do have a reliable teacher. It is the Holy Spirit. Each one of us may read the Bible for ourselves and pray for the guidance of the Holy Spirit as we seek to understand what it is telling us. John 16:13–14 says, "But when he, the Spirit of truth, comes, he will guide you into all truth. He will not speak on his own, he will speak only what he hears, and he will tell you what is yet to come. He will bring glory to me by taking from what is mine and making it known to you" (NIV).

Moses Repeats a Commandment

Moses was the great prophet chosen by God to lead His people out of total bondage, misery, drudgery, and exploitation. He secured their release from terrible slavery. He became God's prophet, speaking God's words to them. Twice after the Israelites were set free he repeats the same remarkable words of prophecy from God about blessing and cursing. We have already read the passage from Deuteronomy 30:15–16 with its promise of blessing. Now read it as Moses repeated it a short time later in Deuteronomy 30:19a: "I call heaven and earth to record this day against you, that I have set before you life and death, blessing and cursing: therefore choose life, that both thou and thy seed may live."

The way every man or woman "chooses life and blessing" is to hear God's voice speaking His Word and believe what is said. He made us. He loves us. He knows how we can be happy.

When Adam and Eve chose to listen to the devil, they were no longer able to live and multiply and be blessed. The beautiful earth placed by God under their dominion passed from their hands to groan under the control of Satan (Rom. 8:22). From then until now, Satan has used that transfer of power to implement his unpleasant lifestyle of endless labor, illness, shame, failure, and disappointment for everyone and everything that lives on it.

Even animals over which Adam was given dominion came under the rule of Satan when Adam did. Under God's program, the lion will lie down with the lamb; but under Satan's program, God's magnificent and beautiful creatures prey upon one another. The introduction of death that resulted from sin caused them to require the protein of another life to replace the cells dying daily in their own bodies. Many could not maintain life except at the cost of another life. So attacking and devouring became the norm—another example of Satan's program of death at work.

It's Hard to Love When We're Miserable

Unless we all reverse that deliberate choice made by our great, great, great ... however many greats ... grandparents, Adam and Eve, we find it hard to love God. We really are not free to. We are so swallowed up in struggles and embarrassment whenever we think about God that we cannot think the God who made us is wonderful and good, so it is difficult to love

Him. If He came to take a stroll with us around our back yard one evening, would we huddle in the bushes like Adam and Eve did, embarrassed and ashamed of what we had done and said that day?

This world as designed and controlled by Satan is so miserable, how can I love the God who gave me life in it without some kind of change and relief? Thank God there is relief available. We *can* learn to believe God and accept His great solution to the problems that Adam and Eve created. Jesus was born on this earth with a plan to do it. He completed on the cross and in His resurrection all the work that plan required to bring us full deliverance from the devil's clutches.

When we learn what really happened through Jesus' Passion and death and accept it, we are redeemed from Satan's control. We can begin immediately to get loose from Satan's drab and dreadful lifestyle. We can be happy enough to be able to love God freely and joyfully.

Make the Choice Now

God has done His part to redeem us and change our lives. The plan of salvation is in place and operational. The work of the cross is finished. The Holy Spirit is doing His part at this very moment, drawing you to choose life ... to choose to believe in the goodness of God and the blessings that follow that choice. Now it is up to you. The choice is up to you. The choice is up to me. The choice lies before us every day that we are alive.

So that you can be saved, Jesus gave His life for you. Now you are being invited to give your life to Him. Every day you are invited to exchange your flawed life for His perfect life. Every day you are invited to do it anew so that it is always fresh and wonderful. The choice to trust God with all your heart and give Him your life is a choice that only you can make.

What are you to choose? You can choose to believe that what the Bible says is true. You can choose to believe what it tells you about Jesus. Believing the Bible and basing your life and all the choices you make on that belief is called "faith." A life of faith in Jesus Christ is a life transformed from hell on earth to citizenship in the kingdom of God. Jesus Himself told us to pray for the kingdom of God to come into being right here on this earth. In Matthew 6:9–10, He taught His disciples to pray, "Our Father which art in heaven, Hallowed be thy name. Thy kingdom come. Thy will be done in earth as it is in heaven." How wonderful it is to think of living a life of heaven right here on the earth. Deuteronomy 11:21 says, "That your days may be multiplied, and the days of your children, in the land which the LORD sware unto your fathers to give them, as the days of heaven upon the earth."

Be Transformed ... Into What?

Maybe no one can explain exactly *how* salvation works in its practical application. It just works! It is a plan that works when we work the plan. It removes all sin from our lives. When we apply it, we are made brand-new again, just like Adam on the first day of human life in the world.

God sees us as perfect. We are made perfect with Jesus' perfection (2 Cor. 5:21). And if I cooperate with the Holy Spirit in any kind of a workable way, God will make the perfection He sees in me express itself in the world as well. In Hebrews 7:25, the Bible tells us that Jesus is a constant and active participant in the process of making God's perfection a reality in my life because He intercedes with God for me all the time. It says, "Therefore he is able to save completely those who come to God through him, because he always lives to intercede for them" (NIV). Isn't that amazing? He not only has provided all I need for perfect salvation in His death and resurrection, but also, He is overseeing the whole process of applying it to my life and interceding for me constantly from His position as resurrected Lord in heaven. I love the beautiful, old King James Bible version of this verse in Hebrews: "Wherefore he is able also to save them to the uttermost that come unto God by him, seeing he ever liveth to make intercession for them" (Heb. 7:25).

My own personal experience has demonstrated that I cannot be restored to original mint condition, the way Adam was when he came "off the assembly line" (so to speak), until some work has been done in my heart and life. We all have had some hard wear and tear. We are pitted and chipped. Some parts do not work right, some are badly damaged, and some are just missing altogether. There is a lot about us that does not work right. Sometimes it seems that just about every part needs to be factory rebuilt. It is very exciting to see the work getting underway.

Second Corinthians 5:17 says, "Therefore if any man be in Christ, he is a new creature: old things are passed away; behold, all things are become new." We are living out another of the great mysteries of the gospel. We have seen that Jesus was fully God as He hung on the cross, and at the same time, He was fully human, the complete living embodiment of sinful humanity. In a similarly wondrous mystery, you and I are seen by God as though we were perfect right now, just as we are this minute, even though many of the characteristics and behavior associated with fallible humanity are all too lively every day of our lives. It's amazing.

You and I are received at the throne of grace by a loving God as though we were perfect ... because we already are perfect with the perfection of Jesus Christ. There is no mixture in "perfect." We have exchanged *all* of our sin for *all* of His perfection. Yet we have just begun the process of change that will go on all the rest of our lives (Rom. 7:15–23). It is indeed a mystery! It is our story when we make a rational decision—when we decide to believe it. It is ours by faith (1 John 5:4).

Each Christian is engaged in a process of sanctification by "putting off the old man and putting on the new" (Eph. 4:22–24). We are working out our own salvation with fear and trembling (Phil. 2:12). We are affirming our faith in the power of the promise that old things have passed away and all things are become new (2 Cor. 5:17). We rejoice in our faith that we were baptized into death with Jesus so that "just as Christ was raised from the dead by the glory of the Father, even so we also should walk in newness of life" (Rom. 6:3–4). We have a whole new chance at life. We have a whole new start.

Unlike Adam and Eve, walking about in God's perfect Garden on a beautiful morning at the very beginning of human life on this planet, we have a chance to think about the questions Adam never got to consider: What does God want me to do? Why did God create all of us? What is His will for our lives? What are His special plans for me and for you as individuals? Where is the real meaning in our lives?

I can know that I am absolutely unique and no one else can be the person in God's plan that He created me to be. I am precious and important to Him. So are you! Good things lie ahead and the restoration work itself is exciting and interesting. When it is through, our destiny with God is glorious. Psalm 8:3–9 states,

> When I consider thy heavens, the work of thy fingers, the moon and the stars, which thou hast ordained; What is man, that thou art mindful of him? and the son of man, that thou visitest him? For thou hast made him a little lower than the angels, and hast crowned him with glory and honour. Thou madest him to have dominion over the works of thy hands; thou hast put all things under his feet: All sheep and oxen, yea, and the beasts of the field; The fowl

of the air, and the fish of the sea, and whatsoever
passeth through the paths of the seas. O Lord our
Lord, how excellent is thy name in all the earth!

Before I can start life afresh, the way Adam did on the
first morning of his life, my whole being has to be healed and
restored—especially my heart. The same thing is true of your
heart and life.

As we go step by step through this study together, I pray that
the Lord will be binding up your broken heart, renewing your
mind, and restoring your whole being to mint condition. Day
by day we shall work our way through the passion and death
of Christ as described in the fifty-third chapter of Isaiah to find
the means of repairing and rebuilding each aspect of your life.
When we are through, you will have a new vision of yourself.
You will see yourself as brand-new again—fully transformed.
You will see how Jesus gives you a new life. With that new
vision and that new life in Christ, you will be ready to become
the precious, unique, successful person God created you to be.

Chapter Eight

Salvation

A Practical Step-by-Step Process

Everything we need for a new life comes to us through the practical step-by-step process by which Jesus takes sin out of our lives and replaces it with righteousness. Being righteous is being functional. It means that we operate correctly, with parts that work together according to God's good plan. Sin, on the other hand, is like a bunch of parts that just won't come together to work properly. Sin makes us all dysfunctional.

If you have a car with an engine that knocks and spark plugs that "miss," you know it is not operating quite the way it should. If it burns oil and the brakes squeal and little rust spots appear, you begin to think of trading it in. When the transmission system, the brake system, or the steering system begins to go, the performance of the whole car is affected.

People are like that. If our social lives, relationships, financial affairs, physical health, or jobs are a little bit out of whack, we cannot expect our lives to run smoothly. We keep trying and trying to make our lives work using Satan's defective techniques for success. All his solutions are designed to strengthen his hold on us. It is not surprising that we fall into line with his program because we have been trained in it all our lives. His plan never works to our benefit, and we fail one way or another over and over again. In each area of our lives, the fallible people who raised us and the sinful world we grew up in failed to teach us the proper operation and maintenance of things.

Just trying harder is *not* the answer. If your car needs repair, driving it more and harder will not correct the problem. It will make it worse. For years I worked harder and harder to make the dysfunctional systems in my life work, instead of realizing that I needed to repair the system. As we have said, doing more of what did not work in the first place will bring continued disappointment.

I could never count the number of people who have assured me that they grew up in wonderful families that loved them and gave them wonderful Christian values. I believe them. I am sure they loved their families and were loved in return. But if we had grown up with God's program working well in our lives, what need would we have for a savior?

We have to get real about this. Even in the most loving and caring of families, our needs were not met. We all have fallen short of the glorious life and the stellar performance that our heavenly Father desires for us (Rom. 3:23).

What we are doing in the process of being transformed by the renewing of our minds is reprogramming the control center that governs our lives. When we have God's program in place, we can be sure that it works right. Certainly the Son of God would not come down here to this earth and endure torture, death, and hell to bring us a plan and program of salvation that does not work very well.

The Lord's new program for us is designed to transform us by healing and repairing every damaged part. After that is accomplished, we'll see what comes next. Meanwhile, it is vital to have all of the physical and emotional healing we need, and it is essential to our peace of mind to know that we are going to heaven and not to hell. If our daily experience of living in this world is to change, we need to stop being conformed to this world and be reprogrammed (Rom. 12:2).

Lots of people stubbornly reserve the right to change their minds when they *want* to. But the truth is that few of us ever do. Most of us *need* to change our minds about things. The trouble is that it is often clear to us how other people need to think and behave differently, but it is very hard for us to see our own need to change. And it is harder still to do the changing. In fact, I believe that it is nearly impossible without God's help.

You may be wondering, *What are some of the foolish but obvious ways I may need to change? What are some examples of how our lives are made miserable?* Here is one example that I have seen often—the perspectives we get on style and fashion.

Let me explain. If I think my world is looking at me with critical eyes because I am not wearing designer clothes, then I am going to go out my door into every new day feeling ashamed and embarrassed when I don't have them. Then in time, if I allow the standards and attitudes in my mind that govern how I make decisions to be programmed by a social world that judges and criticizes the cut of a suit or the style of a dress, I will walk about my life in a state of distress that I have created out of a myth. While it is wonderful to wear beautiful clothes, the superficial ideas we get about style and fashion can make us miserable. Yet these ideas are still easy to recognize as artificial. Other things in life are not so easily understood.

If worrying about the latest style seems like foolishness to you, maybe you are a person who feels humiliated if you are caught with your bed unmade. Perhaps you feel ashamed if you are caught crying over something, no matter how moving it is. Maybe you have difficulty expressing love. Maybe there is no longer anyone trying to express love to you because you are distant or aloof. There are many things in each person's life that need to change.

Is the World's "Gospel Truth" Bad News?

A few years ago, a beautiful and accomplished young black woman moved onto our street with her family. Her husband was a physician, and she was publishing her first book. As we stood chatting by my driveway one sunny morning, I was appalled to hear her describe what had happened to her in school when she was growing up.

As a young teenager in Florida, she had attended an all-black high school. The African American teachers and administrators of that school had not permitted her to enroll in a biology class the year the curriculum normally introduced that subject. The reason was that she was quite dark skinned and the faculty actually told her—right out loud, in so many words—that children with skin as dark as hers were not smart enough to learn biology.

What an awful experience for a child to have. I could have cried. How could Satan get away with such a bizarre lie? How could any lovely young person absorb a hurt like that and go on to success? Sadly, it happens in this world that the devil gets help from all of us to spread his ungospel messages throughout the earth. Jesus explained it this way:

> You belong to your father, the devil, and you want
> to carry out your father's desire. He was a murderer
> from the beginning, not holding to the truth, for
> there is no truth in him. When he lies, he speaks
> his native language, for he is a liar and the father of
> lies. (John 8:44 NIV)

For many children back then, not having any high school biology credits was enough to deny them a college education, since biology was an entrance requirement at that time. Fortunately, my friend fought her way through the system and graduated from college anyway, but clearly, many of her contemporaries had difficulty doing so.

For my black neighbor, the teaching that dark skin meant lesser intelligence was actually spoken aloud and made overt. For many people of every race, messages of inferiority like that one are not so openly stated. Instead, they are absorbed through subtle experiences that shape us without being subjected to rational review. We learn them through a lifetime of cues and attitudes without ever considering that they might not be true.

Certainly my neighbor was anything but inferior in ability. As a published author, she was plainly gifted ... and beautiful and charming as well. The remarkable thing is that the attitude of inferiority that she had encountered lived on through her school years in blatant contradiction to her fine performance. That is a perfect example of the kinds of things that create sinful, dysfunctional people whose lives fall short of the glory of God. It demonstrates very well how the devil's ungospel message works to steal, kill, and destroy (John 10:10).

My neighbor's story is also a perfect example of the things that happened to you that resulted in ideas and perspectives that need to be changed. The circumstances may be different, but the evil intent to defeat you is the same. Many hurtful things happened to you that narrowed your options in life and limited your potential for joy. You may be sure that many experiences in your childhood were designed by Satan to persuade you that you were not very smart, not likable, not admirable, not interesting, not handsome, not beautiful, etc. They were *not* the truth. They were lies. Jesus taught that the devil is the source of lies. We have already quoted the words of Jesus that say of the devil, "there is no truth in him. When he lies, he speaks his native language, for he is a liar and the father of lies" (John 8:44b NIV).

Every person in this world has ideas programmed into his or her mind that are not true. Our lives can never work properly until they are changed. Jesus told us in John 8:31–32 that if we "continue in My word, then you are truly disciples of Mine;

and you will know the truth, and the truth will make you free" (NASB).

Surely our loving Savior is saying that we do not know the truth before He shows it to us. God's Word to us is good news, and it is the truth. Men and women alike, He tells us that we are beautiful, cherished, precious people with unlimited potential. That is the good news the world needs to hear. And that is what the word *gospel* means: "good news." If it isn't good news, then it isn't the gospel truth.

Chapter Nine

———

Free

In Newness of Life

When we understand what the Bible teaches, we'll be free of the terrible kinds of lies that tell a child that dark skin means a person cannot be smart. All of us have been told destructive things that are not true. Most of them are not as preposterous as that absurd lie, but all of them are aimed at damaging us. Some cripple us for life. We need to be set free from the lifelong bondage created by such lies, and the Bible is the great source of truth that can do the job.

The study units that make up the second part of this book are about reworking some of the most fundamental principles on which our understanding of life are based. They are about changing your understanding about yourself and your life. But they deal with much more than understanding. These studies deal with more than mental concepts and learning. They are about changing and healing those deep inner attitudes and feelings and misunderstandings that grow out of hurtful experiences in life. In other words, we are concerned with both thoughts and feelings.

The series of studies we'll be working through together is about changing the way we feel about ourselves and our lives.

It is about changing feelings that are so much a part of us that we think they are the truth. Those feelings hurt and hinder us, but often we do not question them. Sometimes we don't even notice them. We are scarcely aware of the dull sadness that they often produce in our hearts or of the crippling effect that they have on our performance.

Wrong ideas about ourselves and about life become mental habits from which we develop all kinds of actions and ideas that hurt us. They hurt others too. They prompt us to do endlessly self-defeating things. They may reveal themselves in selfishness or abusiveness toward others. The message of the gospel of Jesus Christ is designed to help us change our minds and all of our "instinctive" or "automatic" responses in a sweeping renewal that truly results in transformation. This is a far deeper process than we normally think of when we speak of learning—if we think of learning as acquiring information—but it certainly does include a vital relearning or retraining process.

An Individualized Program for Every Learning Style

The process of profound change that is being described here is formally known as sanctification. Liberation and blessing result from it. It is so vital a theme in the Bible that it is presented and described in many ways:

- In Ephesians 4:22, sanctification is described as putting off the old man and putting on the new man.
- It is described in Romans 6:3–5 as a process of dying to the old life and being resurrected to a new life with Christ.
- Elsewhere, the Bible describes the process of total life change in believers as our being removed from our family of origin on this earth and being adopted into the loving

family of God. Descriptions of these two families form a striking contrast in the teachings of Jesus. He taught His followers to pray to "our Father who art in heaven." He called others the "children of your father, the devil," in whose custody we are raised in a life of bondage and deceit. Growing up, we have been both abusive and abused, as well as deprived, until God adopts us into His own royal family (John 8:44; Eph. 1:6; Gal. 4:3–7; Rom. 8:21 NIV; 2 Peter 1:3–4; 1 John 3:1–2). Once we become a part of the new family, we begin to live a totally different kind of life. It is a life of entitlement and privilege (John 14:13–14; 1 John 5:14–15; Rom. 5:17; Rev. 1:6).

- In Romans 11:17, 24, it is described as a branch that is grafted into another tree. John 15:1 gives us a beautiful picture of ourselves as branches that are entirely dependent on Jesus as the vine. Our choice to abide (live our lives) in that nurturing relationship with Him, drawing life continually as a branch draws life from a vine, shows us where the process of change is leading us (John 15:4–5).

- In 2 Corinthians 10:4–5, sanctification is presented as warfare, with victory growing out of winning battles against enemy strongholds within us that rule and program our lives, assault our thinking, block our success, and try to keep us from knowing God.

- In Romans 8:1–2, Paul describes it as the difference between walking in the flesh and walking in the Spirit. Understanding this transformation constitutes a fascinating lifetime study.

- Paul also pictures it as the contrast between our being prisoners in bondage and our being free (Isa. 61:1; Luke 4:18). We are set free by Jesus from all condemnation after having been prisoners of the law of sin and death.

- In Nehemiah, Jack Hayford,[6] a prominent minister from California, finds the rebuilding of the ancient walls of the destroyed city of Jerusalem comparable to the reconstruction of the human personality from the rubble and ruin of life's traumas. This is also a good way to view sanctification; it makes it clear that sanctification is a process from which transformation results. The resulting transformation of that city from a ruin to a thriving metropolis describes the magnitude of change that we can expect in the life of a Christian. In the introduction of this book, I told of relinquishing to God the responsibility for my own learning and growth. This teaching series was one of the first things that occurred following that prayer. It had a powerful impact on my life.

In Exodus we are told the story of the deliverance of a whole nation out of slavery and into freedom. Many Bible teachers compare the journey of the children of Israel out of Egypt and across the desert to the Promised Land to the process of growth and change that takes place in the life of a new Christian. They point out that everyone begins the journey as a newly freed slave (to sin) and that the mentality of a slave is not empowering. Among other things, a slave may point out that his or her attitudes and ideas are not adequate preparation for a life of victory over giants or for nation building. When we start out our lives as former slaves, to be the head and not the tail, to be on top instead of on the bottom requires an extensive transformation of the way that we feel about ourselves and our potential (Deut. 28:1–13). Yet that is what the Bible teaches us to expect. As newly freed slaves, the Hebrews saw themselves as grasshoppers, and often, so do we. If we'll pay attention to what God has to say in the Bible, all that will change. Transformation can be accomplished. We can look to the history of the Israelites and their journey for invaluable guidance for our own journey with God (Num. 13:33; 1 Cor. 10:11).

- In Deuteronomy 28 and 30, we see that the transformation of our lives that we are studying here is described as demonstrating the contrast between life and death and between blessing and cursing. What a contrast that is! Adam and Eve demonstrate this process in reverse when we see what the introduction of sin into their lives produced. While their bodies did not die instantly, they immediately entered into a completely different experience of being alive on the earth. It was very unlike the abundant life that they previously had experienced.

- In Mark 10:15 Jesus compares the transformation process in the life of a Christian to a child growing up. He tells us that we need to enter the kingdom of God as little children or we cannot enter it at all. So it is clear that we are to begin with childlike trust and without preconceived ideas. Since it is obvious that we have seen many new Christians enter the kingdom of God and remain adults in their bodies, this verse must mean that we are to enter our new lives mentally, emotionally, and spiritually as children who are ready to learn everything about life all over again. When we begin the Christian life as little children, clearly we have both learning and growing to do (1 Cor. 13:11).

What was your early experience like? Were you taught that the color of your skin means that you can never be smart? Probably not. But in all likelihood, you were taught things somewhere along the way that were equally hurtful and damaging. Few people in this world manage to grow up without being shaped and influenced by some form of a lie. That being the case, we all have relearning to do (John 16:13; Phil. 1:6; 2 Cor. 5:17).

As new Christians, we have to sort out the lies told to us all of our lives by the "father of lies" (John 8:43–44). As new Christians, we have to begin all over again to learn what life is all about and how we fit into it. Clearly we did not get all of it right the first time.

Things Are Going to Get Better

Many abusive, hurtful things happen to all of us in our lives, and they damage us. Confusing and untrue things have been taught to us. It is little wonder that we do not work quite right. That is why the Bible tells us not to be conformed to the world any longer. That is why we have to repair and correct the errors in our programming. The pathway to repair is the cross.

I have heard the message that the cross is the answer to life's problems since I was a child, but I did not understand it. I certainly could not make it work. I thought that the cross was to stand there as a continual rebuke for the terrible suffering Jesus had to endure because I failed and sinned over and over. I thought that the cross was supposed to make me try harder to be good all of the time. I thought it was there to give me a clear picture of how God feels about sin … of how angry it made Him … of what He wanted to do to sinners. I did not understand that Jesus died there to *help* me, not to shame or threaten me.

It must have been something like the story of the boy who could not write that we shared previously. For so many years, the gospel message really did not have practical meaning that helped me to deal with each new day. Now I see that the message is practical and meaningful minute by minute.

How does it work? It works as desperate Christians kneel at the cross and exchange the things that are wrong in their lives for the things in Jesus that are perfect and right.

Please stay with me to see how truly wonderful this plan of salvation really is. Let me give you one quick example: We will be studying the verse in Isaiah that tells us that Jesus bore our griefs and carried our sorrows (Isa. 53:4). As a concept, that idea is interesting. But as an experience, it is life-changing.

Once you have knelt at the foot of the cross with a sorrowing heart and felt His love and willingness to take from you that sorrow and experience it for you while giving you His joy in exchange for it, the concepts in these studies can become a transforming way of life (John 16:24; 17:13).

What's It All About?

We find out how the transforming work of the cross operates in our lives by looking at what happened there event by event. All of His life, Jesus was perfectly righteous. Therefore He was never vulnerable to the devil. But the minute He made a covenant with all of us sinners in the upper room, He began the process of taking our sin upon Himself. It took three days and three nights to complete it; but the minute it began, sin was found in Him. Then Satan had all kinds of freedom to go after Him. Using that freedom, the devil immediately incited Jesus' enemies to move against Him, making them his evil instruments to destroy the Lord's ministry and take His life.

Once Satan was free to attack Jesus, he swooped down on Him with a vengeance. Jesus was abused in many different ways and with great viciousness at the hands of His enemies. Before His guilt was established and before His sentence was pronounced by Pilate, our Savior was subjected to assault by the temple guards, to torment and torture at the hands of Roman soldiers, and then to rough handling and abuse by Herod's "men of war" (Luke 23:25; Matt. 27:27–30; Mark 15:16–19; 14:65; Luke 22:63; 23:11; John 18:22; 19:2–3).

Once arrested, Jesus was deprived of everything a person needs for life; He suffered hunger, thirst, nakedness, and the lack of all things (Deut. 28:48). That certainly reads like a description of being cursed, doesn't it? Hanging there on the cross, He eventually lost even the ability to breathe when He could no longer raise His head. Everyone who had the slightest power or inclination to help Him fled. He was completely abandoned and helpless.

There was no rescue mission like the modern Israelis launched at Entebbe to free Jesus from the hands of His torturers. The disciples did not get together a gang to storm the citadel of the high priest. They did not arm themselves and attack the governor's palace where Pilate held court. They took no action to snatch Jesus away during His transfer from Pilate's to Herod's court or to help Him escape during the long walk up to Golgotha. Most of the people of Jerusalem went about their daily lives, ignoring His plight completely. (Their attitude and behavior reflected the same neglect that is common today.)

Jesus was abused, abandoned, deprived, and neglected. He endured it all. By the time He breathed His last breath on that cross, there was not a blessing to be found anywhere in His life. Everything about Him was cursed (Gal. 3:13–14). He took upon Himself every cursed thing for every person who had ever experienced any part of the curse of sin and death. He took every curse from you so that He could flood your life with every blessing that belonged to Him as the perfect and glorious Son of God.

The Bible describes one event after another in which Jesus experienced awful things that are all too common in the world. When you and I give our lives to Jesus, He gives a new life to each one of us. In our new lives in Christ, we can experience heaven's norm—which is blessing—in place of earth's norm—which is suffering.

Our Savior experienced absolutely all of the painful things that are this world's "norm" so that a way could be made for us to experience the opposite kinds of things—the wonderful things that are God's "norm" for us—things that always belonged to Jesus in eternity past and eternity future. That is why He suffered for us. He did it so that He could make a way to bless us. He did it so that He could take the curse out of our lives and replace it with blessing (Gal. 3:13; Luke 24:50–51).

Jesus Helps Us

Jesus took our place as helpless victims of the cruelty of man and of Satan so that God could make a way to help us. He wanted to rescue us from the hands of an enemy whose program was designed to steal from us, kill us, and destroy our lives (John 10:10). It is amazing that we all participate so effectively in the implementation of Satan's program. It hurts us and hurts others, but day after day, we all keep helping him work it out, until God shows us what we are doing.

Even though we all choose the Enemy's program in this world by default, the Lord knows that we do not understand what we are doing (Luke 23:34). God wanted to provide a way in which He could help us without violating our free choice. The way is the way of the cross, the plan of salvation.

The plan of salvation called for much more to be done to Jesus than just the nailing of His body to the cross, just as it provides for saving us from much more than an eternity in hell. Everything that happened to our Savior from the moment of His betrayal until He breathed His last breath was significant. Each thing that happened to Him then forms a part of our deliverance now.

Look at the things that happened to Jesus. Examine them one by one. The Bible tells us that "with his stripes we are healed" (Isa. 53:5). Jesus' whole body was broken and torn by a terrible whipping, a beating by an especially cruel kind of a whip. *His* body was ripped and broken by that whip so that the ravages of disease and trauma in *our* bodies may be healed. His body was broken so that our bodies may be made whole.

As a part of every Communion service we remember again that His body was broken for us. We often hear believers citing the power of the shed blood of our Lord, and it is wondrous indeed. However, it may be that we fail to fully comprehend the full power of what Jesus did for us through the bread that He offers us to commemorate the breaking of His body on our behalf.

Accounts of Jesus' beating describe an event—tradition suggests forty stripes since Jewish law imposes that limitation, but Roman justice appears to have no such limit—that occurred before the actual driving of the nails in crucifixion, and yet, it is *the* event that pays the price for our healing (Deut. 25:3; Isa. 53:5). It shows us that the suffering Jesus endured before the nails were driven into the cross was important to God's plan of salvation.

All of the torture that Jesus experienced all the way through His interrogation and trial appears to be as much a part of the plan of salvation as the execution that occurred on the cross. His beating was something that happened to Jesus that gained a wonderful benefit for us, just like His death and resurrection gained us life. His broken body gains us health, but it did not occur while his hands and feet were nailed to a cross.

If the cruelty of that flogging may be understood as the pathway to our healing, then should we not pay close attention to the other forms of torture He endured? What about the plucking out of His beard (Isa. 50:6)? Or the beating with fists about His blindfolded face (Matt. 26:67; Luke 22:63–64)? What about the torment of wearing a crown of thorns that pierced His brow (Matt. 27:27–30)? Those thorns were hammered down into His head with blows, an experience too horrible to think about (Mark 15:16–19). What do these events gain for you today?

What a Wonderful Savior!

Scripture presents us with a significant series of events that occurred *before* the moment when Jesus picked up that heavy cross and began the long struggle up the hill to Calvary. All through the night before He was crucified, Jesus was subjected to torment and misery of every kind. He was mocked, beaten, and humiliated. He was betrayed, rejected, and reviled. He was brutally interrogated, isolated, and abandoned.

Jesus was beaten in a variety of ways before He ever came under Pilate's whip. The guards struck Him with their fists. He was slapped and struck with rods (Matt. 26:67; 27:30; Mark 15:19). They spit on Him. They tore out His beard (Isa. 50:6). He was compelled to stand before a mob that was shouting for His death and forced to suffer total rejection. When they could have secured His release, they chose Barabbas instead (Matt. 27:21–22).

Along with everything else He suffered, Jesus had to have been cold, for His clothes were taken away (Matt. 27:35). You will recall that during the night Peter warmed himself at a fire in the courtyard where they were interrogating Jesus (John 18:18). Jesus was cold, wretched, suffering, and alone.

Now there is an important point that needs to be made while we are looking at all of the terrible things that Jesus experienced. Without really thinking about the idea that I could be wrong, I always viewed God as being very angry about sin. I saw Him as having strict standards and rules, and I thought that when one was violated His justice demanded that someone suffer punishment to pay for the offense committed. Now I do not see things in quite that way.

Romans 6:16 (NIV) says, "Do you not know that when you present yourselves to someone as slaves for obedience, you are slaves of the one whom you obey … ?" Those words led me to a broader understanding of the reason for Jesus' suffering—of the vicious depravity of it.

By eating the forbidden fruit in the Garden of Eden, Adam and Eve submitted to Satan's will instead of God's will. In the act of obeying him, they "signed on" to be his slaves, just like seamen signing on to an old-time sailing vessel. Once they were committed, there was no escaping the tyranny of the captain until the voyage ended. Similarly, any slave on a colonial plantation was the property of the master, and so were their children after them, until their freedom was given or purchased ... or until they died. The children of slaves automatically belonged to the slave owner, just like their parents. Satan laid claim to Adam and Eve and all of their children after them. From the moment they obeyed him of their own free will, his rules and programs—not God's—controlled their lives.

Everyone must make his or her own decision about what the Bible teaches, but I believe it is Satan's program that demands that every person who violates the rules will be subjected to harsh punishment. Social systems around the world fall into line by enforcing the rules of the system. It is interesting to note that other women may be harsh enforcers of the rules in societies that oppress women. In the same way, it often was other slave taskmasters who drove slave laborers most cruelly.

Satan is the accuser who is nitpicking about our behavior day and night (Rev. 12:10). It is Satan who is looking for reasons to accuse and punish us. God is loving and good (John 3:16; 1 John 4:8; Ps. 73:1; 100:5; 145:9). It is Satan who seeks our blood and our pain. And we are the ones who gave Satan the power to set up the world's justice system to be the way it is. He got that power at the same time that he got all the other kinds of power he possesses to make us miserable. He got it from us (Gen. 1:28). God gave it to us, and we gave it away. The devil lied to us (to humankind) back in the garden, and we believed him and acted on his word instead of God's (John 8:44; Rev. 12:9). He lies to us now, and many of us still believe him—especially about God and His goodness.

Satan's power in the world resulted from the decisions and actions of the first man and woman God made. God gave them the freedom to make those decisions; and He never took back, revoked, or cancelled the freedom that He had given them (Rom. 11:29). So when the time came to set in motion a plan to save humankind from the desperately awful situation we had gotten ourselves into, God did not violate the system that our foolish disobedience had created. He operated fully within the system to deliver us and save us out of it.

God Desires Mercy—Not Sacrifice

God's will for us and His attitude toward us is revealed in the fact that He sent Jesus to provide a way to forgive us (John 3:17). He sent Him into the dreary, nasty stuff that we live with every day to get us out. He sent Him to walk a path that leads to our forgiveness. He sent Him to tell us how to avoid punishment. God sent Jesus to be punished in your place and mine. He sent Jesus to negotiate your formal adoption into His royal family so that you can be loved there as a son or a daughter and receive an inheritance there that is more wonderful than we can imagine (Eph. 3:20–21; 1 Cor. 2:9). And all of it was established for us while we were sinners, before we ever repented in the slightest way. Romans 5:8 says, "But God commendeth his love toward us, in that, while we were yet sinners, Christ died for us."

All of that forms a strong case for the fact that God's justice system is not one of cruelty and harshness (Hos. 6:6; Matt. 9:13; 12:7). Of course, I am not saying that God has not been angry at what the human race has become and what humankind has done. We are made in His image, and the outrage over cruelty and injustice that we feel must be mirrored in His feelings many times over. Certainly He does not suffer a fool willingly. Yet God shows so much mercy and willingness to withdraw harsh verdicts and rescind orders to punish (Ps. 106:15; Jonah 3:10).

The continual unfolding of the goodness of God has come to be very powerful in my life, so it now seems clear that there must be forces at work other than God's vengeance alone in determining the future punishment for unrepentant sinners.

By our obedience to his ungospel, we have given the devil the right to lay claim to us and torment sinners until we give our lives to God. Adam and Eve turned the world over to Satan's program when they sinned. What has happened in it since then has been widely controlled by Satan's rules, unless we deliberately chose to restore power to God.

Of course, God can do anything, but He gave every man and woman the freedom to choose. More than that, He gives each one of us the responsibility for doing it (Deut. 28:15–20). God does not reverse the consequences of our bad choices unless we ask Him to do it. He never takes back the gift of freedom He gave us. The gifts of God are without repentance, and that includes the gift of free choice (Rom. 11:29). When we let Him instruct us, He guides us into all truth (John 16:13). Then we shall know the truth and the truth will make us free:

> And ye shall know the truth, and the truth shall make you free. (John 8:32)

> If the Son therefore shall make you free, ye shall be free indeed. (John 8:36)

Chapter Ten

God Honors
Our Choice

Faith Worketh by Love

God had to find a way to rescue us even while staying within the parameters of all of Satan's rules and control, because we set his regime in power and we have chosen to live under it. It was our sovereign choice to decide whom we would obey. We decided who would be served and whose rules would be imposed. We foolishly chose to eat the one fruit in the garden that God claimed for Himself.

God does not revoke the liberty that He gave humankind to make its choices. And He respectfully operates within the rules of the system we chose when He deals with us (Deut. 30:19). What is more, I believe that He honors our faith in and our affirmation of Satan's system, albeit reluctantly, just as He honors our faith in His Holy Word.

Make no mistake about it: People affirm faith in Satan's program of bad outcomes *all the time.* We proclaim our faith in something bad happening constantly. I believe God enforces our negative proclamations just as He does our positive ones (Prov. 18:21; Matt. 9:29; Mark 11:23). Our heavenly Father is perfect in His respectful treatment of our boundaries and our sovereign choices.

In a sense, the situation could be compared to that of a sergeant who spots his men walking into the middle of a minefield. When he calls to the men and tells them that they must do exactly as he commands, he is not giving instructions out of a power-hungry need to control or because he is taking offense at their behavior. He is trying to help them escape from danger in a way that will not increase it. I now view the prophetic words of the Old Testament law as the record of a wise and caring God laying out for people a path on which to walk. I believe it was a safe path through a minefield until Jesus could get His salvation plan up and running in our lives. It does not represent the arbitrary demands of an irritable God.

Jesus had to pay a terrible price to save us out of our own folly, and He did it without violating the rules and control of the world system into which we put ourselves. He came into the system with us and lived in it all of His earthly life without violating the system our choices created. He overcame the system, but He never violated it. He won a mighty victory over it, yet I believe He conducted Himself within its rules, even though they were depraved and evil, because He had respect for our right to create it. He did not call companies of angels to help Him, even though He could have (Matt. 26:53–54). Jesus never sinned, but He endured all of the temptations to sin that the rest of us have had to cope with in Satan's world. And because He was a genuine part of it and operating within it, He won the right to help us—within its rules and limitations—to escape from its control. God did not violate any gift of freedom He had given us to achieve our salvation.

In summing up what is being said here, I now believe it is Satan who constantly accuses us and claims the right to demand retribution for sin, because we gave him power to do so (Rev. 12:10). God forgives and forgets (1 John 1:9; Isa. 1:18; Ps. 103:3, 8, 12). Every time Satan entices us to sin, he claims a victory and the booty and the control that goes with it. That control includes the power to punish and the right to make us feel guilty.

Of course, I believe that the plan of salvation in which Jesus died for us is so complete and so flawless that God's own perfect justice was fully satisfied at Calvary. At the same time, I have come to believe that Satan's demands were being satisfied at the cross as well, because we gave him the power to make them. God's accounts against us were paid off. Satan's accounts against us were paid off. I believe that our debts to one another and all our offenses against one another were also paid in full. And I believe our offenses against ourselves were wiped away. What a wonder this plan of salvation is turning out to be as we study it in greater depth.

I do not believe that God was the sole author of the cruelty found in the way of the cross. God's sovereignty comes into play as He supports and affirms our freewill choices. So it was not to appease a vicious streak of cruelty in an angry God alone that caused Jesus to die in terrible suffering. All of that was the culmination of a horrible social system in the world that was carried to its awful, evil climax. What a sobering realization it is to see that it was the most "godly" and scholarly men in that social system who were the devil's instruments used to kill the Messiah.

Make no mistake. We have offended a good and righteous God in many ways. We have rejected Him. We rebelled against Him, though He has done nothing whatsoever to deserve our rebellion. Often we have ignored Him and violated the loving and generous agreements He has made with us, even though He honored them down to the last tiny detail. On top of all that, we have done lots of things to one another and to ourselves to make Him angry with us (Jer. 32:35 NIV).

I believe that we are made in the image of God and that our sin, foolishness, and injustice toward one another make God angry at us just as they make us angry at one another. We are like

Him in the emotions we experience and in the reasons why we experience them. But reading such scriptures as Hebrews 10:5–8 and the passage in Psalm 40:6–8, tells me that God did not like what the law required as retribution for sin. The law or covenant that God gave to Moses demands the sacrifice of bulls and goats to take away sins, but the Bible tells us that Jesus set aside the first covenant to establish a new covenant because He did not like the first one. Hebrews 10:5–8 (NIV) says, "Therefore, when Christ came into the world, he said: 'Sacrifice and offering you did not desire, but a body you prepared for me; with burnt offerings and sin offerings you were not pleased. Then I said, "Here I am—it is written about me in the scroll—I have come to do your will, O God."' First he said, "Sacrifices and offerings, burnt offerings and sin offerings you did not desire, nor were you pleased with them" (although the law required them to be made)."

The statement that "without the shedding of blood, there was no remission of sin" (Heb. 9:22) was a truth reflected in the law God gave His people, but was it truth because Satan had the right to demand it—ever striving toward his goal of death—after we gave him the power to make demands on us in this world and claim us for hell in the next? I believe the Bible is saying that God did not like Satan's cruel system of bombarding us with temptations to sin and then accusing us before God and demanding judgment and death for us (like the judgment and death brought upon Adam) when his temptations are successful (Rev. 12:10).

Out of His divine wisdom, God gave us the Old Testament law as His best counsel for operating inside Satan's domain until He could get us out of it through Calvary. For example, God directed Moses to have the priests sacrifice a lamb every night and every morning in the wilderness tabernacle so that there was a continual shedding of blood for the forgiveness of sins. He gave us directions for the best way to cope with the terrible system we found ourselves in after Adam and Eve sinned until Jesus completed the work of the cross. The old law was a way to navigate through Satan's system—to cope in it—until Jesus came to do away with its power to own and control us. Hebrews 2:14–15 (NIV) says, "Since the children have flesh and blood, he too shared in their humanity so that by his death he might destroy him who holds the power of death—that is, the devil—and free those who all their lives were held in slavery by their fear of death."

A Way to Find Grace

Would Jesus have had to die to deliver us from him who has the power of death over us if he had not actually held that power? So it is not God who holds death over our heads, it is the devil. That being true, we can go on to say that when the Old Testament tells us that he who sins must surely die, it is explaining the devil's system, the system we are born into and not necessarily the will of God.

As stated, I believe that in helping us to understand what we are up against, and in instituting the blood sacrifices in the temple, God laid out for humanity a way to find grace in the sinful system that we got ourselves into until Jesus could provide the final perfect sacrifice that meets all requirements. His sacrifice is a way back into fellowship with God despite the sin that grips us in this world.

So after years of coming to know the God of the Bible better and better—since I began reading it firsthand for myself rather than listening only to what others wanted to teach me about it—I have come to believe that the whole depravity of Jesus' torture and death had its roots in Satan's program to kill and destroy and not in the heart of God (John 10:10). Satan meant it for evil, but God meant it for good (Gen. 50:20). God transformed that evil to make it work out for good (Rom. 8:28).

Satan thought he was doing his best work in killing Jesus and destroying His ministry, but God transformed it into *His* best work. God worked it all together for good to rescue us, in order to save us from everything from which we shall ever need to be saved (Rom. 8:28). In other words, God used Satan's own viciousness as it was heaped upon Jesus to secure our complete release from evil's control and to reverse the effects of our own foolish choices (1 John 3:8).

Summing up then, it was our foolish choice to obey the word of Satan instead of the word of God when Eve and then Adam ate the forbidden fruit. By obeying Satan, we gave him ownership of us and thus control over us. By obeying Satan, we put ourselves under a lifetime of instruction in the devil's laws and rules and principles and decrees, all of which brought us more and more firmly under his control.

The devil's rules form the social, business, and economic structure in which the world conducts the daily business of living. When we violate the world's evil rules, the devil demands his justice … and it is harsh. I believe that the Lord lets him do it because He never took back from humanity the free right to choose and we are the ones who put Satan into office.

From Adam onward, no person ever succeeded in avoiding the temptation to sin, to obey Satan, to walk in his evil ways, to keep his evil commandments and his evil statutes and his evil judgments—until Jesus. Jesus made the choice, in this world as a man, to obey God and God alone in absolutely everything He did. With this choice by a man, Adam's choice to obey Satan, and thus to put him in power, was reversed by a man—by the Son of Man, Jesus. Then God's plan of perfect righteousness was reestablished on the earth (1 John 3:8).

All of this adds up, I believe, to show the truth that the Old Testament teachings of "an eye for an eye, a tooth for a tooth, a life for a life" and the harsh judgments they represent spring from the devil's rigid demand for retribution based on his right to rule us (Ex. 21:23–25; Deut. 19:21). They do not represent the heart of God. It was our heavenly Father who sent His Son to die for us. It was Jesus who quoted His Father as saying, "I desire mercy, not sacrifice" (Matt. 9:13; 12:7). The whole idea of God's love and mercy flows through the Bible like a river of life (Pss. 25:6–11; 107:1; 108:4; Isa. 54:10; Jer. 33:11; Eph. 2:1–9; James 5:11; 1 John 4:16–19).

In part, the laws that God lays out for humanity are there to help us to understand what we are up against as we try to live day by day in Satan's regime. It is rather like living under Nazi occupation or an oppressive communist regime. The laws teach us how to cope while we live here. They point out the booby traps hidden everywhere—the large and small rules that permit Satan to punish us because we set him up in place of God and gave him the right to make up the rules.

All of this is not to say that God's perfect justice was not also served at Calvary. It was … totally. And all of Satan's demands also were met. And so was our debt to one another. All of Jesus' torture and death is amazing in that it accomplished so many seemingly impossible things at one time. Pure justice was perfectly satisfied at the cross, but it was love and not vengeance that initiated the plan of redemption and brought Jesus to earth to save us.

Do Pharisees Live Today?

One of Satan's greatest victories was the distortion of God's Word in the hands of the priests, scribes, and Pharisees of Jesus' day. Their study of the Scriptures led them to believe that God was ever ready to judge and punish. They monitored the behavior of others, constantly watching the details of their lives play out. They spent their lives in Bible study and debate, endlessly consumed with details governing things like how and when they washed their hands, how they washed their cups, what they did on the Sabbath, and so much more (Matt. 15:2; Mark 7:1–13; Luke 6:6–11). Their cruel treatment of Christians following Jesus' death demonstrates the full extent of their willingness and ability to enforce a depraved system.

Every generation has to handle the devil's efforts to distort God's Word, just as the Pharisees did. They were deceived. Their attitude was rigidly legalistic. They presented God to the world as easily offended and ever ready to say "Gotcha!" at the least violation. Because they were widely seen as experts in God's law, this harsh perception of God provided the Pharisees with a means to acquire power and status among the people. They were perfectly willing to use that power and status to persuade Pilate to execute Jesus.

Allowing seemingly righteous Pharisees to become powerful in any age is more dangerous than it may seem. When people view God and the world in the way that the Pharisees viewed them, there are difficulties that inevitably arise in any society or culture that prompt folks to look around for someone to blame—for an offender, for the one in their midst who did not obey the rules, for the one who has riled up God and brought judgment and problems raining down on everyone else. This diversion leaves Satan unopposed in his work of stealing, killing, and destroying while people become almost savage in their attempts to identify and punish the "scapegoat" who is blamed for getting everyone else in trouble with God. Righteousness in a nation or a people is not achieved this way.

Love covers sin. It covers multitudes of it. It does not search it out and expose it. Judgment and condemnation expose sin. They search it out and publicize it and, at times, can appear jubilant to find it and spread abroad the news of its discovery (1 Cor. 13:6; Matt. 7:1–2; Rom. 8:1–2). The quest to find, expose, and punish the transgressor is light years distant from the mission of Jesus on the earth (John 3:17).

God's Approval and Blessing

How radically and dramatically different life is for those who choose and walk in God's blessing. Loving and caring and giving are direct routes into God's favor and blessing. The times of greatest blessing upon our nation have been times when we forgave our enemies (Japan and Germany) after World War II and gave generously into projects to rebuild their countries. Those years when mercy and generosity were expressed in American foreign policy were times when there was rapid growth in programs to care for others here at home also: the handicapped, the sick, widows, orphans, the elderly, even those in prison and the mentally ill and retarded. Those years also were years when our country grew enormously in wealth and power and blessing. No other country in the world could match the blessings that were poured out on our country.

World influence abroad and prosperity here at home in the United States of America increased dramatically during and immediately following the times we chose to bless our enemies and not to turn away from the needy people among them (Isa. 58:6–12). It became our national policy not to extract retribution, but rather to help our enemies rebuild their war-ravaged countries and give them what was needed to accomplish it.

The period of history immediately following the Second World War is a striking example of biblical principles empowering a nation. No nation can suffer the loss of its beloved young soldiers and sons without building up strong feelings toward the nations against which they fought. Japan and Germany exhibited a striking kind of inhumanity during that conflict, and our nation defeated them soundly. Yet there was a magnanimous outpouring toward them at the war's end that rebuilt both the social structure and the economies of both nations. At the time that America chose this course of grace toward former enemies and gave generously to them and to other needy nations around the world, our own wealth and position in the world began to soar.

Could it be that a reversal of a public policy that endorses giving to those in need, near to home, and elsewhere tracks along with a downturn in any nation's economy and a diminished status in the eyes of the world? I believe it could. I believe it happens in the eyes of God as well.

Pharisees and leaders in Jesus' lifetime studied God's Word continually as a way of life, but it seems they studied it as a book of rules to be enforced to the letter of the law instead of as a revelation of God's love and grace. Although Jesus pointed out that they did not lift a finger to live that way themselves, perhaps the Pharisees found the enforcement of the letter of the law in the lives of others a personal pathway to personal power, prominence, and influence rather than into fellowship with our heavenly Father (Matt. 23:4; Luke 11:46). The Bible says that the letter kills. Second Corinthians 3:6 (NIV) says, "He has made us competent as ministers of a new covenant—not of the letter but of the Spirit; for the letter kills, but the Spirit gives life." The Pharisees certainly seemed more interested in killing Jesus than in loving Him.

It seems imperative as nations and as individuals to make a decision about the nature of God and how we are to think and behave if we are to be like Him. Throughout history, the rigid and legalistic study of the Bible as a book of rules instead of a revelation of a good God has led humankind far away from the love and compassion Jesus showed to the world. The Pharisees longed for a Messiah, but they did not know Him when He stood before them. They knew the rules, but they did not know the Lord.

Sadly it would appear that humankind ever reverts to the norm. Until the Lord comes back, the norm in the world is Satan's program. A review of history would indicate that the norm is a society that shapes its leaders to rule with the attitudes and policies of the Pharisees. Our nation has shown itself able to choose another course, a course of compassion and generosity, during at least one period of its history. May God help us to walk carefully before Him in these challenging times and to hear and obey His voice today.

It seems important for each one of us to settle these questions: Is God a harsh and judging God, ever enforcing the law? Is He a God who wants us to be harsh and judging and ever enforcing the law? (See Matt. 7:1–5; Rom. 8:1; Matt. 25:31–40; 1 John 3:11–18; Matt. 18:19–22.) Or is He a loving, caring, and forgiving God, who wants us to be loving, caring, giving, and forgiving people?

> By this all men will know that you are my disciples,
> if you love one another. (John 13:3a AB)

Chapter Eleven

Salvation Operationalized

Getting the Program Up and Running

How does this blessed plan of salvation actually work in day-to-day living? In some ways it is like the transfer of vast sums of money through one of the modern means of communication. You may not actually see a truckload of green paper bills shipped from one bank to another when a large money transaction takes place, but an enormously significant event occurs nonetheless. And it is done simply on the basis of words that are communicated, requesting that it be done.

Great riches are transferred from bank to bank on the power of a few written words that are believed and acted upon by the people to whom they are addressed. The same thing is true about our redemption in Christ. When we read the message on the pages of the Bible, we can believe it, receive it, and cause it to come to pass. Or we can reject it and prevent it from happening in our lives.

Great riches of far more value than money can become ours by a brief transaction involving only a few words that begin with a phrase as simple as "Pay to the order of ...." By our simply saying out loud, "Yes, I receive Jesus as my Savior," and meaning it, we bring about an eternal change in our lives. Once completed, that transaction totally changes our legal status in this world and the next.

Through Jesus, God has given us, men and women alike, power to become sons of God (John 1:12). We have the power, by faith, to exchange everything that is wrong (sin) in our lives for everything that is right (righteous) (2 Cor. 5:21; 1 John 1:9). Immediately, we are empowered and guided by the Holy Spirit to begin the process of being transformed by the renewing of our minds (Rom. 12:2; John 16:13). A brief examination of the process by which we receive physical healing will give us a good example of how things work in other areas of our lives as well.

Let's assume that you and I both just strained our backs. Our senses tell us that our backs hurt; therefore, we need to be healed. Though our bodies send us signals of distress or disease, the Holy Spirit highlights words in the Bible, saying that "with his stripes we are healed" (Isa. 53:5).

Because we now trust the Bible and not what we experience in this world to tell us what the truth is, we exchange the old belief that pain in our backs means we have back trouble or that an aching in our heads means we are subject to headaches for a new reality. The new reality says that God wants us well and already has a healthcare plan in place.

Our new belief is that we are healed. We are whole and healthy. We have exchanged the brokenness of our bodies for the wholeness of Jesus' body. We did it by proclaiming our faith in the Bible's words that say we are healed because of the stripes He endured. Put another way, we withdraw the blessing of healing from the account of blessing bought on the cross and deposited in our own names. We do it by speaking with faith our request for healing to be withdrawn from our account in the Spirit and delivered into our lives in the natural arena. That is our "Pay to the order of ..." required procedure.

We usually do not have a literal paper trail involved in the kind of faith transaction that brings healing, but it is a very solid reality in the Spirit. The point is that we actually have to do it. We have to transact the business with God and submit our request by faith (Matt. 7:1–11). We cannot be passive, believing that if God wants to heal us, He'll heal us. He has already made every provision for our healing through the Passion and death of Jesus. Now we must take the initiative. We must act. We must transact the exchange of what is wrong in us for what is right (righteous) in Jesus. The exchange became possible at the point when we believed and received and entered into the covenant our Lord made with us when He said, "This is my body broken for you," and "This cup is the new covenant in my blood."

At this point, let me encourage you to let your mind just soar through the heavens with God like an eagle flying high and looking down on the earth below while you wrap your mind around the idea that you are healed. Let the picture you see of your life become big. Let your understanding of salvation grow huge and wide.

You are healed because the Bible says you are healed. It says that "by whose stripes ye were healed" (1 Peter 2:24). Healing is just one wonderful aspect of the great and total exchange of everything wrong (sin) in my life and yours for everything right (righteous) in Jesus' life (2 Cor. 5:21). Through His torture and execution, Jesus took upon Himself—He experienced in your place and mine—everything from which you will ever need to be saved so that He could give you everything about Himself that was perfect and good in exchange.

Everything that happened to Jesus from the moment He declared Himself in covenant[7] with us during the Last Supper until His resurrection from hell on the first Easter morning forms the basis of a transfer of priceless treasures from Jesus to us (Matt. 26:26–28; Mark 14:22–24; Luke 22:20; 1 Cor. 11:25). Isaiah tells us that "with his stripes we are healed." Think of the value of health that is transferred to us by those words when we believe and receive them as meaning just what they say.

Salvation and everything covered by the plan of salvation came to us by our simply deciding to believe the Bible and saying, "Yes, I believe that, and I receive it for myself." Perhaps you said, "Yes, I believe Jesus is my Savior, and I receive Him." All the other blessings we need are found *in Christ.* They are contained in the plan of salvation, and they are transferred into your account (into your life) the same way that our first understanding of salvation came to us—by believing and receiving, by proclaiming that Bible promises are true and deciding to accept them. Let's look at another example of this exchange.

Are You Lonely?

How are the riches of salvation made ours? How is a particular thing that we need identified as something provided in the plan of salvation, and how does it then become ours? Well, let's just pick out a problem that occurs in people's lives and then look for the answer in Jesus' Passion and death.

Let's assume that your family has just moved to another state and you are lonely and want to make new friends. The thing you need, the commodity or resource or gift in this case, is favor and acceptance by the people with whom you would like to be friends. You want to be accepted by the people that you want to like you. At the same time, perhaps you would like more freedom in your life to cultivate new friendships. Don't we all want more of that? So how do we receive acceptance, favor, and freedom into our lives through the work of the cross?

Salvation from the loneliness part works like this: Jesus experienced rejection in a huge and total way when the people responded to Pilate's offer to free Jesus by choosing Barabbas instead (Matt. 27:15–26). Jesus was not chosen. The people rejected Him. They did not want Him. They were not interested in having a relationship with Him. All those people made it clear that He was not someone they wanted to be a part of their lives. He was rejected, not by one person, but by a whole mob of people at one time. Standing there in front of them with Pilate, it must have felt to Jesus that He was being rejected by everybody.

Jesus endured the pain and devastation of rejection in a total way—absorbing and experiencing it deeply and completely, just as Satan plans for all of us to do. He experienced being without friends. He experienced being alone. He experienced it deeply and completely on your behalf and mine so that He could take upon Himself the fact of it and the feelings of it. He endured the pain it caused and all of the crippling effects that such an experience causes in a person's heart and life. He bore the grief and sorrow caused by that rejection so that He could take it out of your heart into His own (Isa. 53:4). He exchanged His peace and confidence and acceptance for our rejection and grief.

Jesus experienced our loneliness when every one of His closest friends abandoned Him and ran away. He had not a friend or advocate left in the world to plead His cause in that court of terrible injustice. And then, when the whole unspeakably horrible experience was coming to an end on this earth and He hung near death on the cross, His heavenly Father abandoned Him as well—leaving Him to suffer alone—leaving Him utterly desolate as He hung there on the cross to die alone (Mark 15:34). That has got to be one of the most heartbreaking moments anyone ever experienced in all of eternity. Indeed, it may have been the crushing hurt it took to kill the mighty Prince of Heaven. Matthew 27:45–46 says, "Now from the sixth hour there was darkness over all the land unto the ninth hour. And about the ninth hour Jesus cried with a loud voice, saying, Eli, Eli, lama sabachthani? that is to say, My God, my God, why hast thou forsaken me?"

Jesus was forsaken, abandoned, and rejected. Even Peter, one who was so close to Him, denied ever knowing Him. Jesus went through all of that so the sorrow and grief that such experiences cause you and me could become His, and the love and acceptance and honor and desirability that were His may become ours (Isa. 53:2). Clearly, Jesus will always be accepted in heaven; but He went to hell, where you and I belong, so that heaven would give us the welcome due to Him. You receive all that and much more when you receive Him into your heart. You receive all He is and all He has for all eternity.

At the time rejection was experienced by Jesus, the mob of people whom He had blessed and fed and healed chose Barabbas to be released when they could have secured Jesus' freedom. There was no freedom for Jesus. He was in captivity and not free to do anything at all of His own choosing. Indeed, His freedom grew less and less as the hours of His Passion slowly passed, until He was nailed to the cross and His freedom to move even His hands and feet was gone completely. He wasn't free to wave the flies off of the bloody wounds on His face. Hanging there on that cross with blood oozing from the thorns down into His eyes, He was bound, powerless, and helpless. What a way to purchase the freedom we long for in our lives.

Jesus was rejected on earth so that you and I may always be certain that we are accepted into the family of God (Eph. 1:6). That acceptance that Jesus paid such a high price to obtain for us also is to be ours here on this earth. He was spurned and scorned by the entire mob so that the love and favor that should have been His everywhere He went might rest upon us all the days of our lives. We mentioned at the beginning of this example a desire for more freedom to cultivate new friendships, so we are taking note of the fact that Jesus provides that as well. He was bound so that we might be free.

Chapter Twelve

⟶•⟵

Salvation Works *Now*

Salvation is Forever More and More and More

G rowing up, I used to believe that healing happened back in Bible times because Jesus was here on the earth. I thought that the process of getting us all healed would be perfected again when we go to heaven, but that it was not for now. I do not believe that anymore. I know that Jesus purchased healing that is for us today. Acceptance and friendship and fellowship are also for us today. So is favor ... and so is freedom.

We can be comforted about and healed of every painful experience of rejection that has ever happened to us in the past because Jesus suffered it for us. Then even when no other person is nearby, we have the Bible promise that He will never leave us nor forsake us (Heb. 13:5). And as though that were not wonder enough, we are also assured that we shall always, always, always be accepted in the future and be loved by God (Eph. 1:6). This is a belief that has been taken out of the realm of a theological idea and brought right down to the experiences I have today and every day. Jesus was completely rejected so that you and I may be *completely accepted forever.*

How Jesus Meets Our Needs

The example of how Jesus won our salvation from the pain of rejection discussed in the previous chapter is only one of the many needs Jesus met for us on the cross. It follows the pattern we need to understand in order to see how we are saved from every kind of problem in life. Jesus became sin so that we could become righteous. Jesus died so that we may live. Jesus' body was broken so that our bodies might be made whole. He was reviled, ridiculed, and rejected so that we may be received, honored, cherished, and respected. Jesus suffered the lack of all things as He hung naked there on the cross so that we might enjoy vast blessings and abundance through His exceeding great and precious promises and His meeting of all our needs (Phil. 4:19; 2 Peter 1:2–4). Jesus took all that suffering upon Himself—and much, much more—so that He could save us from it all.

Jesus submitted to Satan's plan for His torture and death. In that state of humble submission, He experienced rejection and everything else that happened to Him without sinning in any way. He won the victory over temptation and the devil that we needed to win. That victory is what sets us free. Jesus took the consequences of our defeat so that He could give us the rewards of His lifetime of victory over sin and Satan.

It was our defeat at the hands of Satan in the Garden of Eden that allowed our enemy to conquer and control humanity and put all of us into bondage. Satan deceived us and defeated us, and in so doing, he gained a great deal of control. But Jesus defeated Satan and won back our freedom, even though He was playing the game—fighting the battle—inside the area that Satan controls here on this earth and strictly according to Satan's harsh rules. He won the victory, even though He was operating in Satan's vicious world system the entire time that He was fighting to complete the work of the cross without sin of any kind.

In the Belly of the Whale

Jesus told His followers that no sign would be given to them except the sign of the prophet Jonah, who spent three days and three nights in the belly of the big fish. I believe that those three days and three nights that Jesus is referring to are the three days and three nights that Jesus spent in hell—that is, under the authority and power of the devil in hell. As the prince of this world, the devil gained control of the world's system that has dominated humankind from the day of Adam's sin until Jesus redeemed us. The authorities and powers of this world—the sinful systems and organizations that are in the world—are under the dominion of the prince of this world. They operate in the world largely according to the devil's plans and rules, except in the lives of Christians who obey the Holy Spirit.

Until the time of Jesus' arrest, the evil prince of this world had no hold on our Lord (John 14:30). He had been able to accomplish nothing whatsoever in the life of Jesus to bring Him under the control of sin. Jesus' victory over him was complete. Once Jesus entered into covenant with us at the Last Supper, He was joined with us in our bondage to Satan's systems. Being swallowed up by the evil, dysfunctional systems of this world is like being swallowed by a monster. Can you imagine a Savior who loved us so much that He volunteered for the job?

Using the example here that Jesus experienced rejection so that we could experience full and loving acceptance in the kingdom of God, we see the pattern for how the plan of salvation applies to our daily needs. The plan of salvation is revealed in the Bible and fulfilled at the cross. We search the Bible for the things we need, and then we search through what happened to Jesus at Satan's hand to see how He provides our needs for us. Finally, we believe it and receive it by faith. That is, we "write the check" in prayer and lay claim to the wonderful blessings that are ours in Christ, our Savior, and then we walk in the confident assurance that it is ours. That's what it means to walk in faith.

When I feel rejected, I look through the Bible for assurance that I am accepted by God. And what do I find? I find the lovely words that Paul wrote, telling us in Ephesians 1:6 that God's grace is so glorious that He "hath made us accepted in the beloved." Isn't that a beautiful phrase? By simply receiving Jesus as your Savior, you can be assured that you will never be rejected by God. You are accepted now among those who are beloved of God—and you always will be!

When Jesus took rejection, He took more than just rejection by God. He took rejection by men. It was not God who shouted words of rejection to Pilate as Jesus stood there before the mob. It was people who rejected Jesus and chose Barabbas. When Jesus took rejection for us, He took all of it. He was rejected by humanity and forsaken by God. He took it the way it had to be taken for us to be delivered and saved from it. He took it perfectly. He took it well. He took it completely. He did the whole job of forever overcoming the power of rejection to hurt us or damage our lives.

Again, let it be said that this account that describes Jesus' rejection represents the pattern for how He gives us whatever kind of salvation and help we need. He was rejected so that we might be accepted. We read that in the Bible; we believe it; we affirm it aloud by faith (the Bible says we confess it, which means to speak it aloud and proclaim it as truth); and we trust in God to bring it to pass. That is the process we need to understand. That was the process that brought us salvation (Rom. 10:9–10). *Everything else we need is acquired the same way.*

There is so much wealth available for us in the gift of salvation that Jesus died to give us. He died that we might live. His body was broken that our bodies might be made whole. He became sin that we might become righteous. He was abandoned by everyone and forsaken by God as He hung there so that He could promise us that He would never leave us nor forsake us (Heb. 13:5). He became weak that we might be strong. He was bound that we might be loosed (John 18:12; Isa. 61:1). He was overwhelmed by sorrow that our joy might be full (Matt. 26:38; John 15:11; 16:24). There are so many more ways that Jesus suffered to provide us with the things that we need and the things that our hearts long for. Every way we'll ever need to be helped is covered in God's plan of salvation.

My Precious Covenant with Jesus

All of the pages that follow are my testimony of what Jesus has done for me. I am going to share with you the little notes scribbled all over the margins of my Bible and all of the little, yellow sticky-pad notes I began to use when I ran out of room on the margins. With matchless joy, I share with you all that God has shown me in the beautiful verses of the fifty-third chapter of Isaiah.

As I studied this chapter, it did not take long for me to realize that Isaiah shows us only some—only a glimpse—of what Jesus took to the cross for me and for you and of what gifts He gives us to replace the sin, sorrow, and suffering He takes away. It has been a wondrous unfolding revelation.

I know that Jesus has much, much more to show you personally out of your own Bible study, but what is written here is what He has given me so far. Almost every day He gives me more. It has transformed my life and the world I live in—and the lives of others who have used this as a kind of recovery program from misery and sin. So let's study God's Word together to learn more of what Jesus went to the cross to give us. And let's do it in a structured way so that we really stay with the study until God can establish a re-creative work in us and restore us all to mint condition like Adam and Eve on their first day in the garden.

From this point on, the material is arranged in seven steps, in much the same way it unfolded for me in my own daily devotions:

1. A title is given to each new study topic.
2. A Scripture verse is quoted. (In some cases, only a portion of a verse is used.)
3. A problem situation commonly encountered in life is described.
4. The Bible passage is commented upon.
5. The Bible principle is stated.
6. A verbal affirmation is offered with the suggestion that it be proclaimed as true and reaffirmed over and over, flowing through the day like a refreshing stream to bless all that occurs.
7. It is recommended that you keep a notebook in which to record your affirmations and make brief notes about the wonderful new things God continually shows you about salvation.

Over the period of our studies together, we are going to learn what it means to take hold of God's Word and see that it is the truth no matter how extravagant the promises are. We are going to see that God's Bible promises contain everything we shall ever need (Phil. 4:19; 2 Peter 1:3 NIV). We are going to learn about the power of affirmations—the power of proclaiming God's Word as the truth. Doing it, actually experiencing it, is the only way to know for certain where the truth in life is to be found. When you do, it is transforming.

Saying a promise from the Bible right out loud before all the hosts of heaven, and accompanying its words with a declaration that we believe what we are saying, is affirming God's Word. It is an affirmation. The Bible uses the word *confession* to describe this kind of speaking (Rom. 10:9–10; Phil. 2:11). One well-known Bible teacher describes this process as *proclaiming* God's Word and declares it to be a vital part of the prayer life of every believer. Or you may think of it as standing before God as a prophet in your own life, declaring the Word of the Lord like a king's proclamation of what will be in your life.

Affirming the truth of God's Word can change the climate of our hearts. It can change the world inside our heads, and it can release the power of God in our lives to change the circumstances of the world outside, in which we conduct the business of living. Affirming God's Word is expressing faith. When we learn to express faith consistently, we have the Bible's assurance that we have the power to overcome the world (1 John 5:4). How is that for a solid promise on which to build your life?

Speaking God's Word aloud into our own ears all day long has a surprising amount of power to clear the atmosphere in which we live and replace it with God's love. For the next few days, your assignment—should you choose to accept it—is to give your own ears the opportunity to hear good news come out of your own mouth long enough to cheer you up. To do so will turn your whole life in a new direction. As a matter of fact, it is designed to make you whole, brand-new, and beautiful.

For Emergencies: Try This 21/21 Program

Every day I try to remember to take vitamins. Normally I take only one vitamin C tablet, but if I feel cold symptoms developing, I may take up to four of them; and then again, an hour later, I take four more. It is called a "therapeutic dose." Effective prayer comes in therapeutic doses as well. The 21/21 regime we are about to present on these pages may be viewed as a therapeutic dose of God's Word for people who really need to see change in their lives. It is especially helpful for those who suffer from significant depression or other difficulties like bondage to addictions. It may not be necessary for everyone to follow it every day, but it will offer marked benefits for you if you are having a bad day, and it will bring real change for those who are in serious trouble.

Olympic athletes around the world and others in sophisticated athletic training programs of various kinds use affirmations (positive statements spoken aloud) in powerful ways. Businessmen, salesmen, and ordinary citizens are using positive affirmations daily, hearing their own voices making positive statements that may or may not be based in the Bible. The straightforward use of a daily affirmation probably would be a healthy permanent addition in nearly everyone's life.

Affirmations are an integral part of formal therapy programs of many kinds and are useful in recovery from addiction. If you are earnest about wanting change in your life, this book and the daily affirmations it contains can be upgraded to a program of serious therapy. The more often you repeat the affirmations, the greater will be the change that occurs in your life.

When he uses this material in counseling, my husband recommends that each morning a person should read the daily affirmation three times into a recording device and replay it throughout the day. The first time, record the day's affirmation as a flat statement of fact as printed on the pages that follow. Make the second repetition a statement directed to yourself as though spoken to you by someone else. The third time you record the affirmation, make it an "I" statement (see examples below).

- Example one: "God's promises are true and eternal and unchanging, and every Christian can rely on them completely."
- Example two: "Connie, God's promises to you are true and eternal and unchanging, and you can rely on them completely."

- Example three: "I know God's Word is true, and I rely on His promises all the time."

Notice that there are slight changes in the three versions of the affirmation. If you prefer to change the affirmation only enough to make the second one a "you" statement and the third one an "I" statement, that is fine. However, as you go along in the program, it will become more powerful if you think about it a little bit and personalize the third statement so that it truly expresses what is in your own heart. You may want to shorten the third one so that you can remember it easily all day long. Or you may want to add a favorite Bible verse to support your affirmation. Remember that the Holy Spirit is continually at work in us, helping us to grow in our faith and understanding. It is comforting, encouraging, and powerful to ask for His presence and participation day by day as we work.

Once you have completed the recording process, replay the tape, listening to all three versions of the daily affirmation in the car, while working, at mealtimes, at bedtime, and whenever possible throughout the day. The next morning, just record over yesterday's three affirmations with three new ones and start again. In working with a person who is really earnest about wanting to change his or her life, Charles encourages the replaying of the tape seven times each day. If that seems like a large assignment, remember the number of repetitions athletes build into their physical training programs each day. It will encourage you to actually do the work. If you do, you will see the results you want.

Using this "spiritual" training program, you will affirm your faith twenty-one times every day for twenty-one days—hence, the name *21/21 Program*. It is helpful, indeed powerful, to hear your own voice affirming aloud your trust in the Lord and in the Bible over and over. You are affirming constantly and in detail your faith in what Jesus has done for you. Faith builds steadily. Remember that when you begin a new program of physical exercise, by the end of the first day or two you may feel more tired and not less. But strength builds quickly, and people have reported that they feel a real difference in a few short days.

It is important to note that some people learn best by taking in information through their ears, just as we do in listening to a recorder. Others work much more effectively through their eyes. For folks who operate best visually, it is helpful to write the daily affirmation on a card each morning and keep it handy. If you do this, look at it as often as possible throughout the day. Put the card on your desk, where you can see it easily. Or keep it in your shirt pocket or purse so that you can pull it out and read it every time negative thoughts try to flood your brain. And do remember that even though you may be a strongly visual type of person, there is power in speaking the words aloud; so be sure to include that step.

If you are making a daily recording, you may want to reread the affirmation from your card while you are listening to the tape (though not while you are driving, of course). Writing or speaking aloud along with the intake of ideas through both the eye and the ear will activate three separate lobes of the brain. Everyone is unique and different. You may be best helped by seeing or hearing or speaking each day's affirmation repeatedly throughout the day. Whatever you decide is right for you, please be careful to begin each day by repeating the affirmation for that day aloud, as it is written, at least once. As you go along, you will soon see what is most helpful for you and that is what you should do.

Change the Script Inside Your Head

The value of positive, daily verbal affirmations has been well documented in mental health research. The reason is clear. All our lives negative thoughts tend to run around in our heads, and for some people, these thoughts are believed to be constant. Such negative "voices" are believed to have a powerful effect upon us, even when they contain little truth. The chemistry of the brain and the body can be changed by them so that our physical health is damaged and our performance is impaired by the destructive impact of our own habits of negative thought. To replace them with positive thoughts is not easy. It requires a sustained effort to change any kind of habit, but the results are well worth the investment of any amount of time you may give to it (Rom. 10:8–11).

In addition to the use of daily affirmations, journaling may be enjoyable at the end of each day's study. Just as speaking aloud the words of salvation when we confess Jesus Christ as Savior adds power to the faith that is in our hearts, writing down new ideas will support rapid growth. Please take time to make notes, even if you only copy the affirmation word for word. If you can rewrite it in your own words, so much the better. It will support the work you are trying to do. Jotting down other thoughts will enrich your experience and encourage you later as you look back over your notes.

What follows in the remainder of this book is not intended to replace your regular Bible reading program, whatever that may be. Rather, it is intended to supplant the poisonous ideas of negativity and defeat that run around in our heads all of the time. By using these daily affirmations from God's Word, we can permeate our thoughts with positive reminders of God's good and loving gifts and promises. As we do that, we build our faith. And faith is the key to overcoming everything that we have to deal with in this world (1 John 5:5).

It Works ... *If You Really Do It*

There is a real challenge here for you. You *can* change your life. Do you want to? Do you believe it is possible? The Bible says it is. It says, "Therefore if any man be in Christ, he is a new creature: old things are passed away; behold, all things are become new" (2 Cor. 5:17). Do you want to see that promise work in your world and in your life?

It takes twenty-one days to hatch an egg. Can you give God a few short weeks to change the climate in which you conduct your daily activities from now on? Remember, it is the climate that determines what will flourish and thrive and what will wither and wilt. Have you already spent much of your life dealing with defects and defeats? Are you willing to invest three weeks to see if all that can change? Read a little every day. Speak aloud a new verse from God's Word and say a quick affirmation of faith in that Word all day long whenever you think of it. Beginning today, do it for three weeks, and see what changes occur in your life. Meanwhile, be encouraged by these remarkable words:

> Now the God of peace, that brought again from the dead our Lord Jesus ... make you perfect. (Heb. 13:20–21)

Part 2

A Christian Study Series

A Study Series
Isaiah 53
(New International Version)

1. Who has believed our message and to whom has the arm of the LORD been revealed?
2. He grew up before him like a tender shoot, and like a root out of dry ground. He had no beauty or majesty to attract us to him, nothing in his appearance that we should desire him.
3. He was despised and rejected by men, a man of sorrows, and familiar with suffering. Like one from whom men hide their faces he was despised, and we esteemed him not.
4. Surely he took up our infirmities and carried our sorrows, yet we considered him stricken by God, smitten by him, and afflicted.
5. But he was pierced for our transgressions, he was crushed for our iniquities; the punishment that brought us peace was upon him, and by his wounds we are healed.
6. We all, like sheep, have gone astray, each of us has turned to his own way; and the LORD has laid on him the iniquity of us all.
7. He was oppressed and afflicted, yet he did not open his mouth; he was led like a lamb to the slaughter, and as a sheep before her shearers is silent, so he did not open his mouth.
8. By oppression and judgment he was taken away. And who can speak of his descendants? For he was cut off

from the land of the living; for the transgression of my people he was stricken.

9. He was assigned a grave with the wicked, and with the rich in his death, though he had done no violence, nor was any deceit in his mouth.

10. Yet it was the LORD's will to crush him and cause him to suffer, and though the LORD makes his life a guilt offering, he will see his offspring and prolong his days, and the will of the LORD will prosper in his hand.

11. After the suffering of his soul, he will see the light [of life] and be satisfied; by his knowledge my righteous servant will justify many, and he will bear their iniquities.

12. Therefore I will give him a portion among the great, and he will divide the spoils with the strong, because he poured out his life unto death, and was numbered with the transgressors. For he bore the sin of many, and made intercession for the transgressors.

Study One

⟶⇒●⇐⟶

Facing the Truth

A CHRISTIAN STUDY SERIES

Today I choose to believe that the Bible is true.

THE SCRIPTURE: "Who has believed our message … ?" (Isa. 53:1a NIV)

A PROBLEM SITUATION: We all grow up in human families. Both parents and children are imperfect, so we are not always cared for as well as we should be. Our deepest needs may not be noticed. So by the time we are grown, stress and problems are the norm. It is true in the lives of advantaged as well as disadvantaged people. It is true of everyone.

We all develop the ability to push on through the inner feelings of stress that we often have when confronted with painful or upsetting things. Everyone has to learn how to do it so that we can get on with the business of living. We learn to do it early. It becomes a habit. It is not so easy, however, to learn how to push through the mixed-up ideas we come up with when trying to understand *why* those painful and upsetting things happen to us growing up. Without fully understanding the difficulties with which we struggle, we may spend a long time in adulthood trying to make sense of all the things, right or wrong, that we "learned" as children.

One of the characteristics of imperfect families is that we cannot deal with the truth. We cannot face the truth about how much of our lives do not seem to work right. We cannot admit it to others or to ourselves, so we try to hide it—often in shame and embarrassment.

For example, few of us can face the truth about how much fear we have. It just seems to be there so much of the time. We have fear of failure, fear of rejection, fear of embarrassment, fear of dying, fear of being alone, fear of painful disappointments, and so on. The *feelings* of fear are common to us. We learn to push through them. We learn to do what we have to do in spite of them. But we seldom examine the *ideas* that cause the feelings.

As adults we need to learn how to push through our childhood *ideas* the way that we have learned to push through our childhood *feelings*. The problem is that the way we manage to push through upsetting feelings is by learning not to pay attention to the ideas that come with them. We learn to ignore them. We cannot cope with them because thinking about them adds to the stress.

Facing the Truth

There are lots of things we cannot face. Often we cannot face being truthful about the ways we offend other people. We cannot cope with being truthful about how injured we are by the ways people we love have hurt us. It is hard to admit that little things in life like a forgotten promise or not being heard are wounding. Above all things, that kind of truth threatens the tenuous balance we have managed to establish in all of our relationships. So everyone colludes (that is, agrees without saying so right out loud) simply to ignore certain disturbing truths. We never mention them.

Ignoring things is not the only way that we learn to handle disturbing thoughts. Most of us learn to adjust the truth to make it more comfortable. One result of this lifelong training in dissembling (manipulating the truth for our own unstated purposes) is that we do not accept what other people say as the truth. In blunt terms, we color the facts all the time, so we expect others not to tell us the truth.

As small children, most of us learned that we cannot trust everything that is said to us. Being skeptical becomes such a habit that we scarcely are aware we do it. It is one of those ideas developed in childhood that we seldom push through to see what is behind it.

Often we find ourselves thinking that something being said to us is "too good to be true." In other words, we don't believe it. We do not trust what people say to us. We form the habit of wondering about almost everything, especially the good things that are said to us. We question whether or not it is the truth or how much of it to believe.

One of the sad outcomes of mistrust is that we are afraid to look forward to something wonderful happening. We don't trust our own happy excitement. We harden our hearts to joyful anticipation. We learn to expect disappointment by trying to be prepared for it all the time. When it looks like something could be absolutely wonderful, we draw back and rein in our enthusiasm because disappointment hurts so much. We have learned to be cautious. We have learned to be skeptical. It is so painful to be disappointed that we learn to question anything that seems too good to be true.

When something seems too good to be true, often it really *is* too good to be true—*but not in the Bible.* The wonderful promises in the Bible are just the opposite of all of the things that we have hoped for and have been disappointed by everywhere else. The gifts and solutions promised to us in the Bible are *more* true than our best hopes (Eph. 3:20–21). They are more and better than we think possible (1 Cor. 2:9). They are more wonderful than we, at first, can understand because of our life-long experiences with disappointment in this mixed-up world.

The Bible is such a wonderful book. It accurately reflects, on its own pages, the fear and reluctance people have to receive and trust good news. At a recent Christmas gathering, our son Chip gave a brief devotional in which he underscored the difficulties that people have in accepting good news. Have you ever tried to share the blessing of salvation with someone who told you that God would have to send an angel directly to him for him to believe? I have. Chip pointed out that even when God sends us good news through an angelic messenger, we have difficulty being joyful. Zacharias doubted the angel's message that he would have a son (Luke 1:18). Mary was "troubled" when the angel appeared to her (Luke 1:29). And the shepherds out on the hillside were "sore afraid" when many angels flocked around (Luke 2:8–18). For many of us, good news is hard to accept no matter how it comes.

Soften Up

The apostle Paul wrote a large portion of the New Testament. He tells us in Hebrews 3:13 to "encourage one another daily, as long as it is called Today, so that none of you may be hardened by sin's deceitfulness" (NIV). All of the people who lied to us and disappointed us in the past were sinning. We have been deceived and disappointed so many times by that kind of sin that we have gotten tough. We have grown hard. That hardness leads to death, not life. We must not permit past disappointments to cause us to have an untrusting, unbelieving heart.

In the same passage in Hebrews, Paul writes, "See to it, brothers, that none of you has a sinful, unbelieving heart that turns away from the living God" (Heb. 3:12 NIV). Give God a chance. Give yourself a chance to receive from God the wonderful things that Jesus died on the cross to give you. They will be yours through faith ... and faith means you decide to believe that what the Bible says is the truth and you can live by it.

Only you—no one else in the entire universe—only you can decide to give God a chance to show you that He is real. Only you can allow God to show you that salvation is something wonderful and good. Only you can allow salvation to happen in your own individual life.

At the very beginning of the fifty-third chapter of Isaiah, this great prophet acknowledges the suspicious and unbelieving state of mind found in most of humankind. He asks a question. His question suggests that we may be tempted to discount the good news that is to follow. It suggests that we'll do it in the same way that we do it with other things that look "too good" to us in this untrustworthy, untruthful world. But his question also encourages us to get ready to believe something wonderful. I believe Isaiah's question is God's question to you and to me today: "Who has believed the message?"

COMMENTS: Jesus was fully a man. He was like us in every way ... yet He was God interrupting history by coming into our world Himself to rescue us from harm and danger, from disappointment and distrust. Who can dare to believe that such a wonderful message can be true? Let's take up the Bible's exciting challenge.

Everything in the Bible that is promised to us is obtained "by faith." It is important for us to make a firm and rational decision to believe it, to actively believe it.

Try it. If it is not true, what have you lost? Perhaps little more than the pain of disappointment, and we know from experience that we can survive that. But if it is true, and you do not try it, then think of what you have lost.

I believe, because you hold this book in your hands and your eyes are running over its lines of print, that God has a message especially for you on its pages. I believe that He has personally put it into your hands. He has arranged for you to have it because He loves you and wants you to see how much Jesus loved you when He came to save you. He wants you to know how many good things the Lord arranged to give you when He died on the cross for you.

It Is for *You*!

What does God have for you? He has salvation. He has the plan of salvation. God's plan of salvation has much more to offer than most people ever come to understand. It is absolutely wonderful. No matter what you have heard or think you understand about the Christian plan of salvation, I plead with you to take the time to read through the rest of this book ... and to read your Bible. I believe that it will show you so many good things that God wants to give you and do for you that you will be amazed.

Many people who own computers only understand and use a small part of what the computer was designed to do. That is because they do not understand how much more it offers and no one has taught them how to use it. The plan of salvation is the same way. Most of us understand only a small part of what it is capable of doing for us. We need to study our Bibles the same way that we have to study a computer manual if we want all of the programs to work for us. When Christians take the time required to become "Bible literate," the way we have learned that we must do to become computer literate, there will be a wonderful unfolding of what is there for us. Eye has not seen nor ear heard what has been prepared for us (1 Cor. 2:9).

Salvation Is Perfect

Could a perfect God ask for the sacrificial death of Jesus in a great and dramatic intervention in history that turns out not to work very well? No! It is unthinkable. He is God. His plan of salvation is perfect. It offers salvation for everything from which humankind needs to be saved: feelings of sadness, loss, failure, ugliness, inadequacy, and bondages like addictions or fear or poverty—just everything! Moreover, one cannot imagine God designing salvation to be like a perfect piece of machinery that He could create in laboratory conditions somewhere only to find that He couldn't make it run properly out in the real world.

God is more than able to develop, promote, distribute, install, and operate His wonderful plan at your house and at mine. The salvation Jesus bought for us is complete and perfect, down to the smallest detail. But there is a problem. Most Christian do not cooperate with God long enough to get Christianity up and running!

Our manufacturer's service representative here where we live is the Holy Spirit. During the time that we are working together on this Christian Studies series, we can be assured that we have His total attention. Like a personal coach or trainer, the Holy Spirit will guide us (John 16:13). That is a promise Jesus Himself made to each one of us.

With the help of the Holy Spirit, we will explore the vast—perhaps undreamed of—capabilities of the plan of salvation. Jesus joined His voice to that of the great prophet Isaiah by asking who of us dares to believe this wonderful message (John 12:38). God has also challenged us to do it through the prophet Jeremiah by saying, "Call unto me, and I will answer thee, and shew thee great and mighty things which thou knowest not" (Jer. 33:3).

A PRINCIPLE: Jesus died for you. He died to give you salvation. He died to save you from everything from which you need to be saved. The salvation plan He offers you is a program that works. It is a program designed to reverse the destructive effects of sin and restore you to mint condition so that you can fulfill God's wonderful, exciting plan for your life. The first thing that you must do is decide to believe the good news when the Bible asks you, "Who has believed our message?"

AN AFFIRMATION OF FAITH: "I choose to trust in God. I choose to believe that the Bible is God's Word that is full of wonderful promises put there by God for me. I expect to see God work powerfully on my behalf because the Bible promises He will and I believe what the Bible says. I look forward with joyous expectation to the good things God is doing in my life."

Confident and Trusting

A CHRISTIAN STUDY SERIES

My Father's strong arms protect and provide for me.

THE SCRIPTURE: "… and to whom has the arm of the LORD been revealed?" (Isa. 53:1b NIV)

A PROBLEM SITUATION: Thousands of years ago, David the psalmist wrote, "I was young and now I am old, yet I have never seen the righteous forsaken or their children begging bread" (Ps. 37:25 NIV). I believe he is saying to us that in all his life, he never saw God fail to provide what His people needed. The mighty arm of the Lord gives us confidence and trust in the same way that the strong arms of a good and loving earthly father will do.

Not every child grows up in a home with a loving, responsible father. Many children are abandoned, neglected, or abused. What is Jesus' solution for this problem? He takes upon Himself the hurt and damage resulting from inadequate human fathering and makes a way for us to enjoy the care and love of His own perfect heavenly Father.

Some time ago I saw a Christian television program that showed a group of powerful young men doing great feats of strength. They lifted weights. They split thick pieces of wood. They lifted tables with lots of weight, and even people, on top of them. As each young man did his work, the television camera zoomed in close and showed the great muscles that rippled along his shoulders and upper arms. It was impressive. These strong men doing great exploits evoke the same kind of picture that Isaiah encourages us to think about when we imagine the strong right arm of God undertaking to do something mighty and wonderful for us.

My memories of my father as strong and entirely reliable to protect and provide for me gave me a very secure and comforting sense of safety all the years I was growing up. Never once did I doubt his strength and protection. I was quite grown up before I realized what a blessing and gift that assurance was. Many people do not have that feeling of safety and security. Even in early years, so many people are fearful and do not have anyone to turn to when something threatening occurs.

A good father's strong arm lifts us and carries us in childhood; we may fall asleep on his shoulder. As adults, many of us do not have anyone to turn to when we are exhausted and depleted, no strong shoulder to rest on. A strong daddy always assures us of his ability to provide what we need. He handles tasks that overwhelm us. There are some of us who do not have that kind of loving support now and did not experience very much loving care in childhood. We need to have it. We need it all of our lives.

A loving father picks us up and throws us up in the air. What a thrill I remember that to be. He carries us on his shoulders so that we can see over the crowd. He pushes us on a swing and climbs trees to retrieve kites and balls and kittens. His strength and skill add a cherished dimension to our play in childhood and to everything we do as happy

148

children. Our heavenly Father wants to be everything to us that our human fathers were and everything that they were unable to be.

Our heavenly Father has a strong and mighty arm to provide for us, protect us, carry us, play with us, solve problems for us, and help us to grow in assurance of safety and plenty. Never, no matter how old we become, do we outgrow the need for that kind of a father. If our lives were not blessed by having an earthly father who gave us sure confidence in the strength of his arms, then we above all others need to have the loving and powerful arm of the Lord revealed through His constant loving care for us.

COMMENTS: Have you ever wanted to live in a big house and be the child of an important man with everything wonderful that you need provided in grand style? Have you ever wanted to feel safe and abundantly provided for as a cherished son or daughter? A significant part of the good news of salvation is that when you receive Jesus, that is exactly what happens to you.

One of the most wonderful things about being the child of a very important person is that in childhood or adulthood, if you have a problem, your father can help you. He has resources and influence. He knows people and can open doors. He has priceless wisdom and counsel that are available to his own beloved children at any time of the day or night. He always wants what is best for you so that you do not have to be suspicious or on your guard in your relationship with him.

I believe with all my heart that God designed and created the very idea of the role of a father when the first plans for creating the world came up in heaven so that He could show us what He wanted to be to us throughout our lives. He wants to be a strong protector, a constant help, a mighty provider, and a close and loving parent all in one. There is nothing He cannot do for us. He is almighty. There is nothing too hard for Him (Gen. 18:14; Jer. 32:17; Luke 1:37; John 14:14; Eph. 3:20). Jesus Himself told us that (Matt. 19:26; Mark 10:27; Luke 18:27). All in all, He is the ideal storybook father.

In our previous study's comments and Bible passage, we talked about Isaiah asking us whether or not we would believe the wonderful message. Who can dare to believe that such a wonderful message can be true? Now in today's scripture, he is asking, "Who will see—*really see*—God's power at work in his life?" Jesus quotes Isaiah and challenges us with the same two questions (John 12:38). If I will be a person who chooses to believe God's amazing message of salvation and all it means in my life, then I will be one of the people who sees His powerful arm at work on my behalf. And so will you.

A Beloved Child

At times I long to lay down adult responsibilities so that I can be a beloved child picked up in a father's strong arms and safely carried. It is a wonderful idea, no matter what one's age might be. And that is just what God wants to be for you today. It is all there for us. Everything has been provided. The amazing and wonderful words of the apostle Paul in Galatians 3:26 (NIV) make the matter clear. He says, "You are all sons of God through faith in Christ Jesus."

By taking your place and mine on a sinner's cross, Jesus ceased to experience life in this world as the powerful Son of God; He no longer functioned on earth as the perfect, sinless Son of God. By stepping out of that position, He made a way for us to step into it, into the amazing role of God's beloved son in whom He is well pleased. Jesus offers each one of us the way to become God's beloved child, in whom the Father finds pleasure (Matt. 3:17; 17:5; John 1:12). Jesus died to make it possible for God to take His place in our lives as the perfect

Father we all need. Our job is to make the transaction, to transact the exchange at the cross that makes you and makes me God's child.

Jesus was the firstborn of many brothers (Rom. 8:29). Does this mean that the message is only for the "guys"? Of course not. Paul tells us in the passage quoted above from the third chapter of Galatians that we are all sons of God through faith in Christ Jesus. Since he assures us in the very next verse (Gal. 3:27) that in God's kingdom there is neither male nor female, women are included in the category of sons. God is *our* Father. Jesus said so (Matt. 6:9).

A few sentences later, in the fourth chapter of Galatians, verse 6, Paul explains that "because you are sons, God sent the Spirit of his Son into our hearts, the Spirit who calls out, 'Abba, Father'" (NIV). "Abba" is the personal word that means "Daddy," even today in the nation of Israel. When Jesus taught His disciples to pray, He began by saying, "Our Father," and thus includes each person who prays to God in His name as one of those privileged to call God "our Father."

In His wonderful exchange on the cross for us, Jesus submitted to all of the natural deficiencies in the parenting we experience in this world when, for the first time, He came under the domination of our "father, the devil" during the three days of His Passion (John 8:44). He did it so that we could call a loving God "our Father" (John 8:38–47). He paid a high price for us to have a good Father. May we experience every part of the blessing He intended this exchange to be for us. May nothing He suffered be in vain.

A PRINCIPLE: The strong arm of the Lord is revealed to those who, through faith in Christ, choose to believe God's Word and call Him "Father."

AN AFFIRMATION OF FAITH: "I affirm that God is my heavenly Father. His strong arm accomplishes mighty works on my behalf because He loves me. He has made a place for me in His very own family. That special place, prepared just for me, is mine today and will be mine forever" (John 14:2).

Study Three

Fragile and Vulnerable

A CHRISTIAN STUDY SERIES

Jesus understands because He has been there.

THE SCRIPTURE: "He grew up before him like a tender shoot, and like a root out of dry ground." (Isa. 53:2 NIV)

A PROBLEM SITUATION: We are fragile and vulnerable when we arrive in this world. We are tender and needy ... needing to be nursed and nurtured continually ... needing to be hugged and held and surrounded by loving faces that beam with delight on us. We are like timid little plants that push up fragile shoots of green in a desert. If we are to grow, someone somewhere has to supply the water again and again until our roots grow strong enough to reach deep into the earth and find the water that's there.

Often there is no one able to take care of us. Perhaps no one cares to bother. More often, there is enough care given to keep us alive but not enough for us to thrive. So instead of being robust and full of vigorous life, we are fragile and delicate. Our lives are precarious.

The remarkable words of today's scripture found in the second verse of Isaiah 53 tell us that even Jesus grew up experiencing neediness. "He grew up ... like a tender shoot, and like a root out of dry ground" (Isa. 53:2 NIV). A root trying to grow in dry ground is needy. It needs water.

Neediness is not reserved exclusively for people living in poverty. Wealthy, privileged adults and children also experience deep needs that are not met. Some time ago I watched a rebroadcast of a show about the early life of Gloria Vanderbilt, wealthy heiress of Cornelius Vanderbilt. Though she was born to wealth and surrounded by well-known people, Gloria had a terrible childhood. In the midst of great abundance, little happened to make her feel safe and cherished.

History gives us many accounts of the children of wealthy and powerful people who grew up abandoned to the impersonal care of servants or indifferent relatives. Certainly wealth and prominence do not protect us either in childhood or adulthood. Catherine the Great of Russia may have become one of the most powerful women in history, but her life was one bereft of care and nurture. Thousands of similar stories exist throughout the pages of history.

Rich or poor, obscure or famous, everyone grows up with unmet needs. All of us can remember times when we crawled into our beds at night feeling sad and neglected. We hugged our dogs or clung to a teddy bear or curled up around a pillow for comfort. Often the little heart of a child is broken over things adults dismiss as insignificant.

The universal response of men and women everywhere is to minimize the unmet needs and hurts of childhood. We have to do it because growing up is a demanding business. We can't cope with it when we are upset. So we try to pay no attention to unmet needs and minimize the things we can't ignore.

We may minimize or ignore our own hurts or those of others, but God does not. In His sermon to the people of the little town of Nazareth, where He grew up, Jesus said, "The Spirit of the Lord is upon me, because He hath anointed me to preach the gospel (good news) to the poor." The passage He is quoting from Isaiah goes on to say, "He hath sent me to bind up the brokenhearted" (Luke 4:18, quoting from Isa. 61:1). As the plan of salvation unfolds in the fifty-third chapter of Isaiah, it is clear that it addresses the lifelong needs that begin in childhood and continue as long as we live.

COMMENTS: Jesus grew up fragile and vulnerable—just as we all did—in a system that did not supply all He needed. A plant that sprouts in a desert is trying to grow in a deprived environment, in a place where it will experience thirst. Jesus got no special "breaks" in life because He was the Son of God. He had to cope with everything that we have had to cope with. Surely Jesus experienced hunger, thirst, fatigue, and cold. He was needy and easily hurt, just as we all are. But unlike us, none of that ever made Him sin. It did, however, make Him deeply compassionate toward us (Luke 13:34; Heb. 4:15). Out of that deep compassion, He was able to make a way to rescue us out of a life of pain and unmet needs.

A PRINCIPLE: When Christians are taught about salvation, they learn that Jesus took away the sins of the world. Most of us understand sin to be some kind of offense that we have committed against God or one another. We know that Jesus died so that we could be forgiven for our offenses. As wonderful as that is, we often fail to recognize that there is more than that to salvation. We do not realize that things like our hurts and unmet needs fall far short of the glory (the glorious goodness) of God and therefore are contrary to God's will for us (Rom. 3:23). In other words, they are sin. Missing God's mark of perfection makes them a sin even though no guilt on our part may be associated with them. We may not be responsible for the fact that they occurred in our lives. Still they are sin. Often they result from someone else's sins. Jesus died *to take them away.*

As surely as He died to take away the sins for which I am guilty, Jesus died to deliver me from all sin. Jesus took away the sin of the world—all of it (John 1:29). That means that when my Savior went to the cross, He took all of my hurts and unmet needs with Him. In their place, He gives me His wonderful healing and provision. The healing of my broken heart and the supplying of all that I need are fundamental parts of the plan of salvation. Philippians 4:19 says, "But my God shall supply all your need according to his riches in glory by Christ Jesus."

AN AFFIRMATION OF FAITH: "Jesus understands how I feel. I trust Him when He tells me something because He has been through what I have been through. He loves me, and He died to help me. I give Him all the neediness in my life. I give Him all of my hurts. I trust my Savior to heal my broken heart and supply all of my needs."

Beauty for Ashes

A CHRISTIAN STUDY SERIES

I am desirable, and I am an important person.

THE SCRIPTURE: "He had no beauty or majesty to attract us to him, nothing in his appearance that we should desire him." (Isa. 53:2b NIV)

A PROBLEM SITUATION: The sexual aspect of who we are is so strong and so compelling that I do not think many of us quite know what to do with it at times. When sexuality is dysfunctional, it can bring pain and distress. When it is working properly, it attracts us to the beauty and desirability of the lover we have chosen, and he or she is equally attracted to us. We find one another altogether lovely and desirable.

In its natural course of doing business, this world seems to expend a great deal of effort trying to teach each one of us that we are *not* lovely, *not* desirable, and *not* attractive as we grow up. I am so glad that Jesus explained to us that the world does not deal in the truth (John 8:44). Still, almost all of us believe that particular lie—so many people tend to feel ugly and unattractive.

Over the years, I have occasionally worked with my husband in his counseling practice when requested to do so. I have shared his astonishment in discovering how often even the most attractive men and women have a poor or distorted self-image and see themselves as undesirable and even ugly. Few efforts to undermine our joy have been more successful than this one.

It is hard to deal with life when you feel undesirable and unattractive. When we go through day after day feeling ugly, we seldom get good news about ourselves. It can seem very unfair. Many of us are secretly angry that others appear to be attractive while we do not. We grieve that we are not desirable enough to attract the person who attracts us. It can be a crushing way to feel.

Other problems can stem from this matter of feeling plain and drab. Charles and I have found many individuals in secret pain because of problems related to the inability to express physical or sexual love. It is our conviction that every person must believe he or she is truly attractive and desirable to be able to function well sexually.

If people do not really believe themselves to be attractive, they often do not feel free to express sexuality. People who question their own beauty, whether male or female, may tend to be embarrassed by their sexuality. If embarrassment is present, sexual responses do not flow spontaneously as they should. They become blocked or frozen. When that happens, people seem more apt to do dysfunctional things to permit the release of sexual tension. For example, they may depend on pornography so that the beauty and appeal of another person triggers a sexual response that should result from a sense of their own attractiveness and the realization that it is pleasing to the person they love.

Dysfunctional sexual behavior can be a substitute for feeling beautiful and majestic. Those who engage in it do not experience the wonderful blessing of a shared and reciprocal passion that

God planned when He developed His original idea of sexuality. In the kind of sexual experience that we believe expresses God's design, both partners feel beautiful and powerful. They have a glorious sense of joy, not only in their partners but also in themselves.

The Cross and Sexuality

The King James Version of the Bible translates today's quotation from Isaiah as saying, "He hath no form nor comeliness; and when we shall see him, there is no beauty that we should desire him." Of course, we assume it is written about Jesus while He was in the hands of his torturers. His body was torn by the whip. His beard was ripped right off His face (Isa. 50:6). The rest of His face was black and swollen from many blows. His whole body was torn and loathsomely repugnant. He was stripped of any kind of desirability as a man. Among all the other awful things that He suffered for us, He experienced the vicious destruction of His comeliness, beauty, and desirability. Is it not true that so much of the ugliness found in humankind comes from our woundedness?

Remember that we are saying in this study that the things that happened to Jesus lay out for us a clear picture of the evil plan that God's enemy has in mind for you and me. One by one, they reveal the pattern for the cruel things the dysfunctional systems of the world try to accomplish in every person's life. The systems of this world are designed and operated by Satan to implement his "anti-salvation" plan in our lives the same way he did in Jesus' life as soon as he got Him into custody. That being true, you can see that the world has made it a special goal to strip you of your feeling of beauty and desirability.

Never forget that Satan is a liar. The primary weapons he uses to steal from you are lies. Jesus Himself explained that fact to us in John 8:44. Remember too that sorrow and shame soon quench sweet passion. Sadness and bitterness and pain can wipe beauty from any face. Jesus' plan of salvation addresses all of the ways that damage has been done to our beauty, desirability, and sexuality. It also explains the seeming injustice that some people appear to have beauty that others lack. The world (and remember who is in charge of the world's goals and objectives) teaches us to have significant cultural bias when it comes to beauty and desirability.

COMMENTS: We can choose right now, this minute, to put our faith to work and receive all that salvation provides for us, including beauty, desirability ... and also, majesty. In just the same way that Jesus took away our sin, sickness, and fear of hell, He also took away our unattractiveness and lack of desirability. That is an amazing and wonderful revelation. But as marvelous as it is, there is more!

The son of a king inherits the majesty of his father. He is born to it. As a son (or daughter) of God, so should you. You should move through your life with all of the dignity and majestic bearing of royalty. You should carry yourself as a king or a queen. It need not be done in an overbearing way. We do not "lord it over" one another, but we do carry ourselves with elegance and poise.

How avidly people and circumstances work to undermine all sense of majesty within us. No matter how the world has tried to rob you of the beauty that God created you to have, Jesus restores it to you ... and He does it by taking on Himself all lack of beauty and all lack of majesty and all lack of desirability or attractiveness your unhappy life manages to produce. Then He freely gives you His own beauty and majesty in place of that lack. It makes perfect sense when you think about it. Because we are made in His image and likeness (Gen. 1:27), beauty and majesty must be significant parts of who we are—*every single one of us.*

It is interesting to consider the significance majesty has in this matter of attractiveness and desirability. The powerful business tycoon, the prominent political person, the famous entertainment star, or the glamour queen carry a kind of attractiveness that is compelling. It is a well-known phenomenon that people fantasize about being attracted to people of power and fame and glamour. I believe it is because people who are famous and successful carry themselves in a different way and present themselves in a different way in the world. They wear their bodies in a different way—a way that makes them more attractive, more full of life, more free, and more interesting in every way, including sexually.

Majestic is a good word for describing qualities of confidence, power, and significance. God created man (and woman) in His image and likeness (Gen. 1:26–27). When God made us in His image, it had to mean that He meant for everyone to be majestic, because God is majestic. Jesus is the King of Kings; so if He is to be my King, then I, too, must be a king. Kings are just naturally majestic, and you should be too.

Your Beauty Is Bought and Paid For!

While Jesus was in the hands of this world's cruelest kinds of tormentors, He was stripped of His beauty and also of His majesty. And it happened so that He could provide you and me with those lovely qualities. Just as He took my sin and gave me His righteousness, Jesus took my lack of importance as a person so that I may have a measure of the majesty of God that will mark me as one of His sons (Gal. 3:28).

On that cross, Jesus had nothing to make Him desirable. He permitted that to happen so that He could make a way to give me His beauty. Isn't this a wonderful revelation of His love and care for each person to whom He has given life? And there is so much more that is just as wonderful about what He has done for me on the cross. I have learned that I may see each thing that happened to Jesus as a part of the great exchange that took place at Calvary—including this wonderful promise of beauty.

Let's go over it one more time. It is too wonderful not to repeat. We believe that Jesus took our sins to the cross so that He could give us His righteousness, taking everything wrong so that He could make everything right. We understand that He suffered punishment so we could be absolved of guilt. He laid down His life so each believer may take up a new life. It is all a part of a wonderful salvation.

In this case, what Jesus took upon Himself is my lack of significant personhood (or majesty) and my lack of physical or spiritual beauty and desirability. In return, He has made us kings (Rev. 3:21); invited us to rule with Him (Rev. 5:10); provided crowns for us to wear; and given each of us attractiveness, beauty, and desirability.

There certainly is enough beauty and glory and majesty and radiance residing in Jesus for everyone to be lavishly supplied with these lovely qualities. We have a wonderful and generous Savior, who has things to give us that we do not yet know enough to ask for (1 Cor. 2:9). Our Lord took away everything about you and me that is drab and plain and dull and lackluster, replacing it with radiant glory and beauty.

The author of Hebrews tells us that Jesus is absolutely glorious in every way. He is exactly like God and resembles Him in every way. Hebrews 1:3 (NIV) describes Jesus as "the radiance of God's glory and the exact representation of his being, sustaining all things by his powerful word. After he had provided purification for sins, he sat down at the right hand of the Majesty in heaven."

God is described as "the Majesty," and Jesus is described as His exact representation. So was Adam, who was created in the image and likeness of God (Gen. 1:26–27). Everything right and good about Jesus has been given to us in exchange for all that is imperfect and flawed in us. It has to be in order to restore us to His perfect image and likeness (Gen. 1:27). We find all that we need "in Him," waiting to be exchanged for specific areas of lack in our lives. A generous supply of everything that everyone will ever need to be fully "factory rebuilt" the way that God intended us to be—in perfect mint condition—has been given to us in Jesus Christ. And it comes to us in a free and endless supply. It was poured out upon all humanity when the blood of Jesus (the life is in the blood) was poured out upon the dust of the earth on Golgotha's hillside (Lev. 17:11, 14).

It is wonderful to realize that in this amazing fifty-third chapter of Isaiah, these matters of personal majesty and beauty are dealt with before sickness, sorrow, poverty, and even transgression, iniquity, and sin. It is given an important place in this classic Old Testament account of the benefits and meaning of the atoning work of Christ. When quoting from Isaiah 53, many people begin with verses 4 and 5. Perhaps we will not be so quick to do that in the future. Verses 2 and 3 are precious indeed.

A PRINCIPLE: Jesus became grossly repulsive and undesirable in every way by taking on Himself the ugliness of every person who ever lived so that He could give us beauty; desirability; and lovely, majestic dignity. No matter what the world tries to teach us, the Bible says that God created us to be like Jesus, and that includes everything that is beautiful and desirable. He was demeaned and humiliated, despite the fact that He was God's Son, the Prince of Peace. The Father loved the Son and gave all things into His hand (John 3:35). Yet Jesus made Himself to be as nothing so that He could freely give us all things (Rom. 8:32). Think of it! It's wonderful! "All things" includes beauty and desirability and majesty. There is a new supply of His grace and beauty every morning. Just as the tabernacle priests reenacted the ritual of the sacrifice of the lamb every day, we can receive everything the life of Christ contains new and fresh every day because He was the Lamb without spot or blemish.

God's plan of salvation is so wonderful and works so well that He has perfect confidence in its power to redeem me and make me what I ought to be. He has placed in my hands responsibility to rule and reign with Christ in my own life (Rev. 3:21). In my own special and unique area of life and ministry, the Lord asks me to take charge. I am able to be responsible and powerful because Jesus was stripped of His majesty and power. It happened so that He could give those vital qualities to me.

Jesus was humiliated so that I may carry myself with lovely, majestic dignity. He was debased and disgraced so that my life can reflect the regal bearing of a child of the King ... and yours can too. And just tuck this away in your heart, though it is the subject of future study: Jesus became abjectly helpless, hanging on that cross, so that we might receive power from on high to undergird the majesty we receive from Him (Acts 1:8). This is important because we have great things to do for God in the world.

AN AFFIRMATION OF FAITH: "Jesus was brought low so that I may be raised up. Jesus became all that was ugly so He could make me beautiful and desirable. Every morning I receive a fresh supply of the beauty of the Lord along with His righteousness and grace. All that is lovely comes from Him (James 1:17). God made me in the image and likeness of Jesus, who is perfect. Though I do not 'lord it over' others, I encourage others to carry themselves as I do, in a regal manner befitting a brother or sister of the Prince of Peace. I know that I have significance and value to Jesus, so I am important and precious and beautiful."

———◆———

Welcomed and Accepted

A CHRISTIAN STUDY SERIES

God accepts me and welcomes me as a member of His family.

THE SCRIPTURE: "He was despised and rejected by men." (Isa. 53:3a NIV)

A PROBLEM SITUATION: The most powerful single characteristic that mental health professionals have found in many unhappy families is the all-pervasive denial practiced by everyone in them. I am persuaded that one of the most compelling reasons why all of us are in so much denial is that we are nearly overcome by broken hearts. We are so broken inside that at times our ability to keep functioning is tenuous.

Sorrow and grief would overwhelm us if we allowed ourselves to face squarely and unflinchingly the truth of all that has happened to us and all that it means. Moreover, we cannot bear to face the fact that many people have little love for others and we ourselves may be secretly despised or rejected even by some of those close to us. We may be even more dismayed and stricken to find those same feelings residing in our own hearts.

How can we deal with truth when it is so full of pain and sorrow?

We can't! So we don't!

We practice denial—we hide our faces from the pain we see in those around us. This allows us to practice intolerance and discrimination toward others, and to experience it ourselves. How we all long to be respected and valued and precious to others. And yet, how hard it is to see our fallible fellow creatures in that light, to see them as deserving of the same respect that we want so much.

There is built into each person God has created a deep need and desire to be honored and respected; yet we find many people hard to respect. It is so easy to judge, disdain, or despise another person. Perhaps it is because of race or gender or status or culture ... or maybe those things are just smokescreens for inner repugnance or alienation that we cannot name or understand. Perhaps negative feelings toward others spring from disagreements over political views or religious affiliation or because of behavior, foolish choices, ignorance, unreliability, or even sloppiness or laziness. And yet, how very painful it is to be a person who is looked down upon.

What Goes Around, Comes Around

There is an even more disturbing aspect to this matter of despising another person. To despise someone else, we have to judge him or her. Jesus tells us that we cannot do that except at great peril, for with the judgment we judge, *we shall be judged!*

If the truth were fully known, we would find that few of us could stand the close scrutiny of others. We all need a savior. Thank God we have one. Thank God we have a salvation great enough to deal with every problem and need we have. And one of the more serious problems we fail to recognize is our harshness in judging and criticizing others.

There is an idea that pops up in my mind rather often, an idea that is more than a little bit disturbing. I imagine a clear picture inside my head that all the rules and expectations and judgments I have regarding other people are carefully written down in heaven so that one day all my actions can be reviewed to determine not if they measure up to God's demands—after all, He has already forgiven me everything in Christ—but to the demands by which I have judged and criticized others.

The idea that I will one day have to stand and be judged by my own harsh standards makes the words of Jesus in the Sermon on the Mount in Matthew 7:1 very sobering indeed. He tells us to "Judge not, that ye be not judged. For with what judgment ye judge, ye shall be judged: and with what measure ye mete, it shall be measured to you again."

The people we criticize, we often despise. When we place ourselves in the lofty posture that anyone assumes who despises another, we'd best beware. The day will come when we in turn will be despised. It happens to everyone. Thank God ... again, I say, thank God ... we have a Savior who loves us enough to save us when others despise us and when we are being despicable.

COMMENTS: Jesus was despised and rejected so that I may be accepted and cherished. Jesus was despised and rejected so that *you* may be accepted and cherished.

The leaders and brokers of power in old Jerusalem did not respect or accept Jesus. They hated and despised Him in the most vicious kind of way—enough to kill Him! He fully understood the nature of their evil intent toward Him (Matt. 16:21; 26:2; John 16:30). Jesus allowed Himself to become a helpless victim in their hands. He did it because He knows that is what we often are, helpless victims in the hands of others who are cruel, yet powerful in our lives: a parent, a boss, a teacher, an older sibling, a neighborhood bully, an unethical policeman, a political dictator, or even a spouse. Jesus became powerless, without status or influence, so that you may have status, the status He should have had, and so that you may be crowned with glory and honor (Ps. 8:5).

Everyone who reads Titus 2:15 will find the Bible saying, "Do not let anyone despise you." That is a flat statement of command, isn't it? When you read or hear something like that, do you ask yourself how you can control whether or not someone else despises you? It doesn't sound possible. But consider this: Jesus made provision two thousand years ago for just such a situation. He was despised so that you would not have to be.

How does the fact that Jesus was despised protect you from being despised? Despising a person is a process that requires someone to receive as much as it requires someone to give. You have to *be* despised—you have to accept the idea that you are despised and the feelings that accompany it—for the social transaction to be complete. Don't accept it. Give it to Jesus instead. When no one turns on the faucet, there is no water. If there is nothing connected to an electrical outlet to receive the current, none flows, even though it is all there behind the wall. Nothing happens until we plug in to the power, until there is a flow that completes the circuit. Do not receive the message that you are the sort of person who is despised. According to the Bible, it is not the truth. Believe what the Bible says instead. The Bible truth is that you are loved.

Psychology would tell you that you do not have to accept the attitudes and feelings that come at you from another person who would despise you. A therapist will tell you that you have a choice and that choice gives you a measure of control. Most of us have seen other people discount and reject all kinds of positive feedback and compliments when they were given. They would be happier if they made a decision—allowed themselves—instead to accept the good things being said to them.

We are learning that it is possible to reject negative things the same way, by making a conscious decision not to accept them. We can choose to deflect them to the cross and give them to Jesus. We can consciously and deliberately turn them over to Jesus. Making that choice is a huge help, and many of us probably practice it as a mental exercise throughout the busy commerce of daily living. But at the end of the day, in the quiet moments before we sleep, feelings of hurt and shame, rejection and failure, may try to overwhelm us. Often at those times we are challenged by anger and unforgiveness. When that happens, it is the exchange that Jesus offers us at the cross that is the answer to our problem.

Our secret is that we divert the flow of all that would wash over us to Jesus as He hangs there on the cross in our place. You cannot be despised if you do not receive it even for one minute. When a person despises you, scorns you, hates you, or offends you in any way, you can turn your thoughts immediately to the cross. See yourself kneeling there at Jesus' feet. Picture everything that flows toward you and over you as you experience being despised. Then use the wonderful gift of imagination that the Lord has given you to see a great transfer take place. As you whisper aloud the wonderful Bible promises that the Holy Spirit whispers to you, you will experience our Savior's love as He takes away painful things and heals the brokenness in your heart (John 14:13–14).

Transfer everything that has happened to you over to Him—and with it, all the dismay and shame and rejection and pain—and then all the thoughts that roil around in your mind whenever your memory replays any part of what happened to you. Give it all to Jesus as He hangs there. Exercise your faith that He has the power to take what you give to Him and keep it (Isa. 53:4; Matt. 26:38; 2 Tim. 1:12). Let the full depth of the hurt pour into His heart. Let the full measure of confusion and powerlessness to do better or to do anything over again become issues He owns while you receive the mind of Christ and let the love of God be shed abroad in your heart (Phil. 2:5; Rom. 5:5).

Then, as you kneel there, picture His precious blood falling upon you drop by drop, knowing that all that Jesus is becomes all that you are in the greatest exchange in all the history of the world. His life in all its perfection is contained in His blood, and it becomes yours as it flows over you there at the foot of the cross.

While you are there beneath the cross because someone despises you, make it a special point to receive from Jesus all of the honor and love and respect and acceptance that are due to Him as the Son of God. Those things flow from the cross continually. When you receive Jesus, you receive all of Him. The honor that belongs to Him, the love, the respect, and the acceptance you need are all parts of who He is. When you receive Him, you receive it all.

All of this is one example of what it means when Christians encourage one another to "take it to the cross" when times of stress, hurt, and trouble occur. You can take it all *to* the cross because Jesus took it all *on* the cross. Jesus took all these things for you as He hung there—for you and for every other person who ever lived or will live. You can give it to Him at once.

At this point in reading through this material, one person urged me to clarify what is meant by the phrase "take it to the cross." In addition, he thought it was important to provide a sample prayer that might be prayed when kneeling there, seeing myself in my imagination on my knees on the dusty ground at the foot of the cross. So we have taken his suggestion to heart, and here is the prayer:

> Lord Jesus, I was with a person today who dislikes me, thinks badly of me, and acts as though he (she) secretly makes fun of me. It hurts me. It is embarrassing and humiliating to be with someone who

has this scornful attitude toward me. So I come to You with my pain and shame.

I kneel before You, Lord Jesus, remembering that You hung on the cross covered with shame and humiliation. You were filled with pain. You experienced the same kinds of anguished feelings that I am having. In a mystery I cannot fully understand, Your experience grew to include my experience, my pain and shame and helplessness. I cup my two hands together and lift them to You as though all my pain and shame were literally held within them, and I give everything to You.

As I lift my hands to You, I know that my distress is added to all the other pain You endured on the cross. Because You took it to the cross, it is removed from me, just as my sin has been removed and nailed to the cross with You. You took everything in my life that is contrary to God's will. You were hated and mocked and despised, and that is part of what killed You. Because You have already experienced all those devastating feelings for me, I can be free of them.

You have saved me completely from the hurt and shame of knowing that someone despises me. I forgive the one who hurt me. And Your love fills my heart and makes me whole as I receive Your glory and grace, new and fresh, into my life.

Once this process is in place in our lives—this process of going to the cross to give Jesus all of the large and small things we need to be saved from—it is clear that God really means to provide for all things to "work together for good to them that love God, to them who are called according to his purpose" (Rom. 8:28). It is "good news" indeed to know that when we give Him all of the things we are so glad to be rid of, then we can receive, in place of them, the wonderful qualities and feelings that make Jesus who He is. Our whole felt sense of who we are is transformed. The inner reality that is our conscious awareness is transformed, and the washed and wonderful sensation of inner peace that fills us at the moment of salvation becomes our daily experience of being alive.

Salvation: As Big As It Needs to Be

Jesus' suffering was big enough to encompass the greatest suffering anyone has ever endured. He is able to take to the cross all of the devastation of the most painful and destructive things that ever have happened to you. He takes upon Himself all of the negative impact and puts into your heart all of the positive impact that His perfect life gives Him the right to share. Through the great exchange of Jesus' righteousness for our sin, His blessings for our curses, His freedom for our bondage, God provides salvation from everything from which we need to be saved. *Absolutely everything!*

Whether you are the perpetrator or the victim, God's grace in Christ is great enough to take it all away. You are washed clean, as though none of it had ever happened (Isa. 1:18). Everyone—including the murderer, the prostitute, the terrorist, the rapist, the child molester—everyone can be completely free, as though he or she had never sinned.

One more point. It is interesting to note that the words in Titus say, "Do not let ..." We are admonished not to *let* anyone despise us. Those words imply that *we* have to do it. In John 14:27, Jesus Himself admonishes us not to *let* our hearts be troubled. At the same time, He makes it clear that we do not need to yield to troubling thoughts and feelings, because He has made His peace available to us. He gives us His very own perfect peace to replace the things that trouble our hearts.

Clearly, the Bible says that we are not to let ourselves be despised. We are not to let our hearts be troubled. If we are expected to do that, if we are instructed by the Lord Himself to do that, then we must have the ability to do it.

What is it that we have to do? When we have a need, we have to go to the cross in faith and receive what has been provided there. We cannot just know it or know about it. We cannot just understand it. We have to *do* it. We have to go through the procedures involved in actually doing it. We have to transact the business with God. Understanding it is not enough. We must actually do it. We cannot just wait passively for it to be put into our lives just because we see in the Bible that it is there for us. Faith without works is dead (James 2:20). We have to put our faith into gear and go to the Lord in prayer and transact the business with God.

In other words, we have to act. We have to go get what we need at the cross. We have to say, "Lord, I refuse to let my heart be troubled. I kneel before the cross and give everything that troubles my heart to Jesus as He hangs there. Then I receive from Him His very own perfect peace in exchange." Who among us can pray a prayer like that without weeping in gratitude for a Savior who loves us so much?

Everything we need has been provided. The plan of salvation is perfect. The work is complete. But I have found that it will not be apparent in our lives until we go and get it. We have to transact the business with God and then stand in faith when we are through, making our profession of faith strong and firm, declaring that the work has been done—and done perfectly and completely—by a perfect Savior who gives us a perfect plan of salvation.

I make the circuit of negative power complete by implementing Satan's plan when I let myself receive the scorn of the person who despises me. But I do not have to receive it. Instead, I can go quickly to the cross and plug in to God's plan of salvation instead. In that moment, I complete the circuit of power with God's plan of salvation so that the power of the cross flows into my life and heart. Jesus takes away the scorn, and into my life flows the honor and respect due to our Savior. *It happens because I took action.* We cannot just wait passively for God to provide what we need. Jesus finished His part of the work two thousand years ago. Now there is power in our hands when we act in faith.

Faith is the victory that overcomes the world (1 John 5:4). But faith without works is dead (James 2:20). Faith in gear and in action brings blessings to us from the cross. We have an indispensable role to play in working out our own salvation (Phil. 2:12).

Jesus tells us in Matthew 7:7 that we have to ask, to ask and to actively expect to receive what we ask for. In the next verse, He promises us that everyone who asks receives. What a promise! I believe God would like to give salvation and all of its benefits and blessings to everyone in the world. He does not do it because we have to ask before He will intrude into our lives. Just as we have to ask Jesus to come into our hearts and be our Lord, we have to ask for the benefits of salvation. When we need something, we must ask in faith—the same way that we received Jesus as Savior—and it will be ours. The thing we cannot do is be passive and wait and wonder why God always seems to send His blessings to others.

The Bible says He is King of Kings (1 Tim. 6:15; Rev. 17:14; 19:16). In His kingdom, everyone is a king. That means we take responsibility and rule in our own lives. The Bible is the law of the land and we enforce its decrees by faith in an active way. One law stipulates that everyone who asks receives. Our responsibility is to ask.

Ask! Ask! Ask! Jesus flatly declares that everyone who asks receives (Matt. 7:8). He did not promise that everyone would receive. He promised that everyone *who asks* will receive.

A PRINCIPLE: You can always come to the cross and give Jesus all of the pain you feel when scornful people ignore, despise, judge, or shun you. And you can leave your time of prayer with Him having been given His perfect and total attention, love, and acceptance. Then you can go out into the world carrying yourself with the assurance and confidence of a person who is loved and accepted in the highest and best of circles. From this moment through all of eternity, you may know that you are beloved of God and accepted into the closest kind of relationship with Him as part of His family (1 John 3:1). The Bible teaches us that the degree of our closeness with Him is determined by our choice to seek Him (Jer. 29:13; 30:21 NIV). As we draw near to God, He draws near to us. As we cry out to God, He hears and answers (Isa. 58:8–9 NIV).

AN AFFIRMATION OF FAITH: "Salvation is wonderful and complete. In Jesus, all of my needs are met when I ask. I am noticed, accepted, honored, respected, comforted, healed, and lovingly welcomed into God's presence and family forever. Jesus loves me and takes away all of my sin to free me from everything that prevents me from taking charge and taking responsibility in my own life to reign by faith in God's Word, in His exceeding great and precious promises."

Fullness of Joy

A CHRISTIAN STUDY SERIES

Jesus has a cure for my sadness and pain.

THE SCRIPTURE: "… a man of sorrows, and familiar with suffering." (Isa. 53:3b NIV)

A PROBLEM SITUATION: One of the great questions of all time asks why God allows suffering in the world. For years I asked myself that question. Way back in the early years of my marriage, my husband accepted a position as principal of a school for retarded and handicapped children. I was pregnant with my second child, and suddenly my world was full of people with tragic stories of babies injured at birth or born with defects. It was frightening. It was devastating.

Since I was raised in the home of a minister, my faith in God was intimately woven into the fabric of my life. But what I was seeing in the lives of families with handicapped children shook my faith. In fact, it was the strongest force in my life at that time that drove me to seek answers about God.

During the months of my second pregnancy, I found myself praying often to God about children born with birth defects.

They became the symbol of all suffering in the world. "These children didn't do anything wrong!" I would pray in anguish and maybe with a measure of anger, even fear. "Why did this happen?"

I could see only two possible explanations for the evil and suffering in the world. It certainly was indicative of my immaturity in life to believe that this great philosophical question of the ages had to be answered by one of the two simplistic explanations I came up with: "Either You do not have the power to help," I would cry out to God, "or You do not care." I could see no other possible explanation. But there is another one.

I was asking God a sincere question. In fact, it was one of the most fervently sincere questions of my whole life. And the Bible promises that God will answer us when we call to Him (Jer. 33:3; Ps. 91:15; Matt. 7:8). If you have questions, I encourage you to ask Him about what you want to know. But remember that most of life seems to be a process. God made it that way, so my rule of thumb is that since it takes twenty-one days to hatch an egg (create a little chick), I always try to give God at least that long to accomplish anything I ask of Him. In this case, to answer my questions.

So what was the answer that God finally sent? A very moving one indeed! God cares about the needs of the tiniest sparrow when it is hungry (Matt. 6:26). And He certainly is as powerful today as He has always been. But He gave us the gift of sovereignty when He created us in His image. We often do not realize it, but we have far more power and responsibility to actively choose what happens to us than we realize Deuteronomy 30:19 (NIV) states, "This day I call heaven and earth as witnesses against you that I have set before you life and death, blessings and curses. Now choose life, so that you and your children may live."

All Christians have the power and responsibility in Christ to take themselves out from under the power of evil in this world;

but if we do not use it, then by default we remain in bondage to an evil prince (John 14:30).

At the same time that Adam and Eve sinned by obeying Satan, they became slaves of sin. The children of slaves are also owned by the slave master. Adam and Eve put themselves and all of their children under his control (Rom. 6:16; John 8:34). What happened to Adam happens to us as a race and also as individuals. By obeying the devil day by day, we put him more and more firmly in charge. At every point where he has the power to do so, he puts his program in place.

Satan's program is driven by his goals. They are clear. Jesus tells us in no uncertain terms what they are. Satan, the thief, comes to steal and kill and destroy (John 10:10). He wants to take from us what God has given us. He wants to rule over us. He wants worship (Matt. 4:8–9). He wants power. And he tries to kindle those desires—for adulation and power over one another—in us. He wants to control us. And he does. Until we are saved (rescued, redeemed), the prince of this world runs the show. The only person who ever lived on this earth who evaded Satan's control entirely was Jesus (John 14:30).

When we choose Jesus, we are given an alternative plan for our lives, and we receive the power to implement it. Day by day, we have a choice. But without Jesus' redeeming power flowing continually in our lives, Satan is free to send trouble and tragedy, and we have little ability to resist him. So the answer to my question about why innocent children had to suffer was that humanity's choice of Satan's program of sin and rebellion worked like an election that put him in office—in power. Until we vote him back out of power by electing Jesus as Lord of our lives, we suffer under bondage and oppression.

Getting Free

The Bible teaches us that we have an enemy. Jesus calls that Enemy "the prince of this world" (John 14:30), suggesting that he has more than a little power to rule on the earth. From the first accounts of Adam and Eve being deceived at the beginning of the Bible to the great conflict depicted in Revelation at the end, it is a book about the conflict between good and evil, between Satan and God. It is important to realize that humanity, and not the devil, holds the ultimate power on the earth because God gave us the power to choose.

The devil is presented in the media as weird and powerful, but his primary power is to deceive—to lie and use his lies to create fear. Beyond that power, it seems that he usually has to use us as weapons against each other. Deception and fear keep the devil in power because he has us fooled so well and because he uses us so effectively to cause one another injury, pain, and loss (John 8:30–59).

In large measure, our enemy and oppressor chooses to control us through the power of the social systems, organizations, and groups in which we live. They exert constant pressure on us. They are relentless in efforts to make us conform to the expectations of the groups we are in. It is painful when we fail to measure up, when we do not comply with a system's demand. Why? It is painful because we are punished in all kinds of large and small ways for every infraction of group rules. If we continue in noncompliance, some systems will actually kill us, but most eject us or excommunicate us or make us fearful of being ostracized or shunned. It is frightening when we are rejected and excluded from one of the important social systems in our lives.

The Pharisees of Jesus' day headed up a powerful social system. They were totally deluded. They believed that they spoke for God in the world and perfectly represented His righteousness. And yet they knew God so little and understood His truth so poorly that when the Messiah they longed for stood before them in the flesh and spoke God's truth directly to them, they rejected both the man and His words. They hated Him on sight. And, like all social systems, they were so harsh in their punishments of those who did not agree with them that they were willing to be very cruel. They were willing to be vicious. They were willing to kill.

No argument that Jesus had with the Pharisees over the three-year period of His ministry brought any fundamental change to their rigid system. Some individuals, like Nicodemus (John 3:1–21), were saved out of it; but the system itself could not accept the most perfect presentation of truth and righteousness that the world has ever seen. All of the systems of this world are similarly corrupted by their own power and delusions. All are similarly cruel and designed to implement Satan's goals and not God's. The Holy Spirit is always at work in the world, representing God, restraining evil, and seeking to save and deliver humanity anywhere our choices provide an opening for Him to do so. However, Satan is the prince we have put in charge. Romans 6:16 says, "Know ye not, that to whom ye yield yourselves servants to obey, his servants ye are to whom ye obey; whether of sin unto death, or of obedience unto righteousness?"

Sorting Things Out

One of the challenges of my Christian growth has been the job of sorting through the teachings of my childhood—particularly those of the church. I now realize that some of the things that I thought were the teachings of a good conscience were, in reality, fear produced by the violation of a social system rule. One example comes to mind immediately.

When I was a child, the minister's family always sat in the same pew, right up front, because that pew had a brass plate attached to it that said "Pastor." We were always right up there where everyone could see every little thing we did or did not do. When I wiggled enough to make the old oak pews in our beautiful gothic church creak, my mother would direct one of her "looks" toward me. No words were needed. I knew that I was to sit still. So I grew up thinking that a truly righteous and godly person never moved a muscle in church during the sermon.

The struggles recorded in the book of Acts over the keeping of the law as opposed to the grace offered to us through the cross are perfect examples of the same kind of conflict. Thank God for the promise of Jesus that the Holy Spirit will teach us and show us what we need to understand (John 16:13).

Jesus explained that Satan's long-range goals are to steal, kill, and destroy (John 10:10). Satan uses all of this world's organizations and social systems to assist in accomplishing these goals. We go to work and to school every day, struggling to make our way in these systems all the time. They have vast ability to punish and cause us pain. As much as it grieves Him, God gives us perfect freedom to live and operate our lives in those systems if we choose to do so. But we do have a choice. Jesus tells us that we can be "in" them but not "of" them (John 17:13–16). In many cases, we can work productively and respond within them with grace and wisdom without giving them so much power to control us. However, there are some gangs and groups that we probably need to leave (Gen. 12:1).

Jesus urges us to seek the kingdom of heaven (Matt. 6:33). It is a totally different system. We do not have to choose the kingdom of this world (of Satan). Jesus offers us the kingdom of heaven as the only alternative to Satan's array of systems that exist in this world. An invitation to enter that kingdom is the most expensive gift ever offered. It is the gift of our freedom. It is the gift of our salvation. It was bought by the Passion and death of Jesus, and when we choose it, we are in effect turning away from Satan's "anti-salvation" program. By rejecting the world and its prince, we choose instead the way that God developed to rescue us from the stifling rules and roles open to us in whatever culture we experience growing up. It is also the way that He provides to free us from oppressive religious systems, systems like the self-righteous one that worked so hard to have Jesus executed.

The Sorrow of Other People's Pain

You may not be dealing with the tragedy of a child with a disability in the way that the parents who are mentioned at the beginning of this study were. Thank God I did not have to do that. But all of us cope with our own forms of loss and sorrow. The Bible is God's explanation to me of why He made me, what happened that gets me into trouble from time to time, and what He has done to get me out of it. There certainly is no doubt that I need to be rescued, for life can hold so much stress and sorrow that even the more capable among us find themselves unable to cope with it alone.

Some time ago, I was attending a lecture on family systems. The speaker, Terry Kellogg, made a statement that completely arrested my attention, and I lost track of everything else that was happening while I thought it over. He said that siblings—brothers and sisters in a family—often withdraw from closeness to one another deliberately. They squabble. They build barriers of distance because they cannot bear to be close to one another's pain. Something inside me said, "Yes!"

When we love and care about someone, it is very hard to see that person experience pain. The sadness of a person we love can hurt as badly as our own—sometimes more! Every mother knows that it is true of her relationships with her children. I believe it is the most painful part of the curse of Eve that women deal with (Gen. 3:16).

When we see others hurting and we feel helpless to do anything to help them, we can find it so unbearable that we begin to busy our minds with other things in order to close ourselves off from thinking about it. We decide not to be aware. It is too painful. It may even loom so large that we feel crippled by it and fear we cannot carry on. So we choose not to be familiar with the sufferings of others.

This world does not operate on God's plans and programs. Satan is the author of the social systems that dominate life on earth. That fact is demonstrated by the arrest, torture, and execution of Jesus. If the devil's goals are to steal, kill, and destroy, it is not surprising that sorrow and suffering are commonplace. Closing our eyes and our hearts to the sorrow and pain of others may seem essential to our own survival, but it is a terrible rejection to those who are hurting.

Jesus never closed His eyes or His heart to our pain. He not only is fully aware of our suffering, but also He reaches into our lives to remove it, to take it upon and into Himself, and to carry it away to the cross. That is how He saves us from it.

By the time that Jesus breathed His last breath, hanging there on the cross, He had become sin for us (2 Cor. 5:21). He emptied Himself of His righteousness because He gave it all to us. He emptied Himself of His glory because He gave it all to us (John 17:22). Only sin was left. Sin. Sorrow and grief and everything that comes short of the glory of God. That is what He was. As He hung there, He *was* Sin. He also was pain and sorrow and grief, the way a log becomes the fire when it burns, because those things are far from the will of God for the people He loves (John 3:16). They are a huge part of the sin that rules the world. In every way, sorrow and grief fall short of the glory of God.

Jesus took unto Himself all the sin of the world. He took unto Himself all of the sorrow and all of the grief as well (Matt. 26:38). In Matthew's gospel account, we see that overwhelming sorrow and grief were the first things sweeping over Jesus in Gethsemane after He entered into covenant with us in the upper room (Matt. 26:27–28).

What Jesus did for us staggers the imagination. I like to think that this great exchange is one reason why He went to hell. He had something to deliver back to the place where it belongs. I like to think about all that sin and sorrow and grief being deposited there in hell, where it came from, and staying right there in Satan's domain when Jesus rose from the dead. May it never be remembered anymore.

COMMENTS: Jesus died to free us from our own sin and pain and also from the sorrow we feel at the pain of others. Certainly He was a man of sorrow and acquainted with suffering, just as Isaiah described Him in our study verse. To be rejected and despised causes a deep sorrow to fill our hearts, no matter who we are. Jesus took that sorrow for you (Isa. 53:4). You can come to the cross, give it to Him, and receive His wonderful acceptance in its place (Eph. 1:6). He took every other source of sorrow upon Himself as well, and every form of suffering. Every form!

The conversation Jesus had with His disciples during the last evening of His life on this earth is recorded in the gospel of John. As they talked, He was trying to prepare them for what was about to take place and give them hope to sustain them during the terrible events that they were going to witness. He was trying to help them understand that the sorrow He was about to experience—and that they are about to experience with Him—would make Him able to give joy to all who will receive it (Ps. 126:5). But the disciples did not understand what He was telling them. The apostle John records for us what happened and what Jesus said:

> "In a little while you will see me no more, and then after a little while you will see me." Some of his disciples said to one another, "What does he mean by saying, 'In a little while you will see me no more, and then after a little while you will see me,' and

'Because I am going to the Father'?" They kept asking, "What does he mean by 'a little while'? We don't understand what he is saying."

Jesus saw that they wanted to ask him about this, so he said to them, "Are you asking one another what I meant when I said, 'In a little while you will see me no more, and then after a little while you will see me'? I tell you the truth, you will weep and mourn while the world rejoices. You will grieve, but your grief will turn to joy. A woman giving birth to a child has pain because her time has come; but when her baby is born she forgets the anguish because of her joy that a child is born into the world. So with you: Now is your time of grief, but I will see you again and you will rejoice, and no one will take away your joy.

"In that day you will no longer ask me anything. I tell you the truth, my Father will give you whatever you ask in my name. Until now you have not asked for anything in my name. Ask and you will receive, and your joy will be complete." (John 16:16–34 NIV)

With full knowledge of your sorrow and suffering, Jesus found a way to take it from you—to save you from it. With full knowledge of my sorrow and suffering in life, Jesus found a way to take it from me and save me from it. He gathered it all together out of my life, absorbed it into Himself, and then took it to the cross, experiencing the pain of it in every way as He hung there. Just as we accepted Him as Savior from our sins, we accept Him by faith as Savior from our sorrow and from every kind of sadness and suffering as well.

Just as we receive Jesus' righteousness when He takes away our sins, we can receive His comfort and His joy when He takes away our sorrow and grief. If we kneel at the foot of the cross and leave all of our sorrow there, comfort and joy will flow down upon us as His life flows out in the blood that falls upon the dusty ground beneath His feet ... that falls upon us if we are kneeling there. Ever and always, Jesus Himself tells us that He will give us His very own joy, saying, "I have told you this so that my joy may be in you and that your joy may be complete" (John 15:11 NIV).

A PRINCIPLE: Jesus took away all of my sorrow, reaching right down into my heart and removing it to make room for lots of joy. He endured all of the suffering that should have been mine—that is mine—so that He could always give me comfort.

Jesus saves us from the suffering and sorrow that are the effects of loss, criticism, failure, and defeat, as well as from sickness and sin. Indeed, He saves us from everything from which we need to be saved and rescued. The beautiful, old words of the King James Bible assure us that He does: "Wherefore he is able also to save them to the uttermost that come unto God by him, seeing he ever liveth to make intercession for them" (Heb. 7:25).

There is nothing I need that Jesus has not provided through His death (Phil. 4:19). There is nothing good that He has not arranged for God to give me (James 1:17). There is nothing good that He will withhold (Ps. 84:11). Jesus assures me that nothing is too hard for God to do for me (Matt. 19:26; Eph. 3:20–21; Luke 1:37; Gen. 18:14; Jer. 32:17, 27) and that I can ask my Father in heaven for everything I need (Matt. 7:7–8). I am forgiven and cleansed of all my sins and shortcomings (1 John 1:9); I am free from the sorrow, shame, and guilt that they produced forever.

Today—right here and right now—I can lay all of my sorrow, my shame, and my guilt at the foot of the cross and forget them because the Bible promises that God will forget them (Heb. 8:12; Rom. 10:11). I can receive in place of it all of the joy of the Lord and the unending comfort of His loving-kindness and tender mercy because "the LORD is good and his love endures forever; his faithfulness continues through all generations" (Ps. 100:5 NIV; 136:1; Jer. 31:3). This, all of this, is the good news that is the gospel message to the world. An angel announced it to the world, saying, "behold, I bring you good tidings of great joy, which shall be to all people. For unto you is born this day in the city of David a Saviour, which is Christ the Lord" (Luke 2:10–11). This day and every day, the gospel is always a message of great joy.

> Oh that men would praise the LORD for his goodness, and for his wonderful works to the children of men! For he satisfieth the longing soul, and filleth the hungry soul with goodness. (Ps. 107:8–9)

> The LORD is good to all: and his tender mercies are over all his works. (Ps. 145:9)

AN AFFIRMATION OF FAITH: "Jesus is my very own Savior. He saves me from the effects of sin, sickness, loss, criticism, failure, defeat, and everything from which I'll ever need to be saved. I am forgiven and cleansed of all my sins and shortcomings. I am free forever from the sorrow, shame, and guilt they produce. There is nothing I need that He does not provide. There is nothing good that He cannot give me. Nothing is too hard for God (Jer. 32:17, 27). Forever and ever I have the joy of the Lord and the unending comfort of His lovingkindness and tender mercy."

Loved and Cherished

A CHRISTIAN STUDY SERIES

Nobody is a "nobody" with God.

THE SCRIPTURE: "Like one from whom men hide their faces he was despised, and we esteemed him not." (Isa. 53:3c NIV)

A PROBLEM SITUATION: My husband, Charles, and I grew up in Philadelphia. One of the interesting things we remember from childhood is special excursions into the center of the city on the Reading Railroad's beautiful, silver, stream-lined passenger train called *The Crusader*. While in town, it was a treat to eat at Horn and Hardart's Automat, which was located near the huge downtown Reading Railroad Terminal. As returning adults, we were dismayed to find it served so many sad and solitary homeless people.

After we had lived in Texas for some years, we took our children back to Philadelphia to tour the old colonial city with all of its wonderful historical sites. In the course of the day, we decided to show them the automat as well. Visiting it was an experience I shall not soon forget.

The old restaurant certainly did not look new and ultra modern as it had in our youth. It was not particularly clean or appealing in any way. Everything in Texas seems so clean and new by comparison to the old center of Philadelphia. The worst thing about the automat, however, was not its grimy, drab appearance. It was the sad, lonely old people, sitting one by one, all hunched over at separate little tables all by themselves. They did not talk to anyone. Their eyes seemed vacant, and they stared at nothing in particular. They just sat there eating a limp-looking wedge of pie or a similar snack. No one seemed to be there with a friend. No one spoke to anyone.

As the customers shuffled in and out, I could not help but be overwhelmed by their isolation. Some of those old people went through the entire process of coming in, selecting their food from the automated slots, eating it, and then leaving without having anyone speak a single word to them.

As I watched more closely, it appeared to me that even when they were paying the cashier, the rumpled and frayed-looking old men and women were not spoken to. Indeed, I could see that the woman handling the money made a determined effort not to give any of them even the briefest eye contact. It was as though they did not exist.

For some reason, the fact that no one would even look at them hurt me so badly that I began to feel angry. I could understand that if I had to do business with such sad people all day long, I also probably would try to shield myself from their pain by not paying close attention. Nevertheless, it was upsetting to see them ignored.

When it came time for our family to check out, I decided it was important to make the cashier look at me. Her pattern was simple. She looked down at the ticket, then at the money, and then up to the cash register ... and nowhere else. When we worked our way up the line to her, sure enough, she did the same thing to us. It was so terribly impersonal and cold,

I couldn't accept it. So I smiled. I tried to talk to her. I tried every way I could think of to compel her to look at us, short of standing on my head.

I had asked Charles to give me the money and ticket, and when she reached for it, I held it back. I edged backwards, out of her reach. I raised my voice. I very nearly had a tantrum right there in the checkout aisle, but I could not make her look up into my face. No matter what I did, I could not make her look at me. She absolutely refused to have eye contact with me. I was truly stunned.

What a feeling! Even for me—and I had no lonely deficit like those sad old people eating in that place appeared to have. It was humiliating and painful to find that I could not elicit enough interest from the woman to make her raise her eyes to my face. I felt like a nonperson. It does not take much treatment like that to make you feel like a nobody.

Being Shunned Hurts

When people ignore you and won't look at you even in relatively ordinary circumstances, it hurts. Just think of how it must have been to be nailed to a cross right outside in the open, slowly dying, as the world goes by busily tending to its daily activities. How vividly the uncaring nature of humanity can be seen in the whole panoramic picture of Jesus' death.

Take a moment to imagine how all of that must really have been. Jesus hung there on the cross, and many of the people of Jerusalem must have gone about their lives below Him without really even allowing themselves to know—to really be aware of—what terrible suffering was going on there ... without allowing themselves to know that it was happening to a real person. They averted their eyes. They "hid their faces." They turned away and refused to recognize what was happening to Jesus. They are still doing it today. People in this world choose

191

not to know how others suffer. It is part of the denial that is common to our culture and our world.

Even worse than indifference is the response of those people who choose to be deliberate spectators to cruelty and suffering. Imagine having them find ghoulish diversion in witnessing your execution. To do that, they would have to deny all human empathy. Such people would have to see you as an object and not as a person. They would have to close themselves off completely from feelings of caring about you in any way. Viewing you as an object, less than a human being, is an extreme form of rejection. There is enough senseless violence around the world today to prove that sinful humanity has improved little in two thousand years.

COMMENTS: Many of the people of Jerusalem probably did not know who Jesus was. They did not know what a terrible thing they were all allowing to happen. Is the same thing not true when any person suffers? If we walk by, uncaring, when another person is suffering, do we ask ourselves whether or not that person is a child of God?

There were people who turned their faces away and chose to take no notice of Jesus hanging there on that hill. Others scorned Him. Still others despised Him. They shunned Him. They mocked Him. Never were there people who were more truly "children of [their] father, the devil" (John 8:44) than the people who tortured and executed Jesus.

There are many people in this world who go through day after day being treated as unimportant or less than fully human. If you are one of them, you may always know that Jesus wanted to save you from that kind of distress. He died to heal you from the pain caused by that kind of an experience. He was ignored, shunned, and despised so that He could provide a way to heal you of rejection's pain and its destructive impact on your life.

He died to heal everyone of the pain of rejection, no matter what form it takes.

If you will make a deliberate decision to believe that the simple words of the Bible are true, you may appropriate the part of the plan of salvation that heals you from being rejected, that delivers you from being shunned or despised, that heals you from the pain of being mocked and ridiculed as a nonperson.

When you receive Jesus as your Savior, you may put yourself and your whole life into God's hands. Then you may know that in the same way the stripes Jesus bore on His back bring healing to your body, the mockery He suffered brings you respect, the scorn He experienced makes you an honored child of God. He was shunned to make you welcome and cherished in the family of God.

Because people turned their faces away from Jesus, you can be confident that you will be welcomed forever into the family of God. By believing it, you activate it. It is faith at work. By actively receiving it, you plug in to the power of it the way an electrical cord plugs in to the power source at a wall outlet. Faith is making a deliberate decision to believe God.

Jesus took your place and mine as a son of God who has fallen short and deserves punishment. He allowed Himself to be tormented to death by an uncaring world ... so that we may take His place in life as a pleasing and favored and glorious son—a beloved son, a righteous son of God—who is fed, clothed, and cared for in every way in a loving family, by a loving heavenly Father (Matt. 7:11; 6:31–32; John 17:22).

A PRINCIPLE: Jesus was despised, shamed, and humiliated so that you and I could walk uprightly, have self-respect, and be esteemed. Humiliation was heaped upon Him so that honor might come to you. Knowing how deeply it hurts when no one pays any attention to me, Jesus fully experienced the hurt of having others turn away from Him so that He could heal my sad heart of that very thing. His pain was ignored so that my suffering would not pass unnoticed in this cruel world. All of the people who ignored Jesus' plight caused Him to suffer so that I could know that someone who loves me is always ready to pay attention to me … and to heal me of every hurtful situation when no one paid any attention to me.

AN AFFIRMATION OF FAITH: "I have been saved from the pain of rejection. The same way Jesus took away my sin so that He could give me His righteousness, He took rejection from me so that He could give me His acceptance. I am cherished because He was demeaned and discounted. I am honored because He was humiliated. I am beloved because He was despised. He endured sorrow and suffering so that I may be comforted and healed. Because He was ignored, scorned, and shunned, I am noticed, honored, and welcomed forever into the family of God."

The Cure for Sorrow

A CHRISTIAN STUDY SERIES

I am strong and whole and well and confident.

THE SCRIPTURE: "Surely he took up our infirmities and carried our sorrows, yet we considered him stricken by God, smitten by him, and afflicted." (Isa. 53:4 NIV)

A PROBLEM SITUATION: Sometimes I feel weak and tired. I hurt all over, inside and outside. At such times, even my best efforts produce little, and the world seems happy to punish me. Sometimes people really seem to find a measure of satisfaction in my difficulties and hint that my problems are no more than I deserve. Do they presume that my pain is the result of my stupidity or God's punishment? Sometimes I wonder, for when I feel so weak and inadequate I cannot seem to do what needs to be done.

There are days when I feel so full of sorrow that it is hard to keep trying. If experience working together with my husband, Charles, in his counseling practice (when one of his counselees chooses to invite me) is an accurate measure, then most people have days like that, too. Normally it is not quite safe to admit that we have "down times." Others tend to blame us for our problems, and usually, the world just does not want to hear about them. Certainly introducing your personal feelings of stress or sadness offends others in social situations and is considered highly unprofessional in the workplace.

People are quick to judge and criticize. It is frightening to realize that self-righteousness can assume such monumental proportions that men in the leadership positions in the temple of Jesus' day—positions that were established by God and filled by avid students of the Bible—could repudiate the work and words and ministry of the Savior Himself. It is dismaying to realize that they could see themselves as God's representatives, acting in God's name and for His sake, torturing and striking down the only truly righteous man who ever lived. No wonder Jesus told us not to judge (Matt. 7:1). The most scholarly folks among us are ill-equipped to do it.

So great was the self-delusion of the legalists and power figures in the religious community in Jerusalem that they were entirely unable to recognize goodness and virtue. For them righteousness was obeying their rules—not God's. Although their whole lives focused on the things of God, they were unable to recognize the Son of God when He stood before them (Matt. 23:1–6). Because He did not agree with them, they saw even a perfect man as unworthy to speak for God.

Jesus was a perfect man. On the other hand, I am a person who deserves to be stricken by God, smitten and afflicted. But instead, I who am unworthy to speak for God or act as His representative, am daily doing so with the very power, worth, and righteousness of Jesus Himself. You are, too. We are both called to be His witnesses in Jerusalem, Judea, Samaria, and the uttermost parts of the earth (Acts 1:8). We are able to do that because Jesus took our unworthiness and gave us His own infinite worth and value and virtue in return. What a wonder!

COMMENTS: Why did Jesus take up our infirmities and get under the burden of all our sorrows? Why was He stricken, smitten, and afflicted? Why did all of that have to happen to Jesus? It had to happen for the same reason that Jesus was wounded for our transgressions and bruised for our iniquities. It was a vital part of the plan of salvation. It was a necessary part of any plan designed to save you and me from everything from which we need to be saved.

Jesus was scorned so that we might be honored. Jesus was mocked so that we might be respected. Jesus was despised so that we might be cherished. Jesus was shunned so that we might be accepted in the beloved (Eph. 1:6; 3:14–19; Gal. 4:4–7).

Somehow the people of Jerusalem viewed Jesus' suffering as something He deserved. Perhaps they held that view so that they would not have to worry about the injustice of it. By despising Him, they could protect themselves from being troubled by His suffering. He certainly had no one "keeping an eye on Him" to make sure He was safe and cared for. He died without having care and protection so He could make sure that would never happen to you.

Jesus took up my infirmities and sorrows. That is, He picked them up like a big trash bag all wrapped up and tied together with all of my troubles and flaws inside. He actually took them away. Then He owned them, and they became a part of His life, way down on the inside of who He is. He carried them to the cross so He could make a way for me to get rid of them. I really can get rid of them!

There is no other way on earth for sorrow and grief and shame and guilt to be taken out of a person and exchanged for something wonderful except in the death, burial, and resurrection of Jesus Christ. Oh, we have many ways of trying to cover our sorrows and distract our minds so that we are not consciously aware of thinking about them. We numb our brains and our feelings with many things. We work hard, drink alcohol, use drugs, court danger, or stay frenetic. We seek entertainment and watch television for hours. We do many compulsive things to distance ourselves from our feelings. We may call them addictions or distractions or give them many other names, but we use them to keep from feeling our pain or thinking about the things that cause it. They only partly work. They only work for short lengths of time. Jesus is forever.

So whether your pain is a physical one that affects the way your body feels and works or it is emotional pain that affects the way your mind, feelings, will, or spirit operates, Jesus bore your pain. He took it all. He literally carried it away.

Jesus took on Himself everything that cripples you and me so that we may have His vibrant health. He took upon Himself everything that weakens us and causes pain, all that impedes our progress or interferes with our ability to function, so that we may have His strength, wellbeing, and freedom. He was completely overcome and stricken by the sorrow that He took away from me—and from you (Matt. 26:37–38). But He took it all upon Himself so that He could give you His fullness of joy. He gave us not just an occasional taste of His heavenly joy, but joy to the full. When you are full of joy, there is no room for anything else. "Hitherto have ye asked nothing in my name: ask, and ye shall receive, that your joy may be full" (John 16:24).

We Were Healed at the Cross

The King James Version of today's Bible passage tells me that Jesus bore our griefs and carried our sorrows. The Hebrew words that are translated "sorrow" and "grief" can also be translated "sickness" and "pain." That understanding enlarges the meaning of our study verse significantly. Are you sick or in pain today? The plan of salvation has made every provision for your mental, emotional, physical, and spiritual health.

Jesus took my sickness and pain so that I may have His wellness and wellbeing. By simply choosing to believe it, I can plug in to the power of it and see it operate in my life. What a vast, amazing, extravagant, life-changing piece of information is contained in these brief verses from the writings of the prophet Isaiah.

A PRINCIPLE: Staggering under the weight of the cross on that rough road up to Golgotha, Jesus collapsed with weakness and infirmity because He was operating on my limited strength. Though He was acting in perfect obedience to God, He was inadequate as a human being to do the job He was sent to do. He could not carry the cross, even though that is why God sent Him to earth. Where was His strength? Where was His adequacy? He had given them both to me. He had given them both to you. Jesus was stricken, smitten, and afflicted because He had no power or influence or resources or strength to defend or justify Himself. Why not? Because He had left them all with me when He came to get all of my weaknesses and inadequacies to take them away. Jesus' body was racked with pain so that I could experience wonderful wellbeing.

Jesus took my infirmities to the cross. He took every weakness and inadequacy that I have away and gave me His strength and competence. Jesus took on Himself—right into His own heart—all of my hurts and pain and all of my sorrow and regret so that He could give me His very own joy and satisfaction in God's approval of Him in exchange. He endured having people think He deserved everything that happened to Him and that it was really God's will for Him to suffer, and He did it so that I may be free of the pain of other people's self-righteous condemnation. I can scarcely comprehend how much Jesus has done for me and how much He loves me (Eph. 3:17–19). I am filled with wonder at how complete the plan of salvation is, for Jesus took away to the cross everything from which I long to be free.

AN AFFIRMATION OF FAITH: "Jesus' body was pierced and torn and broken so that He could take away my sickness and give me His wellness. All of my infirmity and weakness is gone, and I am strong and whole because Jesus is my Savior. No one can hurt me anymore through harsh judgments or condemnation, no matter what I have done. Jesus took all that away. Because Jesus died for me, sorrow and pain are gone and the joy of the Lord fills my life forever."

————>●<————

Guilty as Charged

A CHRISTIAN STUDY SERIES

My slate is clean.

THE SCRIPTURE: "But he was pierced for our transgressions, he was crushed for our iniquities." (Isa. 53:5a NIV)

A PROBLEM SITUATION: Did you ever wonder what in the world it means to say you "transgress"? My dictionary says that when you transgress, you break a law or command. It also says that to transgress means you sin or go contrary to or pass beyond a limit or bound. The first dictionary synonym offered for the word *transgress* is "to offend." There are several meanings found in these definitions that are familiar to us.

The first time I visited Spain, Charles was working as a consultant to the Department of Defense schools. He worked long hours, so I had free time for sightseeing trips and tours; but I was on my own. However, the people who teach at American Schools around the world are unusually gracious hosts for folks from home. At one social gathering we attended, everyone began to make suggestions as I planned visits to castles and museums and cathedrals and wonderful outdoor markets.

Before long, my plans became a joint project for the whole group. "Why not take a trip to Toledo?" "Why not visit the Lladro factory?" Now that idea made my eyes light up. I love the graceful porcelain Lladro figurines, but a trip to their factory involved a train ride to another city by myself. Dealing with the large railroad terminals that I was familiar with in New York and Philadelphia caused me to feel a little intimidated about working my way through one in another country. I do not speak Spanish.

Hiding my trepidation, I asked the enthusiastic group of world travelers how comfortable and safe a woman alone would feel in train stations and walking about on the streets surrounding them in Spain. "Oh, very comfortable," they all assured me. A chorus of voices agreed that (in those days) it was safe to travel about anywhere in Spain without fear. It was not like New York, where muggings were common, or like conditions we found in Rome, where purse snatching from fast-moving motor scooters had become an art form.

How could that be true? How could the streets of Spanish cities be safe while other great world cities required constant vigilance? Everyone assured me at once that it was true that the streets of Spanish cities were safer than other cities. Why? Because Spain was at that time just emerging from under Franco's political dictatorship. Justice under Franco was swift and harsh. A thief had his hand cut off. I recoiled in shock.

Now Spain is no longer a dictatorship. And it has been interesting to note in subsequent visits that the streets are no longer as safe from petty thievery and purse snatching.

What do you think about Spanish justice? What do you think is the appropriate punishment for stealing a purse on the street?

The picture comes to my mind of American justice. Police who capture a thief are likely to take him into custody with his hands cuffed behind his back. Does that seem like appropriate treatment for one who steals?

Take a moment with me and use your imagination to consider an interesting question. Suppose you were sitting around a large conference table in the halls of heaven. You are part of a group putting together the plan of salvation. The issue under discussion is stealing. How should redemption be provided for a person who steals? What is the appropriate way to deal with a thief? If Jesus is to be punished in the place of a thief, what should that punishment be?

What could be a more appropriate punishment for stealing than having your hands nailed down to a piece of lumber so that they are useless? Does that punishment fit the crime? If you were putting together a series of punishing experiences so that you had one that was appropriate for every offense ever committed on this earth, would nailing down the hands of a thief be one you would consider?

I believe that the just sentence for every offense was identified when the plan of salvation was formulated. And then Jesus stepped forward and took the place of every offender. The just punishment of every offense was experienced by Jesus during His hours of interrogation and torture, His execution, His death, His burial, and while Jesus was in hell between Good Friday and Easter morning's resurrection.

Jesus' hands and feet were pierced by nails for your transgressions and for mine, and then He hung there between two thieves. Blows were struck on his face and the whip tore His back as punishment for your iniquities and for mine. All of the punishments demanded by the laws of justice that prevail in either heaven or hell were satisfied by the suffering He endured.

In a demonstration of love that virtually passes comprehension, Jesus Christ took upon Himself the punishment for every offense—every offensive act great or small—ever committed on this earth. He took upon Himself the punishment for every minor petty act by which anyone ever committed an offense. He also completely absorbed the horrifying guilt for every major atrocity in history, no matter how great. The burden of guilt that became His defies our comprehension. He took the guilt. He took the shame. He took the consequences. He took the punishment.

Jesus took upon Himself everything about every offense ever committed by anyone who ever lived so that He could give us a new life in which our offenses are completely forgotten, as though they never had existed. And remember this: He took upon Himself, in the midst of it all, the trauma and pain of the victim at the same time that He bore the punishments of the transgressor. Doesn't it bring tears to your eyes to see, more and more, the magnitude of all that Jesus did for us and the depth of love that prompted Him to do it?

Saving Offensive People

Do you know people who are easily offended? Are there people in your life whom you find offensive? People who exhibit an irritating lack of manners are described as offensive. A person who commits a crime also is described as an offender. The person who sexually abuses a child is called a sex offender. When you define a transgression as an offense, it covers many situations.

If I offend, I am an abuser; I am offensive. If I pass beyond appropriate limits, I am violating a boundary. Most of us violate the boundaries of others at one time or another in our selfishness or in our thoughtlessness. We are often quite offensive when we do it.

If I violate a legitimate command, I am rebelling. In each case, whether I am offending or rebelling, I have behaved in such a way that action probably should be taken against me. Yet God will not take action against me or repudiate me for these offenses because Jesus stepped up in my place and accepted full responsibility for all of our transgressions. He accepted the guilt and endured the consequences for my actions so that I may have a fresh, clean slate and start over—so that through repentance and trusting Him, I can be restored to mint condition.

Do I sometimes have to deal with the consequences of my transgressions in this world? Yes, sometimes I do. But far more often, I do not. In either case, the eternal justice of God that rightly should demand retribution for my offenses has been satisfied by one who loved me so much that He bore my punishment, my guilt, and my shame. God loved the world so much that He gave His only begotten Son ... so that anyone who simply believes it is true may have all of the fabulous benefits that belong to the Prince of Heaven (John 3:16). They are ours as a free gift, a freely given gift that is ours by just receiving it. How could anyone refuse it?

What Does "Iniquity" Mean?

Now let's turn our attention to the word *iniquity*. The Hebrew word that is translated "iniquity" in today's fifth verse of Isaiah 53 is defined as meaning "perversity" in Strong's Concordance. Have you ever been offended by a pervert? Have you been accused of being a pervert? Other terms used to explain its meaning are "moral evil," "fault," or "mischief." The Bible tells us that Jesus was pierced for our transgressions and crushed for our iniquities. There are many occasions when we demonstrate an urgent need for salvation from the consequences of those negative behaviors: perversity, moral evil, faults, and mischief. As offenders or as victims, we all need help. We all need the work of a loving Savior in our lives.

All of us accumulate traits and experiences that fall into one or another of these categories by the time we grow up. I certainly did. One of the most shame-producing for me was an

experience that caused me to cringe in shame and embarrassment for years whenever I was reminded of it. You may find my
reaction silly, but to me it was awful.

As a young teenager, I was asked to babysit for a neighbor's
visiting grandchild. The child was probably about ten months
old. Babysitting for him should have been easy, for he was
expected to be napping during the time that his mother and
grandmother were out shopping. It did not work out that way.

I think that the sound of the door closing behind them woke
the baby when his mother left. He began to cry immediately,
so I went into the small first floor guest bedroom and peeped
cautiously over the side of his crib to see about him. The very
sight of me seemed to fill him with distress, and he began to
howl in dismay. He did not know me. He was in a strange place
before he ever laid eyes on me, and he did not like it. It is hard
for me to tell whether he was crying in terror or rage, but he
certainly was crying loud and long.

I had no idea what to do. So after fussing over him and
talking to him and offering him a bottle and singing to him
and trying all the tricks I knew as a babysitter, I decided that
my presence was the problem. I left the room, hoping he would
cry himself to sleep. He certainly did not. He continued to
scream. What a pair of lungs that child had!

I was distraught and began walking back and forth in the
living room, wringing my hands, so to speak, wondering how
long I should allow him to cry before giving up on the idea
of letting him cry himself to sleep. Part of me threw up my
hands and said, "Let this kid cry. He is impossible!" I should
have been ashamed of such an attitude ... and I certainly was
ashamed when I got caught.

After several eternal minutes, I was absolutely terrified to
see a man stalk down the stairs into the living room. He had
on a smoking jacket of some kind and a large cloth around his

neck. I was so startled to find someone in the house that I was speechless.

Clearly, the man was in a rage. In the years since that time my head has told me he was angry at his daughter and wife for leaving him there with an inexperienced babysitter. But then I had no idea of such things. It seemed to me that he caught me in the living room ignoring a screaming baby, in absolutely inexcusable dereliction of duty.

The man was obviously sick. I am sure, as I look back, that he was miserable. He was a physician and had that autocratic way about him that I expected all doctors to have when I was a child. To me, he was terrifying. He strode into the bedroom, picked up his grandson, and began pacing back and forth across the living room. After a few moments, he ordered me out of the house. I was sick with shame.

I now realize that my world as the daughter of a nice suburban Presbyterian minister was a protected one. People seldom did unkind things to me. I was very sheltered. But during those years, I thought that I was working very hard never to do anything that would earn me the kind of treatment I received at the hands of that neighbor. It certainly did not happen to me very often, if at all. I carried intense shame for years because I believed he thought I did something terrible by seeming to ignore a screaming baby. As a matter of fact, it is incredible to me to think of actually telling the story here for the entire world to read. Until this writing, I never told a living soul.

Whether you think my offense was very large or very small is not the point. The point is that it was excruciating for me. The Lord knows just what memories you have of situations in your life that cause you equal distress. Let Him show you where you need His loving ministry. He wants to forgive you and comfort you and wash it all away. No matter what has happened to you—in large things or small ones—over the course of your lifetime, Jesus' plan of salvation provides whatever you need to get over it.

Salvation Covers Everything

All the years of my growing up, I didn't have a very clear picture of what Jesus' suffering and death was all about. I believed that Jesus had to die to show us how terrible our behavior was. The cross seemed to be an object lesson, a terrible demonstration of how severe God thought my punishment should be. Yours, too. I thought my job as a Christian was to try harder and not to make those mistakes anymore. I thought all preachers were admonishing me to do better by urging me to avoid all future offenses in my own strength and ability. I thought that Jesus' death was a huge, horrible rebuke to me. *I just did not get it* that Jesus died to help me, that He wanted to save me from the pain and shame I have felt and from my helplessness against sin.

Calvary was about taking *away* my shame instead of shaming me more. The message of the cross is not "shame on you!" Jesus did not come to add to the shame I already felt or to expose it. He came to take it away.

As a fuller understanding of the meaning of Jesus' sacrifice on the cross begins to unfold, the scope of our salvation grows and grows. Jesus really has provided all that we need through His Passion and death. And I do need help to cope with the things that I have done or left undone that are sin. From relatively trivial childhood incidences of stealing and lying, to exploring sexual things, blaming or falsely accusing, being nasty to our siblings, or breaking things accidentally or on purpose, our offenses encompass all things, including murder. Sometimes we think things are too small to have been covered by Jesus' work on the cross. In other instances we may believe that our offense is too great to be covered by salvation's plan. Neither is true. Jesus saves us from it all.

Sometimes the magnitude of my failures and the things that I have done to offend God and hurt others overwhelms me and makes me feel unworthy to have anything good from God or to accomplish anything good in His kingdom. If I allow my mind to dwell on any of it, I am plunged into such deep shame that I fear I shall never be free of it. I must choose not to let that happen. You must make the same choice.

COMMENTS: Jesus took the punishment for everything in me that *is* wrong and *does* wrong so that I may have the wonderful reward due to Him for being perfect and good. He experienced the stabbing pain of guilt so that I could be freed from its suffering. He was crushed—completely crushed—by all my sin and the overwhelming shame that always goes with it. This short Bible verse in Isaiah that we are studying is so stunning in the goodness and love it demonstrates toward us that I feel all of creation should pause in holy awe and wonder when it is read.

What was due to me was punishment—with chilling fear in anticipation of the exposure and punishment due to me for all the things I have done to hurt other people and to grieve God. Along with this went a lifetime of debilitating regret and then eternal anguish. Jesus took all of that for me—not just the punishment of going to hell but also the shame and exposure that could destroy me in this life.

Though all the hosts of heaven should have been at Jesus' disposal, when He was about to be beaten, no one rescued Him (Matt. 26:53). After it was done, no one ministered to Him or cared for Him or dressed His wounds. That happened to Him so that when I need help or comfort, it is only a prayer away. All the angels of heaven may be sent to help me, even though I do not deserve their help, because Jesus, who certainly did deserve it in every way, took on Himself my unworthiness and relinquished to me all the privileges that go with His righteousness and His position as God's Son.

A PRINCIPLE: Jesus was crushed and bruised because He stood in my place. His body was pierced by thorn, nail, and spear because I stepped over the line and did what was wrong. I was in the wrong completely, but He doesn't reject me or disdain me because of it. Knowing every fault and flaw in me, still He engages fully in a daily, personal relationship with me to help me work out my problems and be successful. Others may not even help a mistreated person who is totally in the right. Jesus made a way to help me when I am in the wrong and deserved to be blamed. Knowing me inside and out, knowing every secret sin and bad attitude hidden inside of me, Jesus demonstrates love toward me tirelessly, all day, every day. Indeed, the Bible says that He intercedes with God on my behalf *all of the time.* Hebrews 7:25 says, "Wherefore he is able also to save them to the uttermost that come unto God by him, seeing he ever liveth to make intercession for them." It is so wonderful!

AN AFFIRMATION OF FAITH: "I am free and clear of all charges against me, even though I have disappointed, disobeyed, and offended God. Day by day the plan of salvation works to change me and everything about me that twists my personality and causes me to offend. Jesus takes away shame and guilty memories that trouble my heart and puts His peace inside of me where those things have been. I am being cleaned and polished and restored to mint condition. I am filled with hope and joy continually because the love of God is shed abroad in my heart by the Holy Ghost, who is given to me."

He Is Our Peace

A CHRISTIAN STUDY SERIES

My heart is peaceful and my body is well.

THE SCRIPTURE: "… the punishment that brought us peace was upon him, and by his wounds we are healed" (Isa. 53:5b NIV).

A PROBLEM SITUATION: The huge number of prescriptions for tranquilizers and mood-altering drugs in this country make it crystal clear that there is little peace in people's lives today. At the time of this writing, the *Houston Chronicle* reported that scientists were finding Prozac in the livers and gills of fish that live in Pecan Creek, a stream located in Colorado. It is astounding that a tranquilizing drug is in such common usage that it would be found in one of the pristine mountain streams in Colorado.

In the normal course of our lives, peace is elusive. Mental health professionals make a direct connection between the widespread use of addictive substances and the difficulty people have as they try to cope with painful feelings. The enormous sweep of interest a decade or two ago in patterns of addictive behavior and its relationship to dysfunctional families in our society further confirms that feelings of distress dominate a large part of our daily experience. People are pressed and stressed. Some become violent. Many become depressed. On every side, it is plain to see that few of us live out our lives in peace.

There is a reason why we are so upset. If we were to follow people through the events of their days, it might surprise us to see how many of the large and small things that happen to us are punishing. Folks are nasty. The people around us often are irritable and easily exasperated. The jangling alarm clock in the morning is punishing. Traffic jams and miserable weather are punishing. People often cannot do all that needs to be done in a day, so we are trapped in situations that we cannot control. The rudeness we encounter and the harshly critical things said and done to us as a part of life's normal routines hurt our feelings far more than most of us are willing to admit, even to ourselves. Disdain, disinterest, criticism, and sarcasm cut us painfully, yet they are an ordinary part of living.

Large and small, young and old, we are all much more battered and wounded by life than we can afford to admit. Our strength and joy and productivity tend to be seriously depleted by a troubled heart, a wounded spirit, and a battered and exhausted body. We need a Savior. We need one badly. And we need one whose plan of salvation covers a much broader scope of need than most of us have been raised to expect from the gospel message. We must stretch and expand our understanding of salvation until it covers everything in life from which we need to be saved.

COMMENTS: In all of humanity, Jesus alone obeyed God and should have earned the right to have His prayers answered. What was due to Jesus as a man living a perfectly sinless life on this earth was a wonderful reward and the privilege of having His prayers answered and His needs met. He truly did earn that kind of treatment from heaven by His perfect performance, but He did not grasp it and hold on to it for Himself. He gave it to you, and He gave it to me.

Jesus prayed in great distress in the garden of Gethsemane to be rescued from His approaching arrest—and no rescue came. Jesus knew that every kind of distress and pain and assault to His body was ahead. In those moments of desperate appeal, Jesus knew what He faced. He cried out to be delivered from His fate, *but His request was not granted.* He was not given what He asked for. He did not deserve to be denied (Mark 14:32–36). He accepted that devastating denial of His plea so that you and I, though we do *not* deserve it, may have our prayers for help and deliverance answered.

Jesus understood what was to happen to Him, and He allowed it. He submitted to all of it so that you and I may be spared—from all of it. He took on Himself all of the terrible consequences of my sin and personal perversity while generously giving me His very own supply of total peace (John 14:27).

Peace and the assurance of answered prayer are not all that the Prince of Peace arranged for us to have. Our study verse from Isaiah makes it clear that Jesus purchased healing for our bodies at the same time that He provided our peace. And He did it at a very great price. To all who will receive it, He freely gives us His very own enduring wellness by taking upon Himself every kind of savage assault on His physical body.

Jesus submitted to the ultimate horror by being stripped naked and nailed to a cross to suffer for hours until He died. But that was not all. He suffered many additional torments and offenses before He ever got there. He endured all of them for you … all of them because He loves you. He did it all because He loves us so very much more than human minds are able to grasp (Eph. 3:14–19). The apostle Peter, who saw His suffering firsthand, describes what happened this way:

He was guilty of no sin, neither was deceit (guile) ever found on His lips [Isaiah 53:9]. When He was reviled *and* insulted, He did not revile *or* offer insult in return; [when] He was abused *and* suffered, He made no threats [of vengeance]; but He trusted [Himself and everything] to Him Who judges fairly. He personally bore our sins in His [own] body on the tree [as on an altar and offered Himself on it], that we might die (cease to exist) to sin and live to righteousness. By His wounds you have been healed. For you were going astray like [so many] sheep, but now you have come back to the Shepherd and Guardian (the Bishop) of your souls [Isa. 53:5–6]. (1 Peter 2:22–26 AB)

By His wounds, you have been healed. Because He was wounded, you are healed. Notice that Peter refers back to the passage from Isaiah that is the basis for today's study. The King James Version of the Bible quotes him as saying that Jesus "his own self bare our sins in his own body on the tree, that we, being dead to sins, should live unto righteousness: by whose stripes ye were healed." Think of it. Jesus' body was terribly broken. He laid His back beneath a whip while His flesh was torn off His bones so that He could make a way for my sick and broken body to be healed. Minute by minute He suffered all of that pain for you so that He could make you well

Can I allow such a price to be paid to give me the gift of healing and then not receive it or not learn how to get hold of it and make it work to bless my life? Such a thing is unthinkable! I pray that my heart will always be open and my faith vibrant so that not a lash of His beating shall have been endured for my healing and then wasted.

A PRINCIPLE: "Jesus was judged guilty for my sin and cruelly punished so I do not have to be. Jesus endured pain, suffering, and every kind of disease (lack of ease, comfort, and wellbeing)

in His body so that He could give me His perfect health. He took all of the shortcomings and all of the inadequacies that trouble me to the cross. He was subjected to every punishing kind of experience so that He could absorb the pain and damage of such experiences for me and instead of me. When He takes them out of my life, He gives me instead His very own peace, His perfect peace that He reached down inside His own heart to find and give to me. He does not distribute a little dab for you and a little dab for me, here and there, a wee touch of it. No! He poured out upon us absolutely all of it, until there was none left for Him.

Jesus gives us all the peace He has to give, and it is vastly more than we'll ever need. From the anguished fretting we feel as we toss upon our beds to the sheer terror that sometimes grips us all, Jesus takes away everything that robs us of peace. He takes away turmoil and stress and gives us His own perfect peace. He takes it all upon Himself to free us from it forever. Every defect that makes us sick or ravages our bodies or minds is taken away and replaced with Jesus' perfect health and peace. He freely gives us all things—all of the good things that make up His wonderful perfection in exchange for all of the miserable stuff that makes us sinners who need salvation.

AN AFFIRMATION OF FAITH: "Peace flows through my life like a never-ending river. My heart is not troubled, for I take all of my concerns to the foot of the cross and give them to Jesus. As I kneel there before my Savior, I receive His great peace. It flows through me all of the time. Along with love and joy, the peace of God washes over me—body, soul, and spirit—in constant blessing."

Finding Our Way

A CHRISTIAN STUDY SERIES

God helps when we get off track.

THE SCRIPTURE: "We all, like sheep, have gone astray, each of us has turned to his own way; and the LORD has laid on him the iniquity of us all." (Isa. 53:6 NIV)

A PROBLEM SITUATION: Sheep never seem to be very aggressive. They do not have dangerous teeth or claws. Bible reference books tend to refer to them as helpless. More than anything, they usually appear to be unaware and dependent. They can wander off into dangerous territory with little knowledge of their own peril. If left unsupervised, they just seem to do what they want to do without wisdom or any sense of being at risk.

I do that. Most of the time, I don't stop to ask the Lord what He created me for or what He wants me to be doing right now. For much of my life, I have had to be in real trouble and need God's help very much before I stop and check in with Him to see what His will for my immediate situation might be. Sometimes I have to admit that my behavior is just not very smart.

I once talked to a man who had responded to a telephone salesman and purchased a diamond as an investment without ever seeing it. He had the cost of the stone charged to a credit card and awaited his purchase in the mail. Soon after it was delivered, he received another phone call. This time the salesman on the other end of the line persuaded him to return the small "investment" diamond and purchase a larger one, again on his credit card. He paid more than seven thousand dollars for it, sight unseen.

When the larger "investment" diamond was delivered, it was encased in a plastic covering on a cardboard mounting. A notice was printed on its mounting, telling the buyer that the diamond must not be removed from the plastic wrapper or it would not be acceptable for trade or sale as the investment piece it was purported to be. Think of that. The diamond the man received could not very well be examined or appraised without being removed from the shrink wrap that covered it.

When a jeweler was finally asked to examine the stone, it turned out to be a real diamond all right, but it was worth only a few hundred dollars instead of the thousands that had been paid for it. The poor man was led along step by step until he was completely taken in by an expensive telephone scam.

All of us make mistakes. All of us are vulnerable to being led like a lamb to the slaughter, and perhaps those of us who are most scornful of the foolishness of others stand in greatest danger of being "conned" ourselves. But the consequences of "dumb" behavior can be very serious. Many of us have been lured into situations that have made us "pay" for the rest of our lives. I am so grateful that when Jesus was doing all the work needed for your salvation and mine He did not overlook the less than brilliant things we all do. His plan of salvation is so wonderful that I have been redeemed from every foolish thing

I have ever done, including being "fleeced." My Savior did not leave out my need to be saved from my own stupidity. All I could ever need in order to be perfectly and completely saved, He did for me.

COMMENTS: Many times in my life, I am too dumb to know what I should do and then do it. Like sheep that go astray, I wander off and lose my way. Left to myself out there, I could lose everything, even my life. So Jesus, my strong and loving big brother, took for me the losses caused by my mistakes. He experienced every kind of loss for me in my place.

Jesus lost everything. He was stripped of everything, including the clothes on His back. When He was hung up there on the cross, He lost even the right to stand upon a square foot of land that could be called the minimum territorial right of every human being. Jesus Christ, glorious Heavenly Prince, entered into the curse of full and total poverty in order to rescue me from all of its terrible tentacles of control.

A vivid description of the curse of absolute poverty, lack, and loss comes to us through the pen of Moses in Deuteronomy 28:48. Jesus took every bit of that curse—hunger, thirst, nakedness, and the want of all things—as He hung there on the cross. He was in want of all things, even the ability to breathe without struggling. He had absolutely nothing, not even a tiny piece of the earth on which to stand. He took upon Himself the curse of poverty and lack completely so that He could free us from it just as completely.

Jesus not only experienced the loss of all things in my place, but also He took the pain and the shame of that loss. He intercedes continually on my behalf to solve all of the problems created by the losses in my life. When I am willing, He leads me and guides me throughout my life, helping me to work out solutions for all of the difficulties that I get myself into (Rom. 8:26–28, 34; Heb. 7:25). All of that is in addition to the fact that He took all of the blame and punishment that our Father should have assigned to me.

Not only did Jesus take the punishment for my mistakes and misdeeds, but also He took the consequences. He took all of the bad outcomes of my misdeeds and mistakes and works in my life to reverse them and bring about good. Romans 8:27–28 states, "And he that searcheth the hearts knoweth what is the mind of the Spirit, because he maketh intercession for the saints according to the will of God. And we know that all things work together for good to them that love God, to them who are the called according to his purpose."

So many of our decisions are just plain dumb, and without the help of Jesus, our lives can become a shambles somewhere along the way. Thank God our Savior took my stupidity to the cross and all of the consequences of my foolish choices along with it. In return for the stupidity He took away, God gives me a spirit of wisdom, embodied in His Holy Spirit (Isa. 11:2; Prov. 2:6). Truly, everything we need can be found in Christ ... in the transaction that we make at the cross, where we exchange all that we are that is sinful and falls short of the glory of God for the qualities and characteristics of Jesus, who is the perfect image and likeness of God. Everything we need to know in order to understand how it all works can be found in God's Word, the Bible.

While I was growing up, my family liked to spend summer vacations on Lake Squam in New Hampshire. At night we would carry flashlights and walk through the chilly woods along paths covered with fragrant pine needles. The flashlights' round, yellow beams lit the path so that we didn't stumble over the huge tree roots and half-buried rocks along the way. The Bible is like those flashlights. God gives us His Word to guide us in all that we do. God's Word becomes a lamp unto our feet and a light unto our path (Ps. 119:105). In addition to all of that, God gives us a sound mind (1 Tim. 1:7). Indeed,

He gives us the mind of Christ (1 Cor. 2:16). As amazing as it may sound, along with everything else my Savior gives me of Himself, I can have the mind of Christ if I will let it be in me. Philippians 2:5 says, "Let this mind be in you, which was also in Christ Jesus."

I do not need to fear taking a wrong turn and going astray again, for Jesus made a way for me to have a new life and fresh guidance to light my way. He will help me when I make mistakes. He is always close enough to guide me if I begin to do the wrong thing (Isa. 30:21). I can never be fully and completely saved and restored to mint condition if the stupidity issues in my life are not taken care of. But Jesus has taken care of everything, so I am free to be bold when exciting possibilities open up to me.

Never Alone

When we make mistakes and do foolish things, don't we feel lonely inside? I don't want to talk about it to anyone because I hope no one notices whatever dimwitted thing I did or left undone. If others already know about the situation, I certainly do not want to remind them of it by talking about things. So I can feel very lonely and isolated at a time when I am upset and probably need to share my distress with someone who loves me and cares about me.

A sheep that has gone astray may be out there all alone. What a stark phrase: "out there all alone." If all of us have "gone astray," then all of us, in some sense, have been or now are "out there all alone." To be alone, to feel lost, lonely, isolated, or unprotected is desolate. If we have all "gone astray," then we all feel a kind of loneliness inside that we may be powerless to cure. That lost feeling, like a frightened child who is alone, is not unknown to even the most competent adult.

Jesus knows us. He understands us at the deepest level, even way down inside where we try to fool ourselves. He knows we feel abandoned and lost sometimes. He knows we feel stupid and helpless sometimes. When He went to the cross for you, He did not forget that painful part of your struggle. He remembered your lonely feelings, and He made provision to save you from them—to save you in every way that you will ever need to be saved.

Jesus became lost, alone, lonely, isolated, helpless, abandoned, and desolate when hanging on that cross. He could have summoned angels to help Him, but He didn't do it (Matt. 26:53). He stayed there for you, because He loves you. He did it so that He could take those feelings and the inadequacies in you that caused them out of your life and replace them with His constant presence and protection. He did it so that He could make a way to save you, to rescue you, to be with you every time you are lost and lonely (John 14:18). Jesus brings with Him the comfort and reassurance that He is "the way"—the way out, the way back, the way through—in every situation.

A PRINCIPLE: Jesus, who was never stupid, foolish, or careless, took on those qualities as a part of Himself so that He could give me His wisdom, understanding, counsel, power, and knowledge in their place (Isa. 11:2). The inherent qualities that lead us astray were transferred from me to Him along with all the rest of my sin and my sin nature, and so were the terrible consequences they bring about in my life. In place of them, I am given His unfailing sense of direction and the marvelous outcomes of wise and righteous choices upon which to build my life (Isa. 48:17).

God laid on Jesus all of my iniquity. He took it off of my shoulders and laid it on Jesus. He has rescued me forever from wandering off to somewhere that is unsafe. In my life, He has become "the way" when I do not know which way to go. He becomes "the way" when I can see no way out of hopeless situations (John 14:6). He is the truth when I am not sure what it is. He is the life that is the perfect antidote for everything dead and dying, even for dying dreams (John 14:6; Ps. 37:4–5). He is always with me (Ps. 32:8; John 14:16–20). He is inside of me forever, from the moment that I invite Him into my heart, so I will never be alone again (Heb. 13:5).

AN AFFIRMATION OF FAITH: "I will never wander off and be lost again. I never have to be lonely anymore. I do not have to feel alone or confused or fear making critical mistakes because Jesus redeemed me from a life ruled by my own stupidity and senseless whims. He guides me by the Holy Spirit and will be with me forever to lead me in all of my ways. He cares for me as a gentle and loving shepherd. Jesus loves me. Surely goodness and blessing 'shall follow me all the days of my life: and I shall dwell in the house of the LORD forever' (Ps. 23:6)."

Study Twelve

———◆———

Speaking with Power

A Christian Study Series

I speak with assurance, saying what I need to say in every situation.

THE SCRIPTURE: "He was oppressed and afflicted, yet he did not open his mouth." (Isa. 53:7a NIV)

A PROBLEM SITUATION: I just hate to get caught in a situation where I feel oppressed and controlled or so intimidated that I cannot open my mouth to do anything about it. I am upset when I am in a social situation in which other people are discussed disparagingly and I do not feel free to disagree. I am ashamed when unkind things about others are said that offend me and yet I do not stand up in their defense. I feel shallow and cowardly. I hate the feeling of being caught in a situation in which I feel used or manipulated or humiliated or stifled and yet I do not have the courage to speak up and put a stop to it. In a job or in social situations, it is easy to disagree with something that is happening and yet feel hesitant to express concern.

225

Whenever I think of this problem—this issue of not being able to open my mouth and speak up or speak out when the situation calls for it—I am reminded of an instance in which my husband found himself so constrained by the power of a group that he concurred with actions taken when he felt he should have challenged them. Charles did not see himself as a person who could easily be controlled. He had tangled with powerful people and did not feel readily intimidated. And yet he was silent at a meeting when he felt he should have spoken out.

During the period of time when Charles was working as consultant to then Texas Governor John Connally, his strength was tested in a variety of ways. A bill that Charles had been working hard to promote prior to his appointment under Connally came up for hearings in the Texas legislature. It was a bill requiring the screening of newborn babies for a relatively rare condition that caused preventable mental retardation.

The Texas Medical Association (TMA) opposed the bill, just as they did any legislation that added to governmental control over the practice of medicine. In this case, Charles and the TMA lobbyist went toe to toe during the hearings, each battling hard for a cause that he truly believed in. Indeed, the considerable influence of the TMA was brought to bear to remove Charles from his position with the governor. Happily, that effort was unsuccessful, and in time, the bill passed. The procedure, screening for PKU, is now universally performed.

Charles' career has been one of lifelong advocacy for improved opportunities for children, especially children with special needs. In that quest, he has testified before many school boards and legislative bodies and worked at the federal, state, and local levels for change. He certainly did not view himself as a "yes" man. Yet a small group of laymen on a local church board proved him wrong.

Charles was asked to serve on the board of a Christian ministry that evolved out of unique community service in a mainline protestant church. As a congregation in good standing in their denomination—not one in which we were then or ever members—the church and minister decided to formalize an organization that supported the community of believers directly involved in ministry to troubled and broken people in the church and the neighborhood. Charles was deeply moved by the selfless ministry they offered to others, to people who somehow fell through the cracks when it came to social services. In time, he was asked to serve on the new board that was formed and did so for some time.

Months passed, and the pastor and program achieved a measure of national recognition. Invitations to preach, teach, and minister nationally and internationally increased. And along with them, the challenges of guiding a "total immersion" kind of Christian service within the church increased exponentially. The pastor was under unrelenting pressure as ministry to all kinds of people flourished around the clock. He responded to it by moving to increase the authority and power of the pastor's role—certainly an understandable reaction. One day at a board meeting, without warning, it was proposed that the organization, which duly had been formed by action of the entire church congregation, vote to reorganize itself. It was proposed that the pastor be empowered to make decisions in the light of his own wisdom without requiring the endorsement of the board or any other agency or individual.

Charles believed strongly that the proposed reorganization would serve to close the ministry in upon itself at a time when it needed to reach outside of itself for badly needed expertise in a variety of areas. He also believed that an increased empowerment of group members—rather than an increased empowerment of the leader—was the best way to support the pastor's vision. The issue was not peripheral. It was central. Should the organization of a growing Christian ministry become more authoritarian and thus closed or remain open to the wisdom of many counselors in problem situations? Charles believed that "where no counsel is, the people fall: but in the multitude of counselors there is safety" (Prov. 11:14).

Charles was troubled by what took place in that board meeting. It was not the proposed action by the minister to accrue power to himself that shocked Charles. Not at all. That is a common reaction for a leader in situations in which the potential for conflict is present. For good or for ill, most leaders seek power to stabilize chaotic conditions when difficulties arise in any group. Rather, Charles was appalled by his own reaction to the proposed board action. He voted in favor of it.

In trying to explain and understand his own actions, Charles described what had taken place in the meeting: First, the proposed reorganization had been explained in detail by an attorney who was a member of the board. Next, there was rather brief discussion. Charles made several comments, questioning the wisdom of such an action. A Catholic priest in good standing in his church served with Charles on that board. During the deliberations, he echoed some of Charles' thoughts by commenting mildly that, in its long history, the Catholic Church had not always been well served by granting absolute power to its highest leadership. He observed that his church had been trying to move in the opposite direction for many years.

After one or two others spoke briefly, the minister stood and addressed the group. Looming as a powerful figure indeed, he made a few comments and then turned to look at each board member, one by one, fully in the face, and personally and individually asked for his vote. The full force of his personality and role as a charismatic leader was focused on each man as he was asked to cast his ballot.

The polling of the board members moved slowly and deliberately around the table. One after another nodded affirmatively, but Charles determined in his own mind to vote in the negative. He was convinced that the group needed to reach out and grow and integrate the gifts and talents of a greater variety of people into the ministry to cope with compounding problems. He did not see the issue as one of need for increased discipline, control, and power, but rather of increased knowledge, wisdom, and participation.

Charles was convinced that when most of the power and authority in any group resides in one individual, its vision is limited to the scope of that person's ability. He believed that a healthy organization makes room for leadership gifted with a variety of strengths and insights. He felt that the entire future of the ministry was at stake. And yet, to his own astonishment, when the full force of the minister's gaze riveted on him, he heard himself voting in the affirmative—approving an action to which he was deeply opposed. The Catholic priest cast the only dissenting vote.

In the stunned moments that followed his vote, Charles sat in that meeting and reviewed his situation. He realized that he was in a group in which he felt so disempowered that he was unable to vote his own convictions. He well understood what the issues were. He has taught organizational theory at the graduate level in two large universities, and he knew that the power in the group that required compliance had silenced him. It had rendered him unable to open his mouth in a situation in which he had strong convictions. That day, he resigned from the board.

Let it be understood that Charles did not resign because he disagreed with the action taken by the board. Women and men of good will often disagree in life. It was not a resignation tendered in anger or in protest against the new organization being formed, though he did oppose it. Nor did he resign because he has lost faith in the validity of the mission and ministry. No, Charles resigned because he was not willing to remain a part of a system that exercised such power over him that he was silenced when he believed that he should speak out.

To be unable to speak up is to resign from personhood. Today's study verse tells us that Jesus was oppressed, yet He did not open His mouth. He was unjustly accused, yet He did not defend Himself. For a Christian to accept such bondage when it is imposed by any system is to relinquish the possibility of becoming the person that God made you to be—or doing what He created you to do. A person cannot give his or her life to the Lord if it already has been given into the control of someone or something else.

Prior to this event at the board meeting, some of the most powerful forces in state politics had mobilized against Charles, both personally to undermine his job and professionally to oppose the programs and projects he advocated. Nothing in that arena had silenced him. Yet the power exercised in the small board of a local church of several hundred members formed a powerful restraint.

Like Abraham of old, who was called by God to leave his country, kindred, and father's house, Charles felt constrained to leave a system that successfully achieved compliance above conviction (Gen. 12:1). Not that he was overtly constrained in his action. He was not. The power in that group was not outwardly enforced. It was knit into the fiber of loving and caring relationships. Yet it was great enough to silence opposition. He was not registering a protest against an individual. Rather, he acknowledged in his own heart the power of that social system over *himself.* As Christians, it is helpful to remember that the Bible teaches that we do not contend with flesh and blood (with people) (Eph. 6:12).

Although we seldom realize it consciously, all of us are in systems and groups that control us in the same way that board controlled Charles. Surprisingly it may be our own families that are riddled with forbidden subjects of which we dare not speak. On the job, at home, or anywhere else, it is often the most obvious problems that we do not feel free to address. Feeling unable to talk about the things that are uppermost on our minds, the problems or hurts or issues about which we care deeply, is a kind of prison in which we endure much pain. It is also a bondage that prevents problem solving and resolution of conflict. It blocks communication and all hope of true peace.

Imprisoned in my Role

This matter of communication is so broad and so vital that it seems important to mention at least one instance in which God has brought liberty and healing to my own life. This understanding, that Jesus took upon Himself the constraints that have controlled my ability to be an open person, has changed me very much. I grew up to be a well-trained placater. I nearly never stated the truth in a direct, flatfooted way. Often in family situations, I liked to tell myself that I was keeping the peace and avoiding conflict when I saw problems, yet said nothing. Sometimes I convinced myself that my opinions would not be received so there was no point in speaking. Or I might tell myself that there could be facts I did not have. I had lots of reasons why I did not speak out frankly in times of debate or conflict. But the truth is that something inside constrained me.

Many times, even today, it is hard for me to speak the simple truth. I tend to placate and conciliate instead. In my lifelong role as placater, I have learned that I keep the peace in most cases not for noble reasons, but for my own comfort and for the stability of the system. I want peace and harmony even when the challenge of divergent views is healthier and certainly more honest. I was surprised and embarrassed by this insight. I had imagined myself to be the epitome of kindness and concerned about the health and wellbeing of others. It was not easy to give up my self-righteous sense of benevolence. It was hard to own my own selfishness in wanting to stifle honesty to avoid conflict because conflict made me uncomfortable.

After all kinds of crises—personal, social, or professional—I am likely to have conversations with myself in which I castigate myself for not speaking up with conviction when I should have. I say things to myself like, "Why didn't I say ... ?" or "I should have said ..." I often feel ashamed of my "namby pamby" responses. When it happens, I feel pain and distress over the ineffectiveness or inappropriateness of my verbal behaviors. In these kinds of situations—as in so many others in my life—I am acutely aware of needing the help and healing of a Savior.

Expressing Love

Being unable to express ourselves and communicate in the world often means that we do not give love and affirmation to others any more easily than we are able to stand up for ourselves or for principles we believe in. Difficulty in sharing what is in our hearts walls us off from others. It causes loneliness and neediness where it need not be. If the positive thoughts we have towards others and the appreciation we often feel and fail to verbalize were given freely, there would be more joy in the world. The entire climate in which we live our lives might well change.

Because sin reigns and humanity is stifled in its ability to speak freely and share in matters of the heart, a major source of emotional nourishment is cut off. Here, as in everything else in life, the plan of salvation recognizes every need in the human heart and makes provision to meet it. Jesus was silenced so that we might be made eloquent. He was bound so that we might be free.

I am glad that when Jesus set about to provide me with everything I need to live a wonderful new life, He did not forget to provide a way out of oppressive, controlling circumstances of all kinds in which I feel powerless to speak or act (Rom. 6:4). I am grateful that He knows how desperate I feel sometimes when I sense something is happening to me or around me and I am not able to say a word. I long to be assertive and strong and able to speak up for myself or others when I know it is important. By myself I often cannot do it. Thank God I can receive by faith (the same way I receive forgiveness for my sins) the eloquence I need to speak the truth in love in every kind of situation (Eph. 4:15).

COMMENTS: Jesus did not stand up for Himself when He was in the hands of the "police." He didn't with the temple guard or the Roman forces under Pilate. He was cruelly abused and savagely beaten by the "justice system" of His day, and also by the "church" (Mark 15:16–20). He experienced the ultimate miscarriage of justice. He was treated like a dumb animal, and it happened to Him at least in part so that I may have dignity and honor in stating my position … and can always be eloquent and powerful in my own defense when I am threatened.

Jesus was tortured and tormented for me. Because He gave to you and to me His divine nature and took on our weaknesses, inadequacies, and sins, He went through His ordeal before the Sanhedrin, before Herod, and before Pilate, operating without the divine authority and power that were rightfully His. Having given up His position as perfect Prince of Heaven, He met the accusations and abuses heaped upon Him as a guilty sinner, as the rankest of sinners.

Because Jesus laid aside His glory to become sin for us, and because He laid aside His great power to become weak with our weakness and powerless with our powerlessness, there wasn't anything He was able to say or do to stop the abuse and mistreatment He received. As a result, I who deserve to be treated that way for all of my perversity, contrariness, and offenses will be protected and cared for by God and by companies of angels (Ps. 91). What's more, because He did not so much as utter a word on His own behalf, I am endued with an ability to speak that draws its power from the presence of the Holy Spirit within me. It gives me an eloquence to defend myself, to present my case, and to have a persuasiveness in all situations that is beyond normal human capacity.

There is another idea to consider. Jesus mentioned in John 14:24 and John 17:8 that He spoke the word(s) of the Father here on earth. In that speaking, there was great power. It was power to proclaim healing, to preach, to raise the dead, and to do miracles like calming great winds and multiplying loaves and fishes to feed thousands of people. When Jesus spoke the words He had heard the Father saying—words that the Father had given Him—then mighty things were accomplished on the earth.

> These words you hear are not my own; they belong to the Father who sent me. (John 14:24 NIV)

> For I did not speak of my own accord, but the Father who sent me commanded me what to say and how to say it. I know that his command leads to eternal life. So whatever I say is just what the Father has told me to say. (John 12:49–50 NIV)

We, too, as believers in the Lord Jesus Christ have the power to speak God's Word with the authority of a son of God and expect to see mighty works occur. The reason we have such authority and power to affirm and speak God's Word in faith and see it come to pass is that Jesus relinquished that right on our behalf. When we pray in Jesus' name, we acknowledge the great exchange that has taken place. We are praying as He would pray, and we are heard as He would be heard.

Jesus said in John 14:12–14 (NIV),

> I tell you the truth, anyone who has faith in me will do what I have been doing. He will do even greater things than these, because I am going to the Father. And I will do whatever you ask in my name, so that the Son may bring glory to the Father. You may ask me for anything in my name, and I will do it.

These amazing words from the gospel of John encourage us to speak out. We need not be silent. We can speak. We can ask. We can ask God for anything. Isn't that an awesome realization? They include another promise that is equally wondrous. We are promised that we can do the works that Jesus did on this earth—and more. Glory to God! And one of the things that Jesus did was to speak God's words and speak them with eloquence and power. So we can gather up our faith and claim this promise as a basis for being able to witness, preach, and teach God's Word *with the anointing and power Jesus had.*

Since we are sinners in this world, all creation knows that you and I do not speak with an authoritative voice in spiritual matters. As the Son of God, Jesus did. As sinners we could not. When Jesus became sin for us so that we might become righteous in Him, He gave us His authoritative voice along with His righteousness. As He stood before Pilate, He gave up the privilege of speaking God's Word with power and authority so that we could have it. Since He could not speak without speaking God's Word, He stood in silence (Matt. 27:12–14). He could have called out to God for thousands of angels to come to His rescue had He chosen to do so. But He did not because He was giving away that privilege to us (Matt. 26:53). Isn't that a wondrous realization?

Now, I believe that though Jesus was fully human on the cross, He was also fully divine. So no matter how much the sinful nature of humankind became a part of who He was, Jesus was still the eternal Son of God at the same time. Whether I retain my sin or give it to Jesus, my identity also remains the same. I am still me. Whether Jesus becomes my sin or not, He is still the Son of God, Jesus Christ.

As God's Son, had Jesus spoken the word of God aloud in the courts of the high priest, Caiaphas, or of the governor, Pilate, He would have spoken with all of the power that spun galaxies into being. "All things were made by him; and without him was not anything made that was made" (John 1:3). So not only was He silent at times before Pilate so that we could be empowered to speak, but also He was silent because had He spoken God's Word with power, He could not have been condemned to death. He would have been so conclusively right and the power of His words would have been so overwhelmingly persuasive that He would have been delivered out of the terrible events that were happening to Him. He certainly was delivered right out of the middle of a mob that was trying to throw Him off a cliff outside of Nazareth (Luke 4:16–30). He had to be quiet. (I personally think that had Jesus spoken the truth in Pilate's judgment hall, His words would have blown every one of those men right over like waves of wheat in the wind.)

Jesus did not speak the Word of God to bring about His own deliverance because He voluntarily relinquished the power and privilege and ability to do it to us. Now we not only have the Word of God, but also we have the power and authority to use it. How vitally important it is that we not only have God's Word but also that we *use* it!

As Christians, we know that we have God's Word. Now let us begin to speak it aloud with greater and greater faith so that it can do the things God wants done on the earth. Let us dare to use God's Word as He uses it to accomplish what needs to be done. God's Word carries within itself the power needed for its own fulfillment. That is clear in the prophetic words given by God to the prophet Isaiah when he said, "So shall my word be that goeth forth out of my mouth: it shall not return unto me void, but it shall accomplish that which I please, and it shall prosper in the thing whereto I sent it" (Isa. 55:11).

A PRINCIPLE: The forces of oppression that afflicted and killed Jesus hurled at Him the worst of everything that had ever been done to anybody. When it was happening, He did not use the power of God's Word to control it—just the way we often do not speak out the promises of God when we are in need. We have the right to speak God's Word like thundering prophecy for our own protection when we are in trouble (Matt. 10:19–20). Jesus stood mute, saying nothing before Pilate so that the right words could pour out of my mouth and yours in times of crisis. He was chewed up and devoured by death so that it would have no more victory over us. He took affliction and oppression so we could be set free and live in joyous liberty and health.

AN AFFIRMATION OF FAITH: "Oppression and affliction have come to an end in my life. Jesus is my Savior from sin. I receive Him anew today as Savior from oppression and affliction. He experienced all of it for me so that I can be free of it forever. I trust Him to show me the right thing to say because His Spirit is always with me to guide me. It is one more wonderful thing that He bought for me through the shedding of His blood. Everything I need for complete salvation is mine in Jesus Christ."

The Sacrificial Lamb

A CHRISTIAN STUDY SERIES

God protects me from bitter jealousy.

THE SCRIPTURE: "he was led like a lamb to the slaughter." (Isa. 53:7b NIV)

A PROBLEM SITUATION: Thousands, no, millions of Jewish people were herded into boxcars in Nazi Germany to be sent to concentration camps and gas chambers during World War II. When I think of it, I am struck by how often death and destruction can come in life to people who seem swept along by tragedy in mute helplessness. It is so like the picture of Jesus submitting to the entire program of torture, humiliation, and death at the hands of vicious priests, lawyers, professors, politicians, and police. How ironic and incomprehensible it seems. Those among us from whom the finest of virtues might be expected (like the priests and Bible scholars who framed and executed Jesus) can end up exhibiting the greatest depravity of all.

Jealousy, the Bible plainly states, was the reason for the dreadful behavior of the Jewish religious leaders who

239

pushed so hard for Jesus' death (Matt. 27:18). Powerful men, jealous of their power, controlled the religious establishment in Jerusalem in Jesus' lifetime. All over the world and throughout history, religious and political leaders have persecuted people out of that same fierce jealousy. Only the redemptive grace of Jesus Christ delivers us all from a sinful nature capable of such cruelty.

Pilate knew the priests and others wanted Jesus killed because they were jealous of Him. What kind of moral weakness was it that made Pilate violate his own judgment of the situation to condemn an innocent man? Whatever it was, wicked men were about the business of manipulating power for cruel and despicable ends during that Passover season two thousand years ago. And through it all, Jesus Christ, the Lord of all creation, without whom nothing on this earth was or has been made (John 1:3), walked toward His death with the compliance of a docile lamb.

COMMENTS: All of the viciousness of all humankind throughout the whole history of the human race lashed at the gentle and unresisting Teacher who had spent His life doing good. Though He wept for the grief of those who lost loved ones, though He loved and received the children—putting His hand lovingly on their heads and praying for them—though He forgave thieves, prostitutes, and the IRS (tax gatherers), fed hungry people, healed the sick and suffering, and brought instantaneous relief to wild and dangerous maniacs, Jesus engendered rage and viciousness from the most prominent Bible teachers and scholars of His day. They permitted the temple guards to torture and harass Him with unbridled cruelty, making sport of His suffering and humiliating Him in every way.

All of the events of Jesus' trial and death violate codes and beliefs upon which we base our claim to civilized law enforcement and justice. Jesus, the Lamb of God, without spot or blemish—without having committed the slightest offense in all of His life on this earth—was completely without advocate or defender, weapon or support, in everything that happened to Him when He came under the control and power of the same systems in this world *that we live under all the time.* What He experienced at the hands of those systems destroyed His body, ended His ministry, and took His life. Those are all the things Satan's systems aim to do to us. As John 10:10 says, "The thief cometh not, but for to steal, and to kill, and to destroy: I am come that they might have life, and that they might have it more abundantly."

A PRINCIPLE: One of the basic principles being presented in this book is the idea that we can look at all of the things that happened to Jesus and know that those same things are a part of Satan's plan to destroy everyone (John 10:10). The same way that cattle are herded into a boxcar to be taken to slaughter, the Nazis herded the Jews onto trains to take them to the concentration camps. It is not God's will for any people in covenant with Him to be exploited, oppressed, or victimized (Deut. 28:1–13; 1 John 5:4). That is Satan's program, but not God's. We are to be victorious over oppression and affliction because Jesus submitted Himself to it on our behalf, and in so doing, He overcame it for us (John 16:33). He took our helplessness against it upon Himself so that He could give us His mighty power to be victorious (Rev. 12:11; 2:7, 11, 17, 26; 3:12, 21).

Like defenseless sheep without claws or fangs, we so often feel helpless. But because Jesus put Himself under the dominion of evil in my place, Satan is no longer able to destroy me—or you. We'll never again be led like a helpless lamb to the slaughter. We have exchanged our weakness for Jesus' vast strength. We are delivered out of the hands of our enemies. Their plans and programs for our destruction no longer have the power to destroy us.

Jesus, who is the Lion of the Tribe of Judah, died like a gentle lamb that was casually butchered. Although all power in heaven and on earth had been given to Him (Matt. 28:18), He permitted His life to be taken just as a weak man would submit without resisting. He was weak with my weakness. I am strong with His strength. "Finally, my brethren, be strong in the Lord, and in the power of his might" (Eph. 6:10). It is His power that makes us strong.

AN AFFIRMATION OF FAITH: "Jesus has taken on Himself all of my weakness, and He gives me His boundless strength. I live my life in close fellowship with Him as a branch lives attached to a vine. Jesus is my Savior. He is my perfect Savior. I receive His wonderful deliverance from the terrible future that Satan's systems try to work out for me. My escape is perfect and complete because my Savior's work on the cross is perfect and complete. I do not have to wait until I die and go to heaven to be free of Satan's power and dominion over my life. I live today in freedom. I seek with joy the kingdom of God and His righteousness all the days of my life."

Study Fourteen

⟶➤●⟶

Eloquence and
Freedom

A CHRISTIAN STUDY SERIES

I wish I had said that!

THE SCRIPTURE: "and as a sheep before her shearers is silent, so he did not open his mouth." (Isa. 53:7c NIV)

A PROBLEM SITUATION: The most frequent kind of work that I have done throughout my adult life is writing. In all kinds of situations and for all kinds of people, I have found myself working to put down on paper the things that they want or need to say. In all these years, you may rest assured that I have spent many long moments leaning on my elbows, staring at a typewritten page, and then later, looking at a computer screen, longing for the eloquence to express in words the things I wanted to say.

Very few of us have the ability to express fully and completely what is in our hearts or on our minds. How much we all are confounded by that lack of ability. As a matter of fact, the Bible includes a fascinating account of the ancient peoples of Babel who are responsible for our communication problems even today. They joined together to build a great tower. Because God was dismayed by their wickedness, He set about to confound their efforts to communicate with one another and thus limit their ability to work together effectively toward evil ends (Gen. 11:1–9).

The Bible clearly states that God recognized that the people of Babel could do anything they set out to do if they could achieve good communication among themselves. So God Himself interfered with their ability to communicate by causing them to be unable to understand one another's languages. It worked then. It still works today.

It is very hard to make life work when we are unable to communicate. Often we find we have difficulty communicating well even with those we love and care about most. The plan of salvation would not be complete, covering every area of need in our lives, if this issue were not dealt with.

COMMENTS: The clinical name for the inability to communicate verbally is "aphasia." As I pray through these affirmations—and I find them a blessing in my own devotional life—I shorten this affirmation to say that Jesus Christ became aphasic so that I may be eloquent and articulate. As a person whose work has been writing, the ability to articulate an idea with words is especially precious to me. Clearly everyone needs to be set free from the inability to make others understand what he or she wants to say.

It was sin, all those centuries ago in the city of Babel, that caused humankind to lose the vital ability to communicate. Jesus Christ reversed the consequences of sin in our lives by taking both the sin and its consequences upon Himself. He gave up all ability to communicate to Pilate, when to do so might have saved Him from horrible suffering. In giving up the ability to communicate, He has restored our liberty to open our mouths and speak powerfully and eloquently—with the eloquence and power that was His very own—by taking upon

Himself the consequences of the sin of humanity that led to serious limitations in our ability to speak to one another and probably to God.

A PRINCIPLE: Jesus took on Himself completely our inability to communicate as He stood silently before the judge who had the power to condemn Him to death. He took on Himself every person's inability to speak and also the desperation and despair we all feel when we see that terrible things are going to happen because we cannot make ourselves understood.

The Bible makes it clear that the whole world labors under a specific punishment that limits people's ability to make themselves understood. Jesus set us free from that handicap and the bondage it creates in all our lives. Once He had taken on Himself every bit of the curse put upon the wicked people of Babel and all humankind since, then Jesus lavishly poured out to us all the great power inherent in Him who is called "the Word" (John 1:1–3).

AN AFFIRMATION OF FAITH: "With great joy and liberty, I express praise and love toward God today. I look forward day by day to glorious freedom in my ability to speak effectively anywhere and to anyone. To my loving heavenly Father and to everyone I meet, I now speak in ways that allow me to express all I need and want to say with clarity and power."

———⟫●⟪———

Shielded and Protected

A CHRISTIAN STUDY SERIES

He was cut off from life.

THE SCRIPTURE: "By oppression and judgment, he was taken away. And who can speak of his descendants?" (Isa. 53:8a NIV)

A PROBLEM SITUATION: It would seem that we all have experienced trauma or abuse at one time or another, often at the hands of unscrupulous people. It has a devastating effect on us at the time it happens, but it has a lifelong effect as well. Being in war or in a fire or robbed or raped or failed in school or abused as a child or falsely accused or shamed or humiliated or losing a loved one or being fired from a job are all examples of terrible traumas that introduce sustained pain into a person's life. It is the kind of pain that lasts a long time after the event itself has passed.

Upsetting events not only are devastating in themselves, but also they change the world completely for the people to whom they happen. Nothing can ever be the same. When you are deeply hurt, you are brought to the realization that the world is not a safe place. Without God's help, there is a sense in which you may never feel quite safe in the world again.

When a frightening or hurtful thing happens to you, life often takes on a watchfulness and dread that a hurt that could happen once might happen again. This attitude is called "hypervigilance." It is fear in continual action. It lays a blanket of oppression over life. It is as though a person is led away into a permanent kind of captivity as a result of a traumatic experience. Such feelings can be very real and constant in the life of a victim, of a survivor, of terror or trauma or hurt. Indeed, the very chemistry of the brain may be altered and the goodness of life diminished—without a Savior.

Thank God we have a Savior ... one who saves us from everything from which we need to be saved. He saves us from the ravages of abuse and post-trauma stress by sponging it up into Himself like a sponge cleaning up the proverbial spilt milk. The world tells us not to cry over spilt milk, implying that there is no point in crying because nothing can be done about it. Not so with Jesus. He saves us from it by absorbing it out of our lives into His own ... by taking it for us just the same way He took our sin and died our death on the cross. In today's study verse, Isaiah foretells the cruel oppression and vicious judgment to which Jesus was subjected in the process of taking our pain and trauma upon Himself.

Take Him Away

Being "taken away" is the phrase Isaiah used to describe Jesus' arrest. It covers what happened to Jesus, first at the hands of the temple guards and then at the hands of Pilate's secular troops. Simply stated, Jesus was arrested and held by violent men. Evidently, the security personnel who served the priests back in Bible days were little better than the military personnel who served the Roman governor, Pilate. Both temple guards and soldiers apparently were free to torment and torture their prisoners with unbridled viciousness (Mark 14:65; Matt. 27:27–31).

If ever there was doubt in anyone's mind about the presence of evil in every area of life, the events surrounding Jesus' death make the point irrefutable. Good behavior is no protection. Jesus' behavior was exemplary in every way, yet it proved to be no protection against oppression and abuse by others.

No group or level of human society can be counted on always to behave appropriately and with honor—not even when dealing with a perfect man. The soldiers certainly did not. The false witnesses did not. Bible scholars, priests, and spiritual leaders of the highest rank who condemned Jesus did not. As a matter of fact, the hand-picked group of Jesus' own disciples included a thief who betrayed Him, and all of them ran away in fear.

Not a single one of us in this world is innocent of offense in our treatment of other people. No one escapes being victimized by cruelty in humanity's sinful ways of dealing with one another. We are all victims. We are all offenders.

Often people who act with cruelty justify their actions because the person being mistreated committed some kind of offense. Yet that cannot be the reason that explains the viciousness in human behavior because Jesus committed no offense. His behavior toward everyone was perfect. Yet He was treated with dreadful cruelty. Jesus was guilty of no offense toward any person, yet He was hated, reviled, and tortured to death—and it was caused by "men of the cloth." Even the most godly training and upbringing along with a lifetime spent in study of the Bible could not protect the spiritual leaders of Jesus' day from developing cruelty, greed, jealousy, and self-righteousness. Let us not read those words lightly. Those qualities could appear in any one of us at any time, without the Lord's help to prevent it.

The best Christian parents, along with the best family background and the finest education, cannot produce automatic goodness in the children. A lifetime of Bible study cannot protect us from abusing people and being cruel or jealous or careless or anything else. Sin is a genetic marker present in all of us. Nothing on earth can save us from sin. Jesus alone has a plan and program that takes it out of our lives and addresses the devastation it produces in both victim and offender.

The experiences of God's Son on the earth demonstrate not only that all of us are on the receiving end of trauma and abuse, but also it shows that not one of us is so "good" that he or she is free of guilt as a perpetrator of abuse.

Judas was personally mentored by the finest man who ever lived. He sat under the best teacher the world has ever known and yet proved himself to be a traitor and a thief. The best educated, wealthiest, most respected, most influential, and most spiritually sophisticated among us are just as capable of depravity as anyone else.

The forces of life in this world are at work not to support our efforts to rid our lives of sin, but rather to maintain its power and hold on us. We all have to partake of the death, burial, and resurrection of Jesus to escape the power of sin into which we are all born. The wonderful news of the gospel is that such an escape is possible.

By oppression and judgment, Jesus was taken away. By oppressive spiritual leaders and political regimes, Jesus was falsely bound and taken into captivity. He was arrested, cruelly tortured, wrongly adjudged guilty of offense, and put to death by the very same spiritual forces that are now actively at work to make your life miserable. You are struggling against the same kinds of situations all the time (Eph. 6:10–18). But as we lay hold of the truth and power of the gospel message, we can be set free from the world's plan and rewrite the life script that determines our destiny.

COMMENTS: As far as we know, Jesus never served on a committee. He never had to make a mortgage payment. He never sat through a long, tedious staff meeting. He never served in the military or sat for examination to be licensed in a profession. He never labored under a harsh, demanding taskmaster. He was free on this earth as no one had been free since Adam left the Garden of Eden. Nothing had a hold on Him. Nothing controlled Him. Nothing stifled Him. No vast corporate structure wrapped it tentacles around His life to control it. Nothing intimidated Him. He wrote His own life script. In closest fellowship with His heavenly Father, Jesus laid out the course of His own life. No oppressive force in this world shaped His life or dictated what He would do or be … until His arrest.

Once the normal, "business as usual" groups that run this world managed to have Jesus arrested and brought under their control, everything changed. When Satan, the prince of this world who shapes policy for those "business as usual" groups, had an opening into Jesus' life to cause Him pain, to interfere with His work, and ultimately to destroy Him, he wasted no time doing it. Sadly, it was spiritual leaders and students of God's Word who became Satan's tools (John 14:30; Luke 22:3).

No matter how noble we think a particular human institution may be, Satan is at work, trying to use it to steal, kill, and destroy (John 10:10). So even though the people who took Jesus into custody were priests who had spent their whole lives studying God's Word and His commandments, Satan succeeded in using them to abuse an innocent man in every cruel way he could devise. The sheer depravity of crucifixion as a form of execution reveals the full extent of the evil of which the "best" of humanity is capable.

Once He was "taken away," once He was arrested, Jesus was no longer absolutely free. Instead, He was in absolute bondage. He was totally alone and at the mercy of ruthless tormentors,

tormentors who were the very people who should have been helping Him, honoring the principles of justice, and protecting His rights. The Lord knows all about the feelings that injustice and abuse create. He experienced them. And He did it for you so that He could take *out of your life* the pain and rage and powerlessness of the abusive event itself, and also the lifelong fear and hypervigilance it leaves behind.

Because of what Jesus did for us through His Passion and death, all of us can come to the foot of the cross and give Him not only our devastation over past suffering but also our fear and dread that it could happen again. We need a Savior to help us cope with the endless need for alertness and exhausting watchfulness, along with all the other feelings like abandonment and shame and worthlessness that are present because no one helped us and no one seemed to care. As we leave all of this at the cross, each one of us can receive in its place Jesus' own power, peace, and protection. What a glorious exchange we make with Jesus at the cross!

Turning it Over … and Over … and Over!

Now that you understand the concept of the transfer or exchange that takes place at the cross and you have had the opportunity to begin applying and affirming God's provision for your life, it will be helpful to review in practical terms the principles of "turning it over" to Jesus. While all of these lavish provisions are available to every believer—and that includes you and me—knowing *about* God's resources will not in itself complete the work. Every believer must make a decision to appropriate or activate the provisions God has made for us through His salvation plan. Knowing about this wonderful plan of salvation, understanding it, and even believing in it is not enough. That is having faith, but it is faith without works. We have to *do* it. We actually have to transact the business of salvation at the cross. We are responsible for going to Jesus and telling Him that we give Him our sin and receive in its place His perfect righteousness.

An automobile may have all of the components and parts needed to take us where we want and need to be, but it will not go until we do something. We can know all about cars and look all day long at the car that belongs to us, believing it has the power to take us on our journey, but we will not get anywhere until we make a decision to open the car door, get in, turn the key, grasp the steering wheel, release the brake, put our foot on the gas, and drive away.

Even a perfect and detailed map that shows the way will not move us one inch unless we take action. In the same way, we must take control of and activate God's wonderful resource plan.

We must choose to change the attitudes of our minds and exchange all of our negative, dreadful thoughts and feelings for the good news that Jesus took them to the cross so that we might be saved from their cruel and devastating effects. The impact of abusive events in our lives may not change or disappear instantly, but they surely will in time as we walk out the plan of salvation and affirm God's wonderful promises every day. Meanwhile, your mind, emotions, and spirit can be free of the events' terrible power to coerce and torment you and control your behavior.

Most of us have heard the saying that "iron bars do not a prison make or solid walls a cage." Often it is not the circumstances but rather how we interpret them that impacts our behavior and the climate inside our own hearts. Every Christian must choose to press on with the decision to appropriate all that Jesus has provided for us and to resist the negative, tormenting ideas and thoughts that rush through our minds.

Upsetting ideas that flood our minds can have the power to displace an attitude of faith if a Christian allows it. Not only that, but also such negative ideas overload the circuits in the brain and use up the energy and time needed to seek out and affirm God's "exceedingly great and precious promises" to meet a specific need (2 Peter 1:3–4 NIV).

Instead of entertaining negative ideas, you might try saying out loud:

> Jesus took my shame and humiliation. He bore my anger and self-pity, my powerlessness and the fear that has resulted from the circumstances of my life. He did it so that I would not have to experience any longer the devastation and torment they have caused.
>
> I turn all these negative feelings and experiences (name them) over to You, Lord Jesus. I thank You for experiencing them in my place so that I can be free of their effects mentally, physically, emotionally, and spiritually. I choose to take a firm stand against every negative, shameful, depressing, fearful, or self-limiting thought that misses the mark of the high calling of God in my life.
>
> The news the world tries to give me is not good news. Thus it cannot be the gospel truth, for "gospel" means "good news." I will not receive this bad idea or entertain this bad news any longer. I reject all of it (name it all). I proclaim instead that Jesus, my Savior, made provision to meet all of my needs (Phil. 4:19) for every situation I must deal with, and I am free of their effects on my life, no matter how things may look.
>
> I have decided to follow Jesus, and I receive His provisions for my life, just the way I received Him as my Savior. I receive from Him eternal life, mental and physical health, financial vitality, social acceptance, and wellbeing and success in every part of my life.

When you have done all this, it is still not over. It is not a one-time remedy. It must become a way of life, a way of thinking that dominates every day's business. You must decide to attack and stand against all the old negative, destructive, crippling messages that bombard your mind and all of the new ones that the world tries to send along with each new situation or challenge in your life.

Repeat the process as often as any negative thoughts persist. If an unwanted thought returns, speak aloud to it, saying, "Stop! Stop! I will not entertain these thoughts. I reject them. I give them no place in my thinking." Next, review the whole work of redemption that Jesus did on the cross, event by event, until you find the particular provision that addresses the need you face. Then describe it in the form of an affirmation, and state it out loud.

Example: If you are rejected and hurt by a person or group, think of Jesus being rejected by the mob and give Him all of the hurt and grief and embarrassment and crippling effects of the event. Then quote a Bible verse, such as Ephesians 1:6, in which we are told that we always are accepted in the beloved, and affirm aloud your faith that you are fully accepted as a beloved member of the family of God (Gal. 4:4–7; Eph. 3:14–18).

Example: If you are faced with a job that looms before you as overwhelming and impossible or it comes at a time in your life when you feel weak or depleted or if you feel that the pain in your life is so great that you cannot do the thing that faces you, then think about Jesus struggling to pick up His cross and carry the instrument of His own execution to the place of His death. Accomplishing the work of the cross without sinning for one single nanosecond surely must have loomed before Him as too much for anyone to do.

As our Savior staggered along the path to Golgotha, He did not have the strength and power of the Son of God to draw upon. It was gone. He had given it to you and to me. It happened when He lifted the cup in the upper room and declared, "This cup is the new covenant in my blood" (Matt. 26:27–28; Mark 14:22–23; Luke 22:20).

Jesus exchanged His strength and power for your weakness and inadequacy as a part of the new covenant He made with you. So He walked up that hill in your weakness; in your pain; and in the most total kind of physical, emotional, and spiritual depletion. Yet He had a place to go that He did not want to go. He faced an overwhelming task that He did not want to perform. And He did it all. He did it all depending only on your weakness, functioning in all of your inadequacy that He was experiencing as His own, struggling with your exhaustion and in your crushing sorrow and grief. He did all that for you … so He could give you relief and deliverance from it all. He did it to make all of His power available to you. It's awesome! What a Savior!

Each difficult thing you face in life is another opportunity for you to go to Jesus and exchange what is wrong with you for what is right in Him. You can answer each negative thought that comes to you with a more rational, positive thought. For example, *Jesus gives beauty for ashes, joy for despair, glory for shame, and forgiveness for condemnation* (Isa. 61:3; John 15:11; 17:22; Rom. 8:1).

Remember that the things we affirm aloud are legally filed in heaven's court in the same way that we file a deed or other document at the local county courthouse. Our verbal affirmation constitutes a legal transaction in the kingdom of heaven. Your verbal acceptance of Jesus Christ as your Lord and Savior was all that was required to secure your eternal salvation. Isn't that wonderful?! God accepts your word. It is the only passport you need to enter eternal life in the kingdom of God. No matter what the origin of your pain or problem, your affirmation of faith secures your freedom in Christ, for He was bound and taken captive to set you free; and whom the Lord sets free is free indeed (John 18:12; Gal. 5:1; John 8:32–36).

Remember that no one is perfect. Do not focus on the negative or elaborate on it. God's mercy toward us endures forever (Ps. 100:5; 107:1). Clinging to perfectionistic ideals and behavior is a great setup for a fall. Perfectionistic behavior can be a curse not only for you but also for others in your life who must bear the brunt of its unrealistic demands. For some people, perfectionistic personal demands represent the best description of the sin of pride. Being free of it may be a wonderful liberation indeed.

Most of the time feeling "bad" begins with the flash of a negative thought (a fiery dart from the Enemy), and we begin to entertain thoughts and ideas about a disturbing situation until we are finally reviewing something that is so painful or shameful or fearful that it washes us under. Then we try to resist it after it has become fully developed and rooted in our thinking, a full-blown problem in our minds.

Turning a thing over to the Lord means far more than simply mouthing words. Get your faith in gear. Make a faith decision based on some of the Bible's wonderful promises. Resolve not to be continually reviewing the negative aspects of life and ruminating on them until they overcome you. Instead, you can choose to consider thoughtfully the goodness of God and the completeness and power of the plan of salvation that Jesus died to provide for us. Let your mind busy itself with a review of how much the Lord loves you and how much He has done for you.

In each instance when you entertain thoughts of hurtful or fearful events in your mind, you are actually replaying them over and over at about six times the rate that you normally speak. So in a very short time, you can create a mental environment or climate that is fertile for the seeds of depression, fear, anger, bitterness, and defeat to grow.

When you turn something over to Jesus by taking it to the cross, you turn it over completely. It is over! You have given to the Lord. Then release it, and let it go entirely and receive the life of Christ flowing from the cross to you. What you claim, what you verbalize, what you visualize, and what you receive from the Lord in place of what you have given to Him is always the opposite of what you take to the cross. It is the very perfect thing required to meet the need. It is what Jesus gave up and gave away in order to carry to the cross your sorrow, grief, sin, and everything from which you will ever need to be saved.

Just as you exchange the shame and guilt of sin for forgiveness and acceptance, you exchange sorrow and grief for joy and peace. Across the board, you exchange life for death and blessing for cursing when you receive Jesus Christ as Savior and Lord (Deut. 30:19). Forever thereafter, those things—life and blessing—belong to you based on a few words you spoke when you proclaimed your faith in Jesus as your Savior.

A Practical Example

Let's construct a little more detailed situation to which the principles we are discussing can be applied. Let's use the kind of situation often encountered by counselors and therapists. Let's suppose that you have a particularly unpleasant and nasty boss (or spouse or teacher or parent or neighbor), who is nicknamed "Bull" behind his back by those forced to work under him. Bull is a man who constantly undermines your confidence. He picks at your work, finding fault and being unjustly critical. He strives to control you or deprive you of the resources vital to reaching your goals, controlling them for himself. Bull is far more like an enemy than a colleague should ever be.

Now let's suppose that during a very important meeting with many of your fellow workers and associates present, Bull attacks you by viciously criticizing ideas and work that actually warrant approval and affirmation, or for ideas for which others were equally responsible. Your surprise and pain would be great. Then suppose no one in the whole group of people you work with finds a positive word to say to support you. The abandonment by everyone present (people you had thought to be your friends) leaves you all alone, as the sole and only scapegoat being blamed and punished for something that may not have been an offense at all.

How does it feel to sit silent and alone, with no one to come to your defense? How does it feel to know that others agreed with you and respect your position and your work and yet they are willing to watch you treated with cruelty and injustice and do nothing?

This scenario grew out of real life events. It is not fiction. It was not "made up." Years of counseling with individuals who have endured painful scenes like the one just described at work, in families, or even in churches, confirm that memories of such painful experiences can recur constantly over months and even years. Mental pictures of such events form and reform over and over, bringing a flood of feelings that can be very hard to handle. Such pictures can be instantly overwhelming and often disabling when they recur in our minds, even years after the event. The thought-stopping techniques offered by the mental health field, the mood-altering habits we employ for ourselves, and all of the other devices to which you turn may help somewhat, but nothing can match the plan of salvation for beautiful healing and restoration.

If you are coping with a situation as damaging and painful as the one described above—if you relive your father leaving, your spouse demanding a divorce, betrayal by a friend, failing in school, being fired, having your home burn, losing a business, or any other devastating life experience—take the biblical procedures recommended here and put them to work. Faithfully use them to bring the transforming power of the gospel to life in every situation. Give Jesus everything that is not right and receive from Him all the goodness and blessing that flows from His life into yours.

For the Really Tough Stuff

For the really difficult situations that come up in life, you are encouraged to verbalize your affirmation right out loud and then write it down as well. If possible, record your affirmation three times in three different forms[8] on a recording device (as previously described) and listen to your own voice speaking faith into your own ears and heart. Picture Jesus going through similarly painful experiences after His capture and actually carrying to His death your personal, individual pain or shame or loss or disappointment or whatever it may be. If a negative picture comes into your mind, quickly develop an image of Jesus in your mind. Visualize Jesus experiencing it in your place, and actively affirm your acceptance of His gift of salvation to you, the gift that supplies the opposite thing you need to be made whole.

Turn all of the negative feelings over to the Lord (1 Peter 5:7). He experienced exactly those same feelings so that He could save you from their devastating power. Jesus also was unjustly condemned and criticized. He was belittled for His work, when He should have been praised. He was viciously attacked and condemned for healing the sick on the Sabbath, when everyone should have been shouting with joy and thanksgiving. He was mocked, scorned, and battered, when He should have been rewarded, respected, and honored. He was abandoned by trusted friends, when He should have been supported and defended. He was denied by those closest to

Him, when they should have come to His aid. He was physically, mentally, and emotionally tormented and abused so that you may be consoled, comforted, and healed; so that you may prosper and flourish in all that you do; so that you may be enfolded in the fellowship of caring, committed friends—brothers and sisters in the body of Christ—and so that you may be restored to mint condition.

Now there is one final, truly glorious step to perfect deliverance and victory. Forgive everyone involved in the painful events that have been so destructive in your life. Follow Jesus in this vital act. You will remember that He prayed in the face of heartless cruelty: "Father, forgive them for they know not what they do" (Luke 23:34).

As a brief aside, let me say that I found the matter of forgiveness very difficult at the beginning. Then, at one point, I got to the place in my life where I could forgive people rather easily because I carried in the back of my mind the idea that one day they would be accountable to God, so I felt I could leave justice up to Him. I guess I thought the Lord would be as angry with those people as I was! He'd make sure they got what was deserved. You can see that I wasn't there yet, was I? But this prayer that Jesus prayed was asking God to give His abusers a free pass, a clean slate, so that they will never have to answer for the offenses against Him. My challenge is to do the same for my abusers. Sometimes I still find it hard. It was only when I realized that I was writing out the rules by which I was to be judged myself someday that I made it a point to pray this difficult prayer of forgiveness on behalf of anyone and everyone who ever abused or offended me (Matt. 7:2; Mark 11:25–26).

Whatsoever Things Are Good …

If you and I continue to go down the same old path, we'll keep arriving at the same old place. When you are focused on something grievous and hurtful, it is setting the direction for your life; and you may be sure that it will be the destination you reach.

Change your course. Set a different direction, and you will arrive at a different place. You'll arrive at a place where you overcome pain and defeat, a place in which you are in control of your thoughts and feelings and they are not controlling you. When your thoughts and your feelings and your behavior reflect the fruit of the Spirit that Jesus provides for you, your focus will be on abundant life and grace and peace—and you *will* get there!

The great prophet Moses speaks the word of the Lord to us this day and every day in Deuteronomy 30:15, telling us that the Lord sets before us life and death, blessing and cursing. In verse 19, He admonishes us to choose life. We must choose. We must actively choose. That is our job. It is our responsibility, and whatever we choose, good or bad, God will honor by making the choice a reality.

Salvation Covers Everything

Now let us consider briefly the second part of today's Bible verse. Nothing in the Bible is there by chance. Today's verse asks us to take what appears to be a radical turn in our thinking in order to consider the last phrase: "And who can speak of His descendants?" What does this verse have to do with us?

Not only does Isaiah talk about the tragedy of the things that *do* happen in our lives, but also he talks about the tragedy of the things that *do not* happen. Salvation covers the pain of what *did* happen *and* the pain of what *did not* happen. Thus, today's study directs our thinking to the special pain and loss in the lives of people who do not have descendants, those who do not have families, those who cope with significant disappointment.

When the plan of salvation was drawn up in heaven, before Jesus was born in that little Bethlehem barn, God did not forget the sadness and neediness of people who do not have children or of lonely people who want to be married and are not.

Jesus was killed at age thirty-three without having the opportunity to establish a marriage or build a normal family life. While the Bible plainly teaches that Jesus came to earth to seek a bride that will one day include many in eternity; nonetheless, while He lived here, He was fully a man and was capable of loneliness. He had the same need for intimacy that all men feel. But He died without having had that need met, and He did it so that He could provide every one of us with a solution for the pain such a loss brings.

People who experience grief and sorrow over not having married or had children can receive comfort and healing by taking their pain to the cross. As you consider all the injustice and humiliation that Jesus endured, take a moment to consider His feelings—the different kinds of terrible feelings He must have experienced as so many devastating things happened to Him. He took all of those feelings on Himself for you. He did not overlook a single one. By experiencing them all, He made a way for you to be free of them.

You can bring all of your painful feelings about the unfairness of life and of fear, dread, loss, anger, and so forth to the cross and give them to Jesus, just as you give Him all of your sin. Then in the same way that He gives you His righteousness in place of your sin, He gives you His peace and joy in just the way you need to receive them.

No one and nothing on earth can give you the gift of peace the way that Jesus can. He tells us so Himself when He says, "Peace I leave with you: my [own] peace I now give and bequeath to you. Not as the world gives do I give to you. Do not let your hearts be troubled, neither let them be afraid" (John 14:27 AB).

When the world gives you something, it simply expects you to take it and use it. When Jesus gives you a blessing, He first takes away everything in your life that could interfere with the full power of His gift to bless you. He clears out of your life everything that could get in the way of the blessing by taking it all upon Himself and owning it fully and completely. Then He gives you the fullest measure of the blessing, right out of His own life, to take the place of what He has removed. He ends up owning our problem, and we end up owning His blessing. Give Jesus your disappointment over not having children and your grief over being unmarried. The plan of salvation includes special provision for you.

The plan of salvation is wonderful. It is perfect. Nothing has been omitted. Nothing has been forgotten. Nothing we shall ever need is missing. Jesus bought and paid for a perfect plan of salvation for every person who will receive it. It is complete. It is free! And it includes His perfect peace! Shalom!

A PRINCIPLE: Jesus suffered every kind of infuriating, corrupt form of injustice known to man. He was illegally and unjustly tried, tortured, and executed. He died without having a marriage or children. He experienced enormous pain and loss and shame for you. Personally and individually, He singled you out, reviewed your life, and prepared a plan to save you from everything in your life that is unjust, oppressive, or marked by great loss or disappointment. He was oppressed and judged guilty, though He was worthy of loving encouragement and commendation, so that you and I, who deserve to be judged and who all too often should be restrained and controlled, may be made free and faultless instead (Jude 24–25).

Because Jesus is my Savior, I will not be devastated by oppression or injustice. No one will cut off my ability to grow and explore my potential or take away my power to build a life of meaningful achievement, particularly in building a rich family life. By faith, I will use the gifts my heavenly Father has given me in a climate of liberty and freedom. Because Jesus was oppressed, harshly judged, and cut off from life, I may have life that is abundant and good and free.

AN AFFIRMATION OF FAITH: "I am growing and growing. I am exploring my potential. I am flourishing in a climate of light and liberty and peace. God gave me the power to build a life of rich achievement and satisfaction. In Jesus Christ I have courage and joy and strength. In Him I am faultless and free" (Jude 24).

Study Sixteen

Vibrant Life

A CHRISTIAN STUDY SERIES

No more standing on the outside, looking in.

THE SCRIPTURE: "For he was cut off from the land of the living; for the transgression of my people he was stricken." (Isa. 53:8b NIV)

A PROBLEM SITUATION: My picture of a zombie is some kind of a creature walking around and doing things but not having any real life inside. This is a pretty good description of the way it can be to try to struggle through day after day without Jesus. To be cut off from the land of the living is to be dead inside, shut out, and blocked off from where things are vital and dynamic and from where life is happening.

On the day he first sinned, Adam was told that he would surely die (Gen. 2:17). Certainly his body kept walking around, but I believe he no longer had the zest and excitement and joy and wonder and vitality that go with being fully alive. God's plan for Adam's life was very wonderful. He was to live in a garden where everything he needed was provided. Sin brought an end (death) to God's perfect provision.

While Adam lived in the Garden of Eden, God invited him to have dominion over the earth and everything in it. A person who has dominion is free and in power so that no other person or creature can dominate or control him or her (Gen. 1:28). When he sinned, Adam chose to discard God's program and try out Satan's instead. Under Satan's regime, Adam didn't have control anymore. He didn't control the earth. The earth controlled him. He began long days of drudgery, trying to produce his daily bread by the sweat of his brow, toiling in fields that are under a curse (Gen. 3:17–19). That is not life. That is not living. That is being cut off from the land of the living.

Adam transgressed and was stricken with a fate that has been lived out by every one of his sons to this day. Eve also was stricken with a life of pain and sorrow because she transgressed (Gen. 3:16). Only when the Son of God, who never transgressed, was stricken in man's place and in woman's place was there hope that the cursed life that is "normal" in this world could become blessed instead.

COMMENTS: As we have seen, Jesus was stricken in every way that humankind has suffered since the beginning of the world. He took on Himself all of our sins, all of our punishments, all of the pain and sorrow that grew out of both the sin and its punishment, and all of the crippling aftereffects that sin has had on our lives. Jesus also took the terrible outcomes of human failure and inadequacy. He was cut off, rejected, belittled, disdained, discounted, and finally killed. All of it happened to Him because the plan of salvation called for Him to experience everything that happens in our lives because of sin.

Absolutely everything bad that has ever happened in the life of every person ever created by God that was the result of his or her own sin or someone else's sin was taken by Jesus to the grave ... and beyond the grave to hell. That is where it belongs. That is where it was spawned, and that is where it should end up. There was no other way to dispose of it in this world.

Before Jesus solved the sin problem, it just kept forming and reforming itself over and over again in every generation. The sin problem strips from all people everywhere the abundance and vitality of the life that God created them to have. Satan's program is one of living death and an endless curse. God's program is one of eternal life and constant blessing.

Moses' Wonderful Message

Through the voice and pen of the great prophet Moses, God Himself spoke to the men and women of ancient Bible times about blessing and cursing, life and death. He speaks the same words to us today. With perfect grace and respect for our autonomy and independence to choose the outcome of our own lives, our heavenly Father sets before us this day and every day a choice between life and death, blessing and cursing (Deut. 30:15, 19). We must choose life daily. And interestingly, we must deliberately choose blessing as well in order to avoid the default choice of a curse. Passive Christians will experience disappointment instead of blessing.

Over recent months in my own personal life, I have been struck by the power we have to choose blessing. The gift of a will with which to choose is a wonderful gift indeed. It is one significant quality that marks humankind as unique in creation. Few of us realize the significance of our ability to choose blessing. A series of events that occurred in my life in rapid succession have persuaded me beyond all doubt that there is real power in choosing to expect blessing and to have an attitude that I am blessed—and also to choose to have an attitude that the troublesome events in life can be transformed into blessing if we invest our faith toward that end. Three examples come to mind immediately.

Surely Goodness and Mercy Follow Me

A friend with whom I often have prayed decided to make a special effort to pray with her two teenage sons every day. They were particularly eager to visit family who were living in another country, even though the cost for four to travel so far appeared prohibitive. For some months the children prayed daily with their mother, believing God to keep His wonderful promises and provide for the trip.

Small prayer victories concerning other matters came into the lives of this lovely family from day to day as they prayed together, so everyone was encouraged to continue looking forward to the special trip they all wanted to take. Then came a shock. With no warning at all, their father lost his job. Everyone was stunned. The whole family began to pray for another one, but one day after another went by, until more than a week had passed. While that is a very short time to allow for job hunting, it seemed long and stressful for the two young boys.

The significant thing about the time following the loss of their father's job was that it gave everyone in the family ample opportunity to voice their faith and assurance that God was still in charge of their lives and still the source of their security. That family invested faith in a request to be able to take a trip together. Their faith was tested. All of us will have our faith tested. Together they affirmed that God is faithful and His promises are true. Despite what was happening, they would continue to believe.

It came as no surprise to those of us who were praying with the family about the trip and about a new job for the father when he was offered three jobs in one day. The one he chose to accept pays him ten thousand dollars a year more—enough to pay for the expensive overseas family vacation they were believing that God would supply.

What is the important thing to note about this family? First, they chose to believe that the thing that looked like a problem and a difficulty could be viewed as a blessing. They chose to believe that God was working on their behalf and would bring good from a situation that looked grim and negative. They chose to accept the job loss as a blessing instead of as defeat and loss. They chose to receive it as a blessing and not as a curse (Phil. 4:19; Rom. 8:28).

Did the daily persevering faith of two children and their mother make an avenue through which God was able to bless them? In Matthew 9:29, the blind men were told that good things happened to them because of their faith. Jesus gave many others the same important message directly and personally (Matt. 9:22; Mark 5:24; 10:52; Luke 7:50; 17:19; 18:42).

A second point about this family is also significant. Both the parents and their children refused to feel cut off from life or separated from hope and joy and peace. There was a peace about them each time they discussed their situation. They chose to continue to be happy and participate in life in a positive way. They chose to believe that Jesus was "cut off from life" in our place and that we could expect the good things and the blessings due to Him because He took the negative program of loss and failure and rejection upon Himself for us. We can choose to expect life and blessing. And we can do it because Jesus chose to put Himself into a position of being cut off from life and stricken by one nasty blow after another for us.

Working Together for Good

Two additional examples come to mind to illustrate that even when bad things happen, we can choose to believe that good will come out of them. Sometimes mockingly called a

"Pollyanna attitude," the decision to expect goodness and blessing to evolve out of bad experiences is based on solid Bible teachings. The story of Joseph is a vivid example.

A wonderful hit Broadway play titled *Joseph and the Amazing Technicolor Dream Coat* has been touring the country for years. It tells the biblical story of Jacob's beloved son Joseph, who was sold into slavery by jealous brothers. Even as a slave, Joseph is well liked. But his owner's wife falsely accuses him of accosting her, and Joseph lands in prison. His life seems to go from bad to worse, but somewhere along the way he learned to choose blessing.

Joseph learned that in trusting God he could expect the bad things that happened to him to be transformed into blessings. The whole story of Joseph's life is found in Genesis 37–50. In Genesis 50:20, he makes a statement to the brothers who kidnapped him and sold him into slavery that shows us how to choose blessing instead of cursing: "ye thought evil against me; but God meant it unto good."

Joseph certainly was a survivor. He rose from the lowly estate of slave and convict to the position of prime minister of Egypt. He performed excellently in that position. Great success was his. Joseph learned somewhere in his traumatic journey from favored son to slavery and prison to the highest position in the land that he could choose blessing, and God would honor his choice and the faith that prompted it by blessing him over and over.

Every person is invited by God to develop a lifestyle of choosing life and blessing in both attitude and affirmation. When we maintain a continual expectation of blessing even when problems confront us, we are living in an attitude of faith that pleases God (John 16:33; Rom. 8:28). The Bible teaches us that it pleases God for us to walk in faith (Heb. 11:6). By affirming our trust in God's amazing promises to us, we are walking in faith. We are continually expressing to God and to all the hosts of heaven and earth that we choose to expect the blessing that God promises we shall have.

We ought to affirm God's promises (speak them aloud with faith) every day, because God told Moses that He puts the choice between blessing and cursing and life and death before us every day. Every one of us has the privilege of affirming our faith in God's offer of life and blessing because Jesus chose death on our behalf and took every curse upon Himself (Gal. 3:13). He did it so that we could have life and have it abundantly (John 10:10).

God's Reward

I mentioned above that three examples came to my mind of trusting God to bring blessings when bad things happen. The third example is the story of a bright, young engineer named Jerry, who was selling chemicals to large paper mills. Along with the products he was selling, this young man provided extensive consultation services to the mills that contracted with him, and he had a great deal to offer in the way of professional expertise.

Jerry and his wife prayed together regularly about his business. They particularly prayed for successful sales to a mill close to their home so that Jerry could have a little more time with his family. Both of them felt an assurance that the many hours of problem solving and exemplary service he had given the mill, coupled with earnest prayer, would lead to the awarding of another contract to Jerry's firm. They were surprised and crushed when it was given to a "cheaper" competitor.

At a point of great disappointment, we make one of life's most important decisions. Will we choose blessing, or will we choose to let our lives be pulled down under the influence of the curses that have oppressed humankind since Adam left the garden? Will we put our faith in God's promises of blessing, or will we put our faith in the world's expectation of disappointment and defeat?

If we want to please God in our lives, we will walk in faith that God's Word is the truth and that His promises are trustworthy in every way. Like a witness on a witness stand, we speak aloud our conviction that God's promises are true. And then we walk out our faith by choosing life. We expect the blessing, so we can afford to relax and have joy and peace fill our days.

Choosing life is choosing to live a dynamic, vibrant life of positive expectations in the face of the problems that confront us all of the time. It is not a promise that no problems will occur. But what it does provide is an enormous energy source of joy and confidence to carry us through the daily problem-solving demands that every person faces.

How was Jerry's choice of blessing in the face of disappointment and apparent failure rewarded? Late one Thursday evening, after Jerry and his family were in bed, the telephone rang. It was the mill calling. In desperation, they were asking for help with the "cheaper" product. Things were not working right. The whole operation was in trouble. They needed more than Jerry's superior product, they needed his expert help immediately. Needless to say, Jerry was awarded the contract after all and worked out their problems as well. God does reward those who choose to trust His promises and diligently seek Him no matter how hopeless things look.

Looking back, it seems so easy to see that it was right for Jerry and his wife to trust God in the face of disappointment. But while it was happening, it was not easy. It was difficult. In this case, both of them said aloud to one another and to others who had been praying with them that they were trusting God despite their disappointment. Both consistently affirmed that what looked like something bad would work out for good. It is not an easy attitude to maintain, but it works.

Salvation Brings Life and Peace

Today's study scripture prophesies that in His Passion and death, Jesus was to be "cut off from the land of the living" and that He was to be stricken "for the transgression of my people." When loss or failure or disappointment or problems occur in our lives, it often seems as though all the life flows out of our bodies and we feel dead inside. We are cut off from life. When a father loses his job, his family may be stricken with fear and embarrassment. When a contract is awarded to someone else, a man is stricken by disappointment and failure. When we make the awful mistakes that everyone makes who ever does anything at all in life, then we are stricken by shame and defeat. Jesus had to be stricken for our transgressions because there have been so many of them.

Have you been stricken by tragedy or defeat or catastrophe— a failure, a loss, a flood, a fire, an injury, a death? Where do we go when such things happen? What do we do with the feelings they cause? How can we get on top of them long enough to begin a program of affirming God's promises? We go straight to the cross and give to Jesus (1) everything we have done, (2) everything that has been done to us, (3) all of our feelings about what has happened, and (4) all of the bad outcomes resulting from what has happened.

The world is happy to tell us that we deserve to be stricken. If they said it about Jesus, who certainly did not deserve it, they certainly will say it about us; but we can proclaim that Jesus was stricken for us. The world wants us to know that we deserve to be shunned and disdained for our failures and mistakes, for our stupidity, or even for our malice. We should expect to have "hell to pay" for what we have done or left undone, but Jesus took all of that in our place. When life strikes a blow against us, we always have somewhere to turn. Because Jesus loves us and went to the cross for us, we will never be cut off, no matter what we have done or failed to do.

A PRINCIPLE: Jesus never transgressed any law, but He was punished so that I, who have transgressed many times, may escape punishment. Jesus never did anything to be ashamed of or embarrassed by, but He suffered terrible shame and embarrassment in my place so that I can be free of it all. Jesus was shunned and rejected so that I can be accepted and respected regardless of what I have done or failed to do. Above all, "you He made alive who were dead in trespasses and sins" (Eph. 2:1 NKJV). Jesus' life was cut off and He died and went to hell, though He had done nothing wrong, so that I, who have done lots of things that are wrong, may experience new life—and experience it abundantly (John 10:10).

AN AFFIRMATION OF FAITH: "I choose life. I choose blessing. Today I choose life in Jesus Christ. I welcome Him like a fresh, new morning as the Lord of my life and the source of everything I'll ever need. I am protected because Jesus was not. He was stricken for my offenses and transgressions so that I may never have to be. Because He was bound, I am free. Because He was stricken, I am safe. Because He was cursed, I am blessed. Because He died, I am alive and I live a dynamic, joyful life. Because He was cut off from the land of the living, I am vibrantly alive! I receive now in this life the vast inheritance that He died to give me. And I accept His marvelous gift of freedom."

Study Seventeen

Gentleness and Truth

A CHRISTIAN STUDY SERIES

The truth shall set you free.

THE SCRIPTURE: "He was assigned a grave with the wicked, and with the rich in his death, though he had done no violence, nor was any deceit in his mouth." (Isa. 53:9 NIV)

A PROBLEM SITUATION: Billy Graham has impacted the world for the Lord as few men have. The mainline protestant denomination I grew up in did not have altar calls at the close of worship. I seemed to feel a sort of vague, but persistent, need for one back then. Billy Graham had one in every service. Many years ago I heard him speak in Madison Square Garden in New York City, and I walked forward with thousands of others to make public my profession of Jesus Christ as my Savior. In that moment, my life was changed forever.

Since the day I professed Jesus as my Savior under his ministry, I have heard Dr. Graham preach many times. When I think back over his sermons, I often hear his voice inside my own head, echoing the words of the prophet Jeremiah: "The heart is deceitful above all things and desperately wicked;

who can know it?" (Jer. 17:9). The word *wicked* is derived from a word meaning "twisted," and the confused ways in which we think and feel are aptly described by that word. The Bible plainly tells us that we have deceitful hearts.

In confirmation of Jeremiah's evaluation, a wide variety of writers of a couple of decades ago such as John Bradshaw, Terry Kellogg, Pia Mellody, Melody Beatty, and Alice Miller, along with Satire, Manuchin, Glasser, Whitaker, and many others, have helped us to understand the complex ways we have devised to deceive ourselves and one another in a very dysfunctional world. Family Systems theorists have shown us that we make it a way of life to deceive others; but more than that, we deceive ourselves.

Among the most helpful concepts taught by the proponents of dysfunctional family systems theory are those that relate to our ability to hide the truth from ourselves. We succeed in doing it, they tell us, because we suppress and ignore vital data that we should be receiving from our feelings. We are careful to stay very busy and occupied with something—anything—to distract us from painful, worrisome, or frightening thoughts and feelings. Every therapist knows that helping clients to face simple and obvious truth can be a long and difficult process. All of us live with myths instead of reality much more than we care to admit.

A particularly vivid example comes to mind of a man who was hiding the truth about himself from himself. The incident touched me deeply, and I have never forgotten it. It occurred following a presentation on family systems, during which the issues discussed stirred obvious feelings in nearly everyone. Despite the fact that he argued quite firmly against the principles of family system dysfunctionality that were being presented, the lecture and subsequent discussion appeared to stir floods of feelings for him. Although his face and voice betrayed intense emotion, he was unable to own or share his pain with anyone during sharing time.

When the session ended and it was time for coffee and visiting, our obviously caring group participant was moved to present an eloquent appeal for Christians everywhere to care much more about and put a stop to the dreadful slaughter of babies that occurs in abortion clinics. Obviously, he was stirred deeply. No one could doubt his sincerity on that score. But when he laid his head down on the serving bar and sobbed, it seemed that his tears were piggybacking on someone else's suffering because his own issues were too painful to examine. Am I suggesting that he should not or did not really care about the babies? Of course not. What I am saying is that he also needed to be free to care about and do business with God about the pain in his own heart. I often have marveled at the unshed tears many of us carry around year after year after year.

Mental mechanisms like denial, repression, and delusion are all ways that we lie to ourselves as a way of life. We like to think that they are present only in the mentally ill, but they are woven into all of our lives. They help us to avoid facing our lives truthfully. We make a habit of minimizing or exaggerating things as a way to deceive ourselves and others about problems and feelings that we cannot cope with. The whole addictive cycle that drives people to smoke, drink, overeat, or abuse drugs (or any one of many other things) grows out of a need to manage a heart full of pain and distress that we are trying to hide from ourselves and the world because we do not know what else to do with it.

When Jeremiah wrote that the human heart was deceitful above all things *and desperate*ly wicked, he was accurately portraying the situation. I have come to realize that there are many times when the inner world of my own heart is the hardest place of all to be completely honest. I am indeed desperate at times, twisting this way and that in my thinking, to evade some aspect of the truth that can only be found inside my own heart.

I have learned that it is difficult to see the truth in lots of situations, so I am unwittingly deceitful. At other times, when the truth is painful or frightening, I deliberately choose dishonesty because I am frightened or because I avoid painful things whenever I can. Sometimes lying is simply the easiest way out.

I am forced to admit that there are at least these four ways that deceit has been a lifelong habit for me, and I believe for all of humankind with me:

1. I often deceive myself about what my real feelings or motives are.
2. Sometimes I am not able to see the truth when it is staring me in the face because life becomes such a complex web of lies for all of us that we lose track of what is real. (I believe that I can see this phenomenon occurring in other people's lives quite often, but it is not so easy to see it in my own.)
3. All too often, I feel cornered and lie because I do not know what else to do.
4. Sometimes I do not tell the truth because I am so ignorant that I don't know what it is. Deceit is often found in my mouth. Are these things true in your life as well? Deceitfulness is a failing common to humankind (John 8:44).

God commanded us "not to bear false witness" (Ex. 20:16; Deut. 5:20). When I think of standing before Him, I feel very relieved to know that Jesus, who was always truthful and fully honest, took all my dissembling (lying) ways and all their consequences to the cross with the rest of my sin. He gave me, in exchange, His ability to see and speak the truth and all of the rewards of perfect integrity.

Oh, Grave, Where Is Thy Victory?

The final end for us in this earthly stage of life is the time when we are lowered into a grave and buried. Rich or poor, that is where we end up. Jesus spent the last day of His life on this earth hanging on a cross between two wicked, pitiful men who represented the dregs of society. He became part of that group by dying their kind of death and because self-righteous men, who were probably as worthy of punishment as either of the two thieves, put Him there. After He died, His body was put into a rich man's tomb and He descended into hell.

Jesus' death perfectly fulfilled Isaiah's detailed prophecy. It also portrays perfectly the pattern of what I deserve. He died as a sinner among sinners. Because He did, I do not have to.

Any knowledge Jesus may have had that He was headed for a rich man's grave gave Jesus no relief whatsoever in His suffering. All of the rich and powerful men of this world may make elaborate provision to ensure that they end up in an impressive rich man's grave, but what comfort can it offer them? Think of the great pharaohs of Egypt, who built mighty pyramids in which to be buried. Whether we are rich or famous, powerful or well educated, brilliant or highly privileged, things in this life work together for an evil end for everyone who somehow misses the gift of salvation that Jesus offers to us all.

The Bible tells us that "all things work together for good to them that love God, to them who are the called according to his purpose" (Rom. 8:28). That is not true for those of us in this world without Jesus. Without God's help, all things work together for evil, just the way we see the things working together toward an evil end for Jesus during His trial, torture, and death. Jesus took upon Himself an evil end so that ours will be good and blessed.

Event by event, Jesus' experiences laid out for us a clear pattern of life in this world. They show us what the normal life script in this fallen world looks like: it is designed to steal from us, kill us, and destroy what is good in us and in our lives (John 10:10). The natural outcome of sin in each life is to set the stage for playing out the devil's program for us and others. Without Jesus, we all become a part of the supporting cast in everyone else's tragedy.

From Baptism to Newness of Life

Baptism is the wonderful way we experience, in a real and concrete way, the exchange in which Jesus' death becomes ours. In this case, the process—that is indeed a mystery and a wonder—is described by saying that we entered into death with Christ instead of saying that He experienced our death for us. Whichever way you choose to put it into words, we know that Jesus was condemned to a sinner's death in your place and mine, and because that happened to Him, it won't happen to us. Instead, we'll live a new life, actually a whole new kind of life. Romans 6:3–4 says, "Know ye not, that so many of us as were baptized into Jesus Christ were baptized into his death? Therefore we are buried with him by baptism into death: that like as Christ was raised up from the dead by the glory of the Father, even so we also should walk in newness of life."

Sin's program is at work everywhere in the world, moving us toward "a grave with the wicked." Its goal is to write a life script of defeat for me and for you. But Jesus lived out that life script for us so that we don't have to. We can rewrite the script to tell a story of triumph and victory.

By experiencing baptism, I enter into Jesus' death with Him so that I can escape the world's program. The world has no more hold or control over a dead person. A dead person is not worried or troubled any more with what this world does to him or her. Once I am dead, the world can no longer reach me. I have escaped the world's control so that it doesn't have the power to write my life script any more. As a Christian, my death already is over and done with. Jesus did it for me. He died my death and gave me His life. I choose to believe that He died in agony so I may die in peace. How I praise Him!

Jesus died so I might live. Because of His matchless gift of salvation to me, my death will not be followed by an introduction to what hell is really all about. He took my assignment to hell and gave me instead His endless (eternal) reward for a sinless life. My future will be an eternity spent as a beloved child in the household of my heavenly Father.

Jesus lived out my terrible life script so that He could make a way for me to live out His wonderful eternal life script of triumph and glory. He assumed my destiny and took my place in hell so that I will have a place in heaven as a child of God. Because He was rejected by humanity and forsaken by God (Matt. 27:46), I shall be accepted and receive a joyous welcome in the kingdom of my heavenly Father.

COMMENTS: Jesus was tortured and executed. He died so that I may live—really live—a rich, productive, and abundant life, a life in which torment has lost its power. He was overwhelmed by the threat of violence as He prayed in the garden. Fear and dread enveloped Him there until drops of blood seeped through His skin like sweat (Luke 22:44). A few short hours later He was viciously assaulted by the reality of that violence, first at the hands of temple guards and then at the hands of Roman soldiers. His life was taken away so that a wonderful new life could be given to me. Though He was gentle, Jesus was treated with violence so that I, who can be cruel at times, may be gentled myself and may know His gentle touch. He was so good that He never told a single lie in His whole life. Jesus was punished though He was good, so that I will not be punished for being bad. How could anyone turn away from that kind of love?

Learn to Love

God does not want us to minimize how much our behavior and attitudes have hurt others. I believe that the Lord wants people to stop hurting and crippling one another and learn to love each other instead. He wants us to stop denying how much we have hurt others and how much others have hurt us.

We must let the hurts we have experienced at the hands of others get as big as they really are so that forgiveness and God's healing can get as big as they need to be. We also must allow the things we have done to others to grow as big as they really are so that our confession and repentance—and the forgiveness we seek from God—can be as big as they need to be. This is an important point and needs to be emphasized. Forgiveness may be a process requiring time because of the phenomenon of minimization in which all of us tend to belittle the situations that require it. That minimization is another example of the deceit that is found in our mouths as we deceive ourselves and others.

Perhaps it is wise to be cautious about well-meaning Christians who want to push us into forgiving others for serious abuses until we are clear about the situations we are forgiving. It is when we fully understand the magnitude of the hurt and we have acknowledged and allowed ourselves to experience all of the suppressed devastation it has caused us that we are able to forgive "big enough" to bring the full healing we need. Some people have struggled with the need to forgive for a long time. For them, it may be that the natural tendency to minimize how much hurt the abuse or abandonment or deprivation or neglect has caused them also minimizes the magnitude of the forgiveness needed.

In doing my own work in regard to the dysfunctional family systems that have shaped my life, I learned that many things I have done caused greater hurt and offense than I had any idea of, especially in the lives of my four children. I have come to see that I tend to ask God for a thimbleful of forgiveness to cover an oceanful of offense. By the same token, I find that I minimize hurts others cause me by pretending that I really do not care or by saying, "Oh, it was nothing." As a result, I may offer others a thimbleful of forgiveness for an oceanful of offenses.

It has become clear to me that forgiveness seldom brings a long-lasting sense of liberation and peace without full recognition of the depths of the hurt or the intensity of the feelings caused by it. Rationalization, minimization, or denial of our hurts will set the stage for continuous or recurring negative feelings and behavior. The reason is that they are all ways we have to avoid telling ourselves the truth. The truth is the only way to do business with God.

God's grace is sufficient to help us to forgive when it seems impossible to do so. After we have truthfully acknowledged the full measure of devastation that we have experienced, then we can appropriate the full measure of forgiveness required. Permitting ourselves to know the full truth of how much things have hurt us is a painful process that most of us prefer to avoid. As we work at forgiving, just thinking about what has happened may cause us to experience the hurt all over again. But it is an important part of the healing process that sets us free. When we can kneel at the cross with full honesty about our pain, God's wonderful plan of salvation sets us free as His liberating forgiveness flows to us and through us to others.

Anyone who has seen the movie *The Passion* knows that it is painful to think about what happened to Jesus and to know that it happened to Him because of what we have done all of our lives. And yet, because it did happen to Him, we can expect to receive the wonderful treatment and blessings that He should have had, both in heaven and on earth, because of His perfect performance in every area of His life.

A PRINCIPLE: Jesus told us that He is "the way, the truth, and the life" (John 14:6). Jesus became the *way* for me to be saved when there was no earthly, natural way open to me. He put Himself in a place where there was no way of escape to be found from the terrible death and punishment that loomed ahead. In the garden of Gethsemane, God turned a deaf ear to Jesus' pleas for help and deliverance so that I will never be in a spot with no *way out*, in which I cannot call upon God to rescue me (Luke 22:42).

Jesus is the *truth*, but He was treated as a liar. He was stripped of honor and respect so that I could have both. Jesus was nailed up there on the cross before the whole world, carrying the guilt, blame, and shame that a liar always has, so that I could be completely transformed. We live in a world filled with such complex webs of lies that most of us scarcely know what the truth is about ourselves or anyone else (Matt. 26:59; John 8:44). His sacrifice enables me to be viewed by God, humanity, and myself as a person of impeccable integrity and honor. Just consider for a moment how wonderful that is!

In John 1:3–4, the Bible tells us that all things were made through Jesus and that in Him was *life*. Jesus gave life to everyone who is alive. He *is* life, yet life was taken away from Him so that it could be given to me. Jesus was put to death, becoming the object of terrible violence, so that I may be restored and healed of the effects of all the violence done to me and through me all of my life. Isn't all violence a pathway to death? Jesus was covered with sin and shame so that I could be righteous and crowned with glory and honor. These priceless benefits are a free gift to me, simply because I receive them in faith.

AN AFFIRMATION OF FAITH: "I am alive. My life is brand-new every morning. Jesus is my Lord, and because of Him, I live a new life. In Him, I have a way out of every problem, and He shows me the truth about what is going on. I believe in my heart and confess aloud with my lips that Jesus is my Lord. He crowns me with glory and honor. All of the priceless benefits of His free gift of salvation and all of the power it contains are mine. Jesus is my Savior and daily gives me His love and gentleness and beautiful, crystal pure honesty. He directs my life in paths of His righteousness every day. He will continue to do so all of my life, until I go to heaven with Him."

That's the Truth

A CHRISTIAN STUDY SERIES

It's hard to thank God that I am angry.

THE SCRIPTURE: "Yet it was the LORD's will to crush him and cause him to suffer." (Isa. 53:10a NIV)

A PROBLEM SITUATION: I get so angry with people sometimes that I feel an impulse to slap them. It doesn't happen often, but if people press me hard, I would have to admit that sometimes in my heart I'd like to flatten them. I certainly do not say so most of the time. As a matter of fact, I usually hide such angry feelings. I am very seldom fully honest about my feelings, not even with myself. But I guess that God knows all about them anyway.

I am sure that God does not like all of my reactions to the things that happen day by day, but I also believe that He would like me to "live in reality" about myself and my behavior. I find feelings to be a hard part of reality to handle, both my own feelings and those of others. I am particularly dismayed and upset by anger.

Since I have shared with you that my own anger and anger in others upsets me, it should come as no surprise that the very idea that God could be angry is chilling indeed. It has always been deeply disturbing, even frightening, to read that it was the Lord's will to crush Jesus.

The King James Version of the Bible translates Isaiah 53:10 as saying, "Yet it pleased the LORD to bruise him; He hath put him to grief." That is an even more disturbing translation than the New International Version that we are using here in our studies. And the New American Standard Bible says, "But the Lord was pleased to crush Him, putting Him to grief." Does it trouble you to think of God being *pleased* to crush His own beloved and innocent Son? God is described here as treating Jesus as though He were angry with Him, even though Jesus specifically said that He always did those things that pleased the Father (John 8:29). Always!

What are we to make of this matter of God's hostility toward Jesus ... a feeling that He wanted to crush Him and cause Him to suffer? I must say it again: What a deeply disturbing idea! God was angry with Jesus because Jesus absorbed into Himself—soaked up, if you will—everything about me that made God angry. Jesus stepped into my place and received in Himself first the sin that was mine and then the consequences for sin that should have been mine. God's anger is one of those consequences. Jesus took the anger of God for me ... for you and for me and for all humankind (Heb. 12:2). I'll admit at this point that I have to stretch to wrap my mind around this idea. Probably because I'd really rather not think about the matter at all.

Old Testament prophets tell us over and over again that God was angry and bitterly disappointed with people in general (and I think with me in particular) for a long time before and after Jesus was born. So His feelings demanded expression.

As one example of His anger as it is revealed through the words of His prophets, look at the following two verses from Ezekiel:

> He said to me, "Have you seen this, son of man? Is it a trivial matter for the house of Judah to do the detestable things they are doing here? Must they also fill the land with violence and continually provoke me to anger? Look at them putting the branch to their nose! Therefore I will deal with them in anger; I will not look on them with pity or spare them. Although they shout in my ears, I will not listen to them" (Ezek. 8:17–18 NIV).

The people were doing many evil and appalling things. The most horrifying was the practice of sacrificing their children to idols (2 Kings 23:10; Jer. 32:35; Ezek. 20:31; Isa. 57:5; Hos. 13:2). Anyone who doubts the capability of humankind to be vicious and depraved needs only to read about what was done to Jesus, the one person we know to be totally innocent and good, or to look into the rituals of human sacrifice throughout history.

Another vivid passage illustrating this point about God's anger is found in Exodus. While Moses was up on the mountain with God, receiving the tablets with the Ten Commandments on them, Aaron and the people were making a golden calf to worship down below. Let's read about how God reacted:

> Then the LORD said to Moses, "Go down, because your people, whom you brought up out of Egypt, have become corrupt. They have been quick to turn away from what I commanded them and have made themselves an idol cast in the shape of a calf. They have bowed down to it and sacrificed to it and have said, 'These are your gods, O Israel, who brought you up out of Egypt.'
>
> "I have seen these people," the LORD said to Moses, "and they are a stiff-necked people. Now leave me alone so that my anger may burn against

them and that I may destroy them. Then I will make you into a great nation."

But Moses sought the favor of the LORD his God. "O LORD," he said, "why should your anger burn against your people, whom you brought out of Egypt with great power and a mighty hand? Why should the Egyptians say, 'It was with evil intent that he brought them out, to kill them in the mountains and to wipe them off the face of the earth'? Turn from your fierce anger; relent and do not bring disaster on your people. Remember your servants Abraham, Isaac and Israel, to whom you swore by your own self: 'I will make your descendants as numerous as the stars in the sky and I will give your descendants all this land I promised them, and it will be their inheritance forever.'"

Then the LORD relented and did not bring on his people the disaster he had threatened. (Ex. 32:1–14 NIV)

I believe feelings of hurt and anger that are not expressed go somewhere inside us and reside there. Without salvation's method to free us from them, I think they have their effect on us even when they seem long forgotten. Just as it happens with people, I believe that God's feelings sought expression.

We are created in the image and likeness of God. His feelings, like our feelings, ask for expression. Though He did not always pour out the wrath He felt, I believe it was present in Him somewhere until Jesus provided the way for all of it to be expressed. Jesus understood that, and His death was the time and place when God's anger spent itself. Jesus took for me the full measure of all God's wrath, even though it caused Him to suffer terribly. He did it so that later He could see my life set right and be pleasing to God (Eph. 5:6; 1 Thess. 1:10).

Not only have I made God angry, but also I have failed and disappointed Him in so many ways that His plans for me could not work out. But Jesus did not disappoint God. He did not fail to fulfill God's plan for His life, and because of His perfect performance, He has made a way of salvation for me. He took my failure and gave me His success. Now I have another chance to see God's beautiful plan for my life fulfilled because I am not operating from a base of failure but one of success.

Are We Like God About Feelings?

In Exodus 20:5 God tells us that He is a jealous God. Jealousy is a powerful and compelling human emotion. God is revealed in the Bible as having many kinds of feelings. He has wrath. He is jealous. He hates. The Bible says He hates things; six of them are listed in Proverbs 6:16. He can be grieved. He rejoices over His people. He feels pleased about things. You will remember that He announced from heaven that He was well pleased at the baptism of Jesus, His Son. And above all, He loves us.

All through the Bible, God tells us truthfully and in detail when He is angry with us. Page after page of the Old Testament writings of the prophets express God's feelings about human behavior. God is truthful and open about His feelings with people with whom He has a relationship. It is an example that we might do well to follow.

Along with a full account of how He feels, God tells us what He wants and expects in the relationship that we have with Him and what He requires in order for that relationship to grow and be healthy and strong. Those same prophets make it all very clear. Willingness to be open and truthful and real about what we want or believe we have to have in a relation-ship to make it work is something counselors know to be very helpful in successful relationships.

God tells us in no uncertain terms what we need to do to be in an unbroken fellowship (intimacy) with Him. He models it in page after page of prophetic writings throughout the Bible. Few of us are strong enough or courageous enough in our relationships to be honest and open. God has honored us by being transparent about how He feels and what He thinks about us and about our relationship with Him.

Who among us is able to behave with the kind of integrity that God has exhibited through His prophets in striving with humankind to establish a fellowship based on honesty and openness about feelings? If my experience is typical, most of us would prefer to hide in the bushes like Adam and Eve when God comes on the scene (Gen. 3:6–10). But when it is all said and done, miserable, self-pitying, selfish, abusive humanity persists in its contrariness.

What can we do with the constantly recurring frustration and rage caused by the stubborn refusal of other people to listen to us? What can we do when others make no effort to understand what we are trying to say? Very frequently, indifference occurs in our relationships with one another. It hurts. It is very costly. It leads to endless difficulties that could be avoided with an effort to pay attention to one another. God must surely find the same intense frustration and disappointment in His relations with us as well. How can we deal with these and other feelings? How does God deal with them all? Where can such feelings go—ours or God's?

In all of their sound and fury, they spend themselves upon Jesus!

Why Does God Allow It?

Have you ever talked to someone about God and had that person tell you that he or she did not understand how God could have made humankind to be so miserable and mean? I certainly have had that conversation. The fact is that the Bible tells us that even God Himself is dismayed by the nasty, selfish, ugly ways of humankind. In Genesis 6:5–6, we are told, "God saw that the wickedness of man was great in the earth, and that every imagination of the thoughts of his heart was only evil continually. And it repented the LORD that he had made man on the earth, and it grieved him at his heart."

It seems clear that the Bible is telling us that God is surprised and hurt by the things we think and do. I do not think He ever expected us to behave the way we do toward one another. In Jeremiah 19:5, God expresses total horror that the people were sacrificing their children to idols and tells them that it never entered His mind that they could do such a thing. Clearly these verses show that the sin man dreamed up and then actually committed was greater and more horrid than anything that ever entered the mind of God. Surely that settles once and for all the idea that the evil and suffering in the world originates with God.

As the wicked behavior of men and women unfolded more and more on the earth, God must have experienced growing horror … and great anger. One beloved person after another beloved person was hurt by others. It began with the very first family when the very first child ever born to anyone on the earth murdered the second child that God gave Adam and Eve (Gen. 4:1–2). What must our heavenly Father have thought and felt looking down on their lives and seeing the pain and struggles they caused one another?

Did God consider whether or not He should wipe humanity off the face of the earth to stop the suffering? He certainly did. As we have seen, He entertained that idea very openly. After all, He had done it once, and only Noah and his family survived. At another point of extreme exasperation, God told Moses to get out of His way; He wanted to destroy the whole nation of Israel. Moses interceded, and God's anger was contained

(Ex. 32:9–14 NIV). But one fact is clear: We have made God angry—and not just now and then, but over and over. Our petty, nasty, cruel, and unkind ways upset God, and rightly so.

I certainly would not want God to look with indifference at situations in which someone has hurt me or done me a great injustice. And yet when I have hurt someone else whom He loves, I want Him to view the situation with compassion and mercy. I want Him to be vitally concerned about what happens to me. A people hopelessly caught up in sin are a people who are both offenders and victims.

By the time Jesus was born, people had been grieving God and hurting one another for thousands of years, and God had much reason for anger. What was to happen to those feelings? Where could they be expressed and how? What does a loving God do with His own anger? It was all poured out on Jesus—down to the very last tiny bit of that almighty and awesome anger. Jesus took it for us so that we would experience only the love and approval that God the Father expressed toward Jesus. Because Jesus freely gives us His own glory and goodness, God looks upon us with the pleasure of a loving Father, who said, "This is my beloved Son, in whom I am well pleased" (Matt. 3:17).

Isn't the plan of salvation wondrous?

More! More! More!

If Jesus had taken only the bruising from God described in today's Scripture verse, it would have been as much salvation as most of us ever thought possible. But God planned more. As we are learning in this study day by day, God's marvelous plan of salvation has yet more and more wonderful blessings for us.

Not only did Jesus take upon Himself all of God's anger toward us, but also He took on Himself all of our anger toward one another. The full impact of all the hostility, rage, hatred, malice, and bad feelings that anyone has ever had toward me was experienced by Jesus. He also experienced all of those feelings that I have had toward others. Jesus fully experienced everything ugly or indifferent that any one of us ever felt toward another person.

Along with all the sin and pain and sorrow and grief that He experienced in my place, Jesus took on Himself all of the aggression and vicious, malignant vengeance hiding in our hearts toward one another. *And even beyond that*, He took all of the bad feelings of shame and self-hatred and self-destruction that we direct toward ourselves. What a cosmic burden of hostility for one person to absorb. Jesus took it all.

Actively Accept It

Since Jesus endured so much because it pleased the Lord to bruise Him, it is important to understand that we must transact business with Him about it. It is no more automatic that Jesus will take away our anger and bad feelings than it is automatic that He will take away our sins. Salvation isn't just dumped on us. We have to choose to accept it. We have to come to the cross with our sins, repent of them, give them to Jesus, and then receive His forgiveness and His righteousness in their place. The same thing is true of our bad feelings.

We have to come to the foot of the cross with our hatred, our rage and anger, our bitterness, our malice, and all of our bad feelings and give them to Jesus. We do this by faith. It is an act of faith. It is an act of choice. There is nothing passive about it.

When we have given Jesus all of the negative stuff that makes the inner world of our own thoughts and feelings so bitter, then we accept by faith His love, grace, mercy, compassion, and peace. We receive them as blessings that are freely given to us. We receive them also as qualities of character within us that change the way that we feel and act toward others. With them in place within us, we can go away from the cross endued with power from on high to be like Jesus in every situation.

All of the wondrous process of release and relief from negative feelings coming to us *from* others and from the constant inner pressure of negative feelings that we have within us *toward others* shows us one more way in which the salvation of Jesus Christ saves us from everything from which we need to be saved.

COMMENTS: Could you accept the fact that God meant humankind to experience lovely, joyful feelings and created us in such a way that our positive feelings are to be expressed—hopefully and in endless rejoicing, praise, awe, wonder, and delight? However, our relentless persistence in negative behaviors and attitudes creates constant negative feelings inside of us and in others alongside the positive ones. So the flow of expression of feelings turns destructive. What to do?

To take away our capacity for feelings is to take away our joy. To express them freely and completely toward one another when they are negative is to be hurtful and counterproductive. So Jesus, our perfect Savior, who saves us from everything from which we need to be saved, permitted Himself to become the target of all the negative feelings of God and man for all time and eternity. In doing this, He permits us to keep our capacity for feelings with all their wonderful potential for good and for exhilarating life and still provides a way to cope with their negative side.

The Awesome Answer for My Rage

After years of trying to come to grips with the idea that God was pleased to bruise Jesus, I share with you here—albeit, with a kind of awe and trepidation—my current level of understanding. This aspect of the sufferings of Jesus on our behalf has to do with the management of rage and anger. I feel more and more confident that the solution to managing the rage, hatred, and bitterness we all sometimes feel is to give it to Jesus. In a sense, those words have become a familiar cliché that we hear all our lives in church. When that is the case—that is, when the power and scope of a spiritual truth is swallowed up in a cliché—there has to be a revelation by the Holy Spirit for the full meaning to be restored. In this case, those words "it pleased the LORD to bruise him" contain one of the most powerful concepts for good living that God has to offer humankind.

I have participated in more than a few professional training workshops and lectures for counselors and therapists with my husband in which professional methods for anger reduction were presented and discussed. They are helpful to people, and I would not minimize their value one little bit, but they are far from a complete answer. Jesus does provide a real and practical method for dealing with anger—a perfect answer.

The most striking anger reduction method anyone could ever imagine is contained in the gospel accounts of the beating and torture of Jesus Christ. In practical terms, that means that Jesus received and experienced in His own body and also in His own heart and spirit the full expression of all the rage and hatred that ever existed in a human heart or in the heart of God. All of it spent itself upon Him, down to the last little bit, until it was absolutely gone:

- Jesus was slapped and spat upon. *(Have you ever itched to slap someone?)*
- His beard was ripped from His face. *(Have you ever felt angry enough to do a thing like that?)*
- He was mocked and scorned and ridiculed. *(Do we express anger through mocking, scornful words?)*

- His hands lay under the hammer as nails were driven in.
- Blow after blow was struck until the nails held His feet to the cross.
- Brutal thorns were wrapped around His head and then hammered down.

Buffeted and battered, Jesus received and experienced in His body the full expression of every person's lifetime of rage plus all the anger of God. Jesus received it all in a very concrete kind of way. We are suggesting here that it may be given to Him in the same concrete way.

Let me take a moment to lay out for you the most powerful anger reduction experience ever known. It is offered by the Christian faith to any believer. It was years, literally years, after God showed this to me before I could bring myself to share what I understood God to be showing me, much less to try it out for myself. It was even longer before I could talk aloud about it with any freedom. As a matter of fact, the experience I had in which God showed this to me provided some of the first insights I had to the real practical application of Jesus' Passion in the realities of everyday life.

Let me share with you the situation in which the first revelation of this aspect of the Passion of Christ was given to me. A friend (I hasten to say it is one who does not live anywhere in the Houston area) and I were visiting in my bedroom when a whole sad story of her husband's infidelity came pouring out. I was astonished, for this woman is among the loveliest and most talented women I know. She has been a wonderful mother. What was the matter with her husband?

After the first shock, there followed a sad morning of one unhappy story after another and then a long period of shared grief. Finally we came to the point of praying together. As the prayer began, I truly wondered if there was any answer to the pain that seemed to fill that room. I was furious with my friend's husband. What an idiot I thought he was. What a jerk! What kind of a wife did he think he deserved if this lovely woman was not enough for him? I could almost experience the way it would feel in my arms and shoulders to slap him.

Somehow as I struggled to find words to pray in such an atmosphere, a picture formed in my mind. I saw my friend holding a long leather whip in her hand high above her shoulder. I saw her arm come down and strike one blow and then another and another across the back of her kneeling husband. His head was down, and his body convulsed with each blow. Then the moment seemed locked in a kind of silent wonder when he turned his face toward me. I gasped. It was not her husband. It was Jesus. It was Jesus, still and yielded, doubled over there, absorbing the full force of her fury as she struck Him over and over.

Even as I write these words, tears spill as I remember that moment. There *is* an answer for the deepest kinds of pain that people can experience. Even the kinds of pain and sorrow that seem to have no cure have been provided for in the Passion and death of Jesus, our Lord. When the Bible tells us that Jesus bore our sorrow and carried our grief, you may know that He did it perfectly. He did it completely. He did it well. He understood every kind of sadness the human heart could ever know, and He made provision for our salvation from it. What a Savior! What a wonder!

It Is a Real Experience

When you are overcome with feelings of anger, rage, or a desire for vengeance, imagine yourself literally taking hold with your own hands of the whip with which Jesus was beaten. Clench your fist around the handle of the whip. Grip it hard. Experience in a kinesthetic way the feeling of that handle in your hand. Then raise your arm and strike a blow. Then another.

As the lash falls, be in the moment when the blow is struck, tearing away the flesh. Imagine the person who is the object of your anger there in the place of the one being whipped. Let the rage inside of you open like an air bag and bring down your arm to administer in full force the anger you feel. Once. Twice. How many times? Then at the perfect moment of His choosing, let the Holy Spirit show you that the humble figure there beneath your whip is Jesus. Jesus took that place as the object of your wrath.

The weight of the whip being lifted ten and then twenty and then thirty times—again and again—over the Lord as He presented His back beneath it brings home the reality of His suffering for me in a way that nothing else in my experience can match. It expends those raging negative feeling and uses them up. It takes them away.

As awful and gruesome as it may seem to be, I believe that it is a spiritual reality and truth that Jesus did take your anger and wrath, and mine, upon Himself in all that He endured. And He took God's as well. On the one hand, who can bear to think they were perpetrators of such an atrocity as the whipping of Jesus? On the other hand, it is unbearable to think that such suffering could have been endured and then wasted. Let us derive the blessing and benefit of deliverance from rage and anger that Jesus bought for us at such a price.

Jesus took God's anger toward us. He took on Himself the full magnitude of God's anger and frustration at people who will not obey His wise and loving counsel or trust in His goodness no matter how many times He proves Himself or His wrath toward a people who are willing to be so unkind and unloving toward one another, who are capable of utter depravity. He took our anger toward one another. And He took my anger and rage at myself—and there is plenty of it. Jesus took it all.

In the same process in which He absorbed all of God's anger toward us, Jesus suffered to make a way for you and for me to expend all of our powerful feelings without hurting anyone else. He made a way to take upon Himself the anger and aggression we deserve *from* others and the anger we have *toward* others every day of our lives. All of it was poured out in the many kinds of cruel abuses absorbed by Jesus in the course of His trial and execution. All of it was dealt with and taken away. Now true and perfect reconciliation becomes possible between us and others—and between us and God.

A PRINCIPLE: Because Jesus became sin with my sin, I am righteous with His perfect righteousness (2 Cor. 5:21). I know I have new life in Christ—the life of a favored son or daughter who has done everything right (Matt. 3:17). I have all of the blessings and privileges that Jesus' perfect obedience should have brought for Him. They are mine because Jesus took the consequences of all my guilt and shame and all God's legitimate anger toward me.

Because of what Jesus did for me, I have the biblical right to expect to see a good life and long days (Ps. 91:16), to be blessed with children (Ps. 127:3–5), to have prosperity and success (3 John 2; Deut. 29:9; Joshua 1:8; Isa. 48:18) in all the work of my hands, and to live a life marked by lasting fruitfulness (John 15:16). Because He walked into danger, I am safe in His unending approval and love.

All of the anger that God had toward people's meanness and stupidity—toward all of the continual choice of things that were not good for themselves or others, in spite of all of God's warnings and teachings—all of that was poured out on Jesus instead of upon all of us who deserved it. Once God's anger was spent and His justice was satisfied, He could lavish upon us the same love that He has toward His Son, Jesus, who never offended or disappointed God in any way. At first, most people have to stretch to believe that God loves us as much as He loves Jesus, but the Bible says He does (John 17:23). Please invest the time and effort necessary to read and reread that beautiful verse until the Holy Spirit makes it real in your heart.

Because His perfect Son was punished, a place was made in the Father's kingdom for us to enjoy the role of a perfect and pleasing son. It is ours as a free gift and received by faith alone because Jesus took your place and mine as a rebellious, disobedient, and foolish son who lost his birthright, forfeited his place in heaven, and should have ended up in hell. Like a loving older brother, Jesus stepped into our place before our angry Father so we could receive in exchange His place as a favored, beloved, obedient son.

Jesus restored us to the perfect condition of Adam and Eve before sin entered the Garden of Eden. He restores us to mint condition, making it possible for us to relate again to God as they did when walking with Him through the garden in the cool of the evening. Jesus provided a way for us to rejoice in intimate fellowship with our loving heavenly Father forever.

AN AFFIRMATION OF FAITH: "I am alive in Christ. I am God's beloved child. I have all of the blessings and privileges that Jesus' perfect obedience brings because Jesus took the consequences of my guilt and disobedience; and along with them, He took all of the legitimate anger that God had toward me. The absolute perfection of Jesus Christ was marred by my terrible sinfulness so that my imperfection may become perfect with His perfection. I will see good life and long days. I will be blessed with children, prosperity, and success in all the work of my hands. I am safe in His unending approval and love. I am righteous with His perfect righteousness. God loves me as much as He loves Jesus, and I praise Him with all of my heart!"

God's Will Is Good

A CHRISTIAN STUDY SERIES

How to win the blame game.

THE SCRIPTURE: "And though the LORD makes his life a guilt offering he will see his offspring and prolong his days, and the will of the LORD will prosper in his hand." (Isa. 53:10b NIV)

A PROBLEM SITUATION: Large things and small ones happen in our lives that cause us regret and pangs of guilt. Often we just blush with embarrassment, but sometimes a significant loss results for us or for others and we are troubled by our feelings. It was something of a wonder for me to realize that Jesus had comfort and help to offer us in every kind of situation, including this one. I share the following story, not because it is hugely significant, but mainly because it just happened and also because it is so 'ordinary' a kind of embarrassment that we might not think to involve Jesus.

Yesterday my husband, Charles, and I met our daughter Melissa for lunch. Over the years, we have met her many times and always look forward to particularly interesting and delightful conversations. Her life is very busy and remarkably eventful. She always has engrossing stories to tell. However, this lunch was to be a little different from the rest.

Our lives are busy, but we are not always constrained, as others are, by a formal office structure. We do not have a prescribed lunch hour every day, so no one is offended when we return a few minutes late. Because of that freedom, more often than I care to confess, we permit ourselves to be distracted by a phone message or some other happening so we arrive late for an appointed meeting. Yesterday was an example of our disorganized and inconsiderate behavior. We were not simply late leaving for lunch … we were late!

When we pulled into the restaurant parking lot, Melissa got out of her car and walked over to meet us as we got out of ours. I wouldn't want to say that steam was coming out of her ears, but the overall impact of her approach gave that impression.

"Mother! Dad! I have been waiting for you twenty-five minutes. I called you three times before I left to drive over here to be sure you were really leaving, and I *still* waited half a normal lunch hour for you to arrive. This happens so often with you. It means I miss half our lunchtime together. That is a loss."

Charles and I stood together by the hood of our car like two naughty children with our heads down, wanting to stare at our shoes instead of into her snapping eyes.

"Now I do not want to ruin our lunch, so I decided to confront you two out here in the parking lot. I just cannot go in there without telling you how upset I am. I am very angry. This is not the first time. Not at all. This is a pattern. You have to stop doing this to me. And furthermore, I think you both owe me an apology!"

She paused in a long, highly charged moment, awaiting our humble words of contrition, and I found myself sorely tempted to giggle in embarrassment and shame. There was no doubt that Charles and I were guilty. Guilt rested on us like a heavy pall. It was not a happy feeling.

Needless to say, we apologized. Moments later, we walked in to the restaurant and enjoyed our usual warm and interesting time together with no further mention whatsoever of our offensive behavior. I'll admit to being proud of her ability to put the matter behind us and have a good time together. Nevertheless, it was much on my mind as I considered it all in relation to this study material that I happened to be working on and its practical applications.

While the incident may seem relatively inconsequential in the course of human events, it was major for us. We do not often have interchanges like that with our children. What is more important, it pointed out an offensive behavior pattern we clearly need to change. In addition, it underscored one of the tragic things about guilt. There is no way a person can reach back in time to undo a guilty act. It is sealed in its unchangeability in the past, and all we can do is try to cope with the various negative outcomes of the offense. Never on earth or in eternity can Charles and I give Melissa back the twenty-five minutes we cost her. That is the fundamental nature of guilt.

Because I am so involved just now in the writing of this book, the painful and embarrassing incident with my daughter took on particular significance. The whole happening made me grateful again, but in a new way also, for the gift of salvation that Jesus has given to each one of us. Our children do not take us to task very often, and it was a painful happening. Without Jesus' wonderful sacrifice as our guilt offering, there would have been nothing for me to do with the embarrassment and guilt I had while standing there in the hot Texas noontime sunshine. Even if I were to make the most determined resolution *never* to be late again, and even if I succeeded perfectly in keeping that resolution, the offense cannot be undone.

A guilty act can never be changed, but my regret and guilt *can* be taken away. More than that, I can pray in faith for the circumstances created by my offense to produce something good for everyone involved (Rom. 8:28; Gen. 50:19–22). Based on the Bible's promise, I can believe that God is able to work all things together for good.

Is being late a small thing? Maybe—and maybe not. It doesn't matter. Shame is shame and guilt is guilt. When your heart is full of either one, it does not feel like a small thing. Without Jesus, all of my guilt for large things and for small things would be a built-in part of me—forever. I'd have been forced to add yesterday's guilt to the already heavy burden of all the other guilty acts of my lifetime and carry it always. Even when I am forgiven by the person I have offended, there is no *natural* way that guilt about something I have done can be taken away. I did it, therefore I am guilty.

How grateful I am to know that despite the need for repentance and reform in my life, I have somewhere to go to free myself from the burden of guilt—all of it. Thank God there is someone who is willing and *able* to take away my guilt. There is someone who is willing to take it off of my weary shoulders and *carry it away* … forever.

I have confessed my offense against my daughter to Jesus and asked for and received His forgiveness as well as hers. Because His plan of salvation is perfect and because He is able to implement that plan in my life perfectly, I shall never have to touch that guilt again. That's a miracle. It is a miracle as freely available to you as it is to me. It is available for every offense ever committed in the entire world. You have the same indescribably loving Friend and Savior, who is willing and waiting to lift your guilt onto His own broad shoulders and relieve you of it, no matter *what* you have done.

COMMENTS: The sacrifice of Jesus on the cross was the perfect guilt offering, one that meets every need we shall ever have for a guilt offering. No guilt is so great that it cannot be covered by the greatness of our guilt offering. Taking away guilt is one of the most wonderful things about salvation. Day by day by day, the new guilt I incur because of my shortcomings and offenses is taken away every time I kneel at the cross.

Growing up in church I thought that Jesus' work on the cross focused almost entirely on removing guilt. I believed that when a new believer acknowledged sin, then he or she was forgiven. However, it seemed to me that once I was forgiven, I was expected to shape up and do right. After all, a terrible price was paid for my forgiveness. Once I was able to see that, I thought I should do better. I should understand that I am expected to do better. So back then it seemed that the very next time sin reared its head, I found myself carrying the familiar heavy guilty burden all over again. I was ashamed to ask forgiveness again! In actual practice, the peace of feeling guilt free was short lived.

It took me years to realize that I was not going to overcome the sins and failures that produce a guilty burden just because I knew I should. Until I learned to do it by faith and dependence on God instead of by my own struggle, sin was going to overcome me (Rom. 7:18–25). Meanwhile, every day of life, you and I can go to the cross and leave the guilt itself and the guilty feelings it produces with Jesus. His forgiveness flows over us like a never-ending stream (1 John 1:9).

Jesus Takes Away More Than Guilt

Even during all of those years when I thought that the primary thing salvation offered me was deliverance from guilt and fear of punishment, the Christian faith was wonderful. But now, as we are seeing in this study, Christianity offers us much more than freedom from guilt. The beautiful covenant we have in Christ offers us so much more than removal of guilt and punishment so that we can set out on a lifetime search of the Bible to find all of the good things that are ours at the foot of the cross. What we will find there is "forevermore" ... never less than we need, but always more.

As one way of exploring more of what is provided at the cross, we are going to take time to look at God's instructions to Old Testament priests about the sacrificial rituals that they were responsible to perform. Armed with the knowledge that Jesus Himself was the perfect sacrifice in every sacrificial ritual, we can allow each one to demonstrate for us its own aspect of what His death accomplished.

In ancient Bible times, the priests worked day in and day out to carry out all of the detailed rituals of worship that God required. They are mentioned often in the Bible, but they are described in detail in the book of Leviticus. Performing the prescribed rituals demanded full-time commitment on the part of the priests and others who worked in God's house. Why did He require so much? The answer to that question is very exciting. Every single ritual act demonstrates in a practical, experiential way its own understanding of what the coming Messiah would offer us through His death.

Pages and pages of the Old Testament are required to describe the different rituals and sacrifices that made up Jewish religious life. If you pinch off the pages in the Bible between your thumb and forefinger that are devoted to God's instructions about ritual sacrifices, you will see what a big chunk of the Bible it really is. It takes many pages to show us and teach us all of the benefits of our salvation; it took many examples and separate rituals to help us learn what all of those benefits are. A study of all the activities of the priests begins to reveal the true scope of the plan of salvation.

The priests who served God in the tabernacle had numerous duties in addition to the offering of sacrifices, but we are going to take the time here to consider one list of six kinds of sacrifices found in one brief passage from Leviticus. While far from complete, the list offers a fine overview of the plan of salvation.

There are so many wonderful things that Jesus did for us through the sacrifice of His own life that this study will be longer than the others. If your time is limited, you may want to break this topic into several segments. Looking at one or two of the six types of ritual offerings at a time may allow you to explore in detail the rich symbolism to be found in each one.

Jesus Is the Offering God Offers Us

The book of Leviticus outlines in detail various kinds of ritual sacrifices that were regularly offered by the priests in the tabernacle or tent built by Moses in the wilderness. Since each one of us fulfills the role of priest in the tabernacle of our own hearts, we are blessed when we grow in our understanding of those ancient rituals and search for their meaning in our lives (Ex. 19:6; 1 Cor. 3:16). As we have said, each one illustrates a different aspect of the plan of salvation and helps us to understand what the cross means in practical, everyday terms. For us, Jesus becomes the offering in every ritual.

In Leviticus 7:37, six kinds of sacrificial offerings are described. They are (1) the burnt offering, (2) a grain offering, (3) the sin offering, (4) the guilt offering, (5) the ordination offering, and (6) the fellowship offering (called in the King James Bible "the peace offering"). Remember,

- Jesus is our burnt offering.
- Jesus is our grain offering.
- Jesus is our sin offering.
- Jesus is our guilt offering.
- Jesus is our ordination offering.
- Jesus is our fellowship offering (our peace offering).

The apostle Paul talks about "the unsearchable riches of Christ." The phrase "unsearchable riches" is a way of saying that the wonder of all that Jesus did for us is so great that it cannot be fully searched out. While it may be true that it can never be fully understood in this life, we can understand a lot more than we do now. Every new insight brings blessing and benefit.

When we get to heaven and hear the combined testimonies of all the people Jesus has saved, and hear of all the needs that were present in all their combined lives, then we may have the full picture of what Jesus did for us through His sacrifice. However, we know right now that God's plan of salvation is wonderful—beyond everything any one of us alone can imagine. No wonder its glorious message caused hosts of angels to fill the heavens with joy on that long-ago Christmas night when He was born!

The Burnt Offering: The first chapter of the book of Leviticus begins at once to describe the offerings that are to be made in the tabernacle. The first offering it discusses is the burnt offering.

The ritual of the burnt offering requires the priest to kill a perfect male animal and burn it on a large, square, outdoor altar. The animal's death serves to make atonement for the person who brings the animal to God's house and offers it to God. Its blood is to be sprinkled on the altar by the priests, and then the animal is to be skinned, cut up, and placed on the altar, and all of it is to be burned (Lev. 1:9). Jews today still honor this commandment of God symbolically in their yearly celebration of Yom Kippur. "Kippur" is a plural form of the word translated "atonement."

Did you ever think about the fact that it must have been a lot of work for those priests out in the wilderness to perform the ritual of the burnt offering? It was hard physical labor. For example, it requires effort and strength to slaughter and butcher a bull, even a young one.

Sometimes I find it hard to discipline myself to read the Bible and pray as part of my daily devotions. How would I feel if I had to wrestle with a bull, kill it somehow (in an age before guns were invented)—perhaps with a knife or a sword or a spear—skin it, and then cut it up? Serving as a priest was not an easy job.

I am grateful that you and I can rest comfortably for our daily devotional time in the place where we like to study and that once we are settled there, we can just read about this sacrifice without having to do the actual work. I appreciate the men who labored decade after decade and even century after century serving God through rituals designed—at least in part—to help you and me understand salvation all of these years later.

God thought this ritual sacrifice was so important that every morning of every day, God had His priests begin to lead people through the steps of killing, cleaning, cutting up, and burning this offering on a fire big enough to consume it (Lev. 6:12–13). What is more, it had to burn all night (Lev. 6:9). In Leviticus 6:13, God tells us that "the fire shall ever be burning upon the altar; it shall never go out." The next morning another sacrifice went on the altar. The sacrifice was always there, and the process was always working. It is aglow today in the tabernacle in our own hearts.

God's priests worked hard. The things they did are described in the New Testament (1 Cor. 10:6, 11) as having been written down to serve as examples for us. The effort we have to expend to study God's Word and learn what these rituals have to teach us seems minimal compared with what God required the people of Israel to do.

God's Incinerator

When I was a child, air pollution control was nonexistent. People living in the suburbs or in the country could burn their own trash. Many people had a big, rusty metal container that looked like an old oil drum hidden off in a corner of the back yard. It was called the "incinerator." As often as every day at our house, wastebaskets were taken out the back door and down to the end of the yard behind the rose arbor to be dumped into the incinerator. Usually the last piece of wastepaper was lit by a wooden match struck on the side of the drum and dropped on top of the trash. Wastepaper did not accumulate.

God has a wonderful waste disposal system that is available to us every day of our lives. Its purpose and use is partially explained by a study of regular sacrifices and offerings required in the tabernacle built by Moses.

This first ritual sacrifice in which the sacrifice is cast into the fire and completely burned up gives us a vivid reminder that Jesus went to hell for us so that we would not have to spend eternity there. This ritual sacrifice illustrates for me that aspect of the plan of salvation. Justice was done as far as I am concerned because I was "in Christ" when He died and descended into hell to be punished for me.

The Bible teaches that we are "in Christ" and that He is "in" us. In an interesting quotation from Colossians 1:26–28, we can see that both unique and wondrous states of being are mentioned:

> ... the mystery that has been kept hidden for ages and generations, but is now disclosed to the saints. To them God has chosen to make known among the Gentiles the glorious riches of this mystery, which is Christ in you, the hope of glory. We proclaim him, admonishing and teaching everyone with all wisdom so that we may present everyone perfect in Christ.

We are in Christ. Christ is in us.

I have received and publicly acknowledged Jesus as my Savior. Therefore all of my whole and completely dysfunctional, sinful self was contained inside of Jesus, experiencing death right along with Him on the cross. That is why: (1) sin's claims against me were met, including those regarding all of the destructive things I did against myself, eroding away my potential and banishing the minute-by-minute joy in life that God intended us to have; (2) Satan's claims on me were satisfied (his goal is to kill me after stealing from me and destroying everything in my life); (3) other people's claims against me for sins and offenses against them were met; (4) and, above all, all of God's claims against me were satisfied. I was in Christ and I died for my sins on the cross *with* Him because I was *in* Him.

I am part of the group that belongs to Jesus. Everyone in it has the privilege of close fellowship with Him. Does it seem strange to think of being "in" Him? Perhaps that takes on an aura of spiritual mystery to you … and perhaps it should. But remember that when God created marriage, He used it to demonstrate to us that two people who love one another can become so close that they are said by God to be "one." There is a precious unity in a loving relationship.

Romans 6:3–4 explains that we are in Christ, baptized with Him into death, buried with Him, and our old man is crucified with Him: "… don't you know that all of us who were baptized into Christ Jesus were baptized into his death? We were therefore buried with him through baptism into death in order that, just as Christ was raised from the dead through the glory of the Father, we too may live a new life" (NIV).

How I love that last phrase. It all happened in Jesus so you and I may "live a new life." Isn't that thrilling?

So as we see in our imaginations the picture of Christ as the burnt offering sacrificed in the courtyard of the wilderness tabernacle, we can see ourselves in Christ. I am in that bullock or that lamb when it is slain and when it is burned. We were killed there. All of the corruption, sin, guilt, and shame contained within our bodies was disposed of in the flames on that big brass altar.

It is because we are in Him that the sinful nature that is dysfunctional and causes so much pain and loss can be completely consumed by the flames. How wonderful. What a joy. What a liberation! The burnt offering symbolizes for me that the old, sinful, dysfunctional person that I was—whose whole life was a performance, trying and failing to live up to what I wanted and needed to be—died. Whoever and whatever you were before you were saved is gone forever. A whole new you, a you that is like Jesus, came to life when you accepted Jesus as your Savior. We see the clear symbol of this when a person rises up out of the waters of baptism.

As Christians, we learn to see ourselves as crucified with Christ. Then we have a truly amazing privilege that allows us to take up our cross every day (Luke 9:23; 14:27) and follow Him. That means that we can reenact our salvation every day. As often as—and as long as—we need to be forgiven of guilt and failure, the cross is there for us. Like the priests who made the sacrifice every single day, our salvation is a fresh, new reality every morning and every evening of every day (Lam. 3:22–23).

As we participate in Jesus' death every day, we can see a continual process in place that removes from us everything from which we need to be saved. It removes everything we need to be free of. It removes everything that needs to die and be gone. How wonderful to know that everything I am ashamed of is removed in a concrete, practical, and real way. It is burned totally and thus gone completely. The gospel message that Jesus is our burnt offering is "good news" indeed.

The Grain Offering: All of the different ceremonial sacrifices reflect Calvary in a different way. Each one unfolds a different aspect of Christ's redemptive work. The very number and variety of different ceremonies specifically laid out by God to Moses shows us again and again how broad the scope of salvation really is. In the grain offering, we see that Jesus Himself is the truth and that He reveals the truth to us. Revelation and understanding are given to us kernel by kernel through the Word of God as seed or grain planted in us to grow and bear fruit (Luke 8:11; Mark 4:20).

The other five sacrifices listed in Leviticus 7:37 are not like the grain offering. Each of the others requires the shedding of blood by taking the life of an animal: an ox, sheep, goat, or fowl. The grain offering does not require the shedding of blood. As we study a little more here, we'll see that this is an important difference.

What is the significance of the grain offering, and what is the significance of its difference from those offerings that require the death of an animal (the shedding of blood)? Let's begin by reading some things that Jesus told us in which He describes Himself as bread, an end product that is composed primarily of grain:

> And Jesus answered, "I tell you the truth, you are looking for me, not because you saw miraculous signs but because you ate the loaves and had your fill. Do not work for food that spoils, but for food that endures to eternal life, which the Son of Man will give you. On him God the Father has placed his seal of approval." Then they asked him, "What must we do to do the works God requires?" (John 6:26–28 NIV)

This is an interesting question being asked of Jesus. It seems to reflect the mentality of a people who are thoroughly indoctrinated into a system that demands conformity to rigid rules. It seems to reflect the belief that any power figure—and certainly God is the ultimate power figure—will require "works" because all of the power figures in their lives have required "works" of submission to rules and controls. To me, this question reflects the universal difficulty that all people have in comprehending God's grace. I believe this to be a vital insight into the unconscious expectations we all tend to have that makes the full grace and glory of the gospel difficult to understand and then difficult to believe.

And now continue reading: "Jesus answered, 'the work of God is this: to believe in the one he has sent'" (John 6:29). To believe … to have faith … to accept what the Bible says as true; to believe in Jesus is to believe that the Bible tells us the truth about salvation, kernel by kernel, word by word, verse by verse. All of salvation is a gift requiring only faith. It would take a supernatural demonstration of power for these well-trained legalists who are talking to Jesus to give themselves permission to receive a simple message of God's grace. Elsewhere Jesus told people that they would not believe without signs and wonders (John 4:48). For people with this kind of spiritual orientation and training, the gospel message seems too simple, too easy, and too good to be true. They were afraid to trust in it, even when it was told to them from the lips of God's Son, Jesus, Himself.

The next part of John 6 says, "So they asked him, 'What miraculous sign then will you give that we may see it and believe you? What will you do? Our forefathers ate the manna in the desert; as it is written: "He gave them bread from heaven to eat."'" (John 6:30–31 NIV). Keep in mind as we read this passage of the Bible that bread is the result of people's handling of the grain. God invites the priests to present the grain offering in the form of various kinds of bread (Lev. 2:4–8). Reading further, we see that "Jesus said to them, 'I tell you the truth, it is not Moses who has given you the bread from heaven, but it is my Father who gives you the true bread from heaven. For the bread of God is he who comes down from heaven and gives life to the world'" (John 6:32–33 NIV).

Clearly, the bread of God is Jesus. Jesus is the Word of God. Jesus is the Truth. As we have already said, Jesus described the Word of God as a seed (Luke 8:11). Every "kernel" of God's truth may be viewed symbolically as a seed—as a part of the grain from which to make the bread.

Many seeds together form a quantity of grain. Grain threshed and ground becomes flour. Flour with water (a biblical symbol for life and also for the Word), oil (the anointing of the Holy Spirit), salt (to prevent corruption), and the sweet herbs for flavor, all combine to form dough or bread with which a grain or cereal offering may be made.

It would appear that God's people were able to prepare the grain offering in various forms of bread, such as loaves that were baked, cakes in a pan, griddle cakes that were fried, wafers, and grains that were toasted or roasted (one would presume that this was rather like popcorn). Though the form that it takes or the way that it is handled may vary from time to time or from situation to situation, each kernel ground into the flour carries the truth of Jesus Christ.

While the burnt offering described above was totally burned, other offerings were eaten by priests and worshipers. In Leviticus 8:31, the Bible tells us that "Moses then said to Aaron and his sons, 'Cook the meat at the entrance to the Tent of Meeting and eat it there with the bread from the basket of ordination offerings, as I commanded, saying, "Aaron and his sons are to eat it"'" (NIV).

Feeding upon the sacrificial bread that makes up the grain offering could be described as the process by which God's Word is translated from the dusty pages of a Bible on a shelf into a dynamic life force inside us. We receive His Word and make it a part of us the way the bread we eat becomes a part of our bodies.

Many Bible teachings present Jesus to us as the Bread of Life. Since He is the Word made flesh among us, He is the Word of God represented in parables and teachings as the seed or kernel of grain from which bread is made. It is easy to find in the words of Jesus Himself confirmation that He is this grain offering. At every Communion service, we hear Jesus' voice echoing down through the centuries in the words of Paul who wrote:

> For I received from the Lord that which I also delivered to you: that the Lord Jesus on the same night in which He was betrayed took bread; and when He had given thanks, He broke it and said, 'Take, eat; this is My body which is broken for you; do this in remembrance of Me.' (1 Cor. 11:21–24 NKJV)

Bread was given to each disciple by Jesus in the upper room as part of establishing a new covenant with them and with each one of us. That covenant has been renewed over the centuries with both the bread *and* the wine (representing the shedding of blood). It takes *both* tangible substances to commemorate Communion in our churches, even to this day. So the Word (bread) and the blood (wine) come together in the new covenant made with each one of us at Calvary. Thus we see the need for both the grain offering and the blood sacrifice.

Still we have the interesting question to consider: why did God ordain a separate and distinct sacrificial ritual around bread? To me it seems that the critical point of action in the sacrifice of the grain lies in the *choice*—the decision made by each believer to receive and believe the truth contained in God's Word. This is what we do when we receive Jesus Christ as Savior. We make a life-changing choice, and the critical action is ours. In each of the other five offerings, the critical point of action is the shedding of the animal's blood in death, and the critical action is what Jesus does.

Whatever Jesus did for us in offering the plan of salvation and paying the price to make it work, it is what we do in deciding to accept Him and believe what He has said—what the Bible, God's Word, says—that makes it all actually happen for us as individuals. The critical point of action in receiving salvation is an act of each individual person's will. We either receive it and make it a part of us like bread we eat or we do not. The power lies in our choice and our action in receiving the truth of the gospel message first. Nothing provided in any of the sacrifices with the shedding of blood will benefit us unless we receive God's Word that is calling us to salvation. All of the benefits of the blood sacrifices that follow are dependent on our first decision to receive the truth about Jesus.

Salvation was provided through the burnt offering when Jesus' whole life was destroyed for us like the offering is consumed by the flames. Then we must accept the word or the message or the testimony of that salvation to make it real in our individual lives. When both have occurred, the bread and the wine (the Word and the blood) have both been applied. After that is taken care of, there are four other sacrifices that paid the price for many, many additional benefits that can be ours if we will but receive them by faith.

Working Out the Plan

Where are we now in this process of comparing the different ritual sacrifices to the happenings in our own lives as we work out the plan of salvation? First, we have accepted the Word of God about salvation and then we entered into death with Christ so that our old self is dead. Now Jesus said that we have been given the power to become the sons of God (John 1:12). What an interesting process that is, both to experience and to study. What do the next four blood sacrifices have to tell us about how it will happen?

First of all, the sacrifices were performed by the priests. As we have said above, all of God's people are described in Revelation 1:6 as priests. Equally clear are the words in Exodus 19:6, in which the Lord tells Moses that He wants His people to be a kingdom of priests unto Himself. When we receive Jesus, He comes into each believer's heart, which then becomes His cathedral or the tabernacle in which He dwells (1 Cor. 3:16). We are all to function as priests in the tabernacle of our own hearts. So it is our job to do the work of the priest to offer these sacrifices—to make them happen in living reality, as part of the daily business of living.

You and I are called to officiate as the sacrifices are reenacted day after day and season by season. It was the priest who actually made the ritual happen in the natural world of human experience in the courtyard of the tabernacle in the wilderness. It was the priest who stood near the smoky altar with his feet in the blood-soaked dust of the desert floor and translated the commandment of God into a vivid, actual experience—a grimy, sweaty, labor-intensive, human experience.

The true spiritual reality of the sacrifice of the Lamb for us all is not supposed to exist as a musty doctrine. It is a genuine, true happening in the world of personal experience. It is not lost in the past or hidden in the future. It is reality now.

The Sin Offering: The third offering, after the burnt offering and the grain offering, is the sin offering. When we accept Jesus, we receive first from Him full pardon and deliverance from all of our sin *and* from the sin nature that is incapable of anything but continued sin. As soon as He comes into our hearts, Jesus becomes an integral part of our being. He is like new DNA in every cell that makes us who we are. Paul describes it by saying, "I live, nevertheless not I, but Christ liveth in me" (Gal. 2:20).

The great creator of the universe lives inside of me. What a wonder (John 1:3). That is not to say that we lose our identity and Christ occupies us like some kind of alien being who takes over our bodies. God doesn't want us to cease to express our identity and our individuality. If He had wanted that, He could have cloned Jesus over and over, creating millions upon millions of exact replicas of Jesus by simply speaking them into existence the way He created stars and planets and galaxies. Nevertheless, when Jesus comes into our lives, we are a part of

Him and He is a part of us forever. So when that first burnt offering is laid on the altar and burned, it represents Jesus' sacrifice for our sins and we are in Christ as a result. We enter into death with Him there (Rom. 6:3–6). Our sin is taken into Himself by Jesus and then consumed by the flames as the lamb is burned on the altar.

All of your sin is gone forever, and so is mine. Glory to God! However, after we are saved, we still do dysfunctional things. We still sin. We are like Paul, who said in Romans 7:14–25 that he still did things he did not want to do. Not only did Paul have difficulty ending behaviors he did not want, but also he found himself at times unable to do the good things he really wanted to do. So sin was still a matter that needed to be dealt with in his life, even though he was saved and no longer a person who was capable of nothing else *but* sin.

The price had been paid for Paul to go to heaven, and he was no longer doomed by his complete inability to overcome sin. But the transformation of his personality that would allow him to be healthy and righteous and good was a process that had only just begun. Although Paul had been given the power to *become* God's son, all of his behavior did not perfectly reflect God's will the way Jesus did while living on this earth as God's perfect Son (John 1:12).

I understand the things written in Leviticus about the sin offering as having to do with our blunderings and our ignorance. It discusses the things we are unknowingly guilty of. I am glad that Jesus has a plan for taking care of things I do not know about or understand. Jesus has taken care of everything for us.

Everything about sin that needs to be addressed has been taken care of through the death of our Savior. Now we are walking out the retooling or reprogramming inside that will make us capable of righteousness. We are learning. We are growing. We are developing, and we are doing it as free, sovereign men and women. In the meantime, provision has been made for all of the times that we will revert to patterns of behavior and attitude that are not yet reworked.

The Guilt Offering: The story I shared today about being late for lunch with our daughter illustrates something very important about sin. I offended her by being late. Thank God she loves us and she forgave us. After our confrontation in the parking lot, we had a good time together over lunch that day, and our offense was never mentioned. But that did not change the fact that I had caused a waste of twenty-five minutes of her life in which she was just sitting in a hot car, not free to accomplish anything worthwhile. I can never give that back to her. So even if the flaw in my character that makes me habitually late is forgiven—and even if I am completely changed from this day forward—that twenty-five minutes is gone forever. As I see it, sin is the flaw in my character that makes me tend to be late all of the time. The guilt comes from the pain, loss, and suffering that my sin causes for others—and even for myself. Both the sin and the guilt need to be dealt with if I am to be completely "saved."

The sin offering accomplishes changes in who I am so that my flaws no longer make me "miss the mark" all of the time and so that my personality and performance are no longer unacceptable to God, to others, or to myself. Because of this aspect of Jesus' offering of Himself, sin no longer reigns in my mortal body.

Writing in Leviticus, Moses seems to me to be saying that the guilt offering covers wrong things and offenses that I deliberately and knowingly do. Even more importantly, the guilt offering addresses the consequences or the outcomes of sin. I believe that to be true because instructions are included in the Bible concerning the matter of making restitution. We are instructed to restore what was lost with interest (20 percent interest to be precise). The interest is all about the cost or consequence of the sin.

The guilt offering addresses the consequences of sin, the pain and loss that sin causes—and the shame I would feel over my guilt without it. John and Paula Sanford have taught that the matter of making restitution with interest should be taken seriously by Christians today. They believe that the love and grace it would represent to people would honor God and bless the world. Making restitution also provides a welcome balm to our own souls. I hope that you have had the opportunity to enjoy their fine materials.

The sin offering dealt with the offense itself, the evil, the weakness, the dysfunctionality, the things we did that we should not have done, and the things we left undone that we should have done. Long after it has been committed, the consequences or outcome of sin can shape events and character in the lives of all kinds of people. The outcome of sin is guilt. How wonderful and loving and good is a heavenly Father who deals not only with the sin itself, but also with its consequence: guilt.

Working Together for Good

When Jesus takes away our guilt, our guilt is gone. That sounds like a simplistic statement, but it needs to be made. Jesus' work as our Savior is perfect. He succeeded in doing what He set out to do. He has taken away our guilt completely. And there is more.

Jesus is so wondrous in His role as guilt offering that He is able to take the worst and most awful things that I have done and that have been done to me and make them work together for good ... and not for the evil that Satan plans. As a part of salvation, Jesus takes away the guilt and makes things work out for good and not for evil.

Do you have the courage to ask God for yourself whether or not our salvation is really great enough to make the sin in your life and in the lives of those you have offended "work together for good"? It is up to God Himself to confirm for you by His Spirit and out of His Bible the truth of what is being said here:

> Likewise the Spirit also helpeth our infirmities: for we know not what we should pray for as we ought: but the Spirit itself maketh intercession for us with groanings which cannot be uttered. And he that searcheth the hearts knoweth what is the mind of the Spirit, because he maketh intercession for the saints [us] according to the will of God. And we know that all things work together for good to them that love God, to them who are the called according to his purpose. (Rom. 8:26–28)

If the Bible had said only *some* things could be worked together for good, we might have to keep some of the agonizing guilt that our sin causes us, because some of the bad outcomes would have to be accepted. But He did not say *some*. He said *all*. There is nothing that God cannot work together for good, because He is that kind of a God. He is that kind of a wonderful God. And His plan of salvation is that kind of a wonderful plan.

When our love for Him and His love for us is the foundation of our lives, when His offer of salvation is joyfully accepted, and when His purposes and will are finally recognized as the only path to joy and good living, our faith in the fact that all things work together for good is in gear. In this state we live in blessing. Every day we choose to live in blessing (Deut. 30:19).

More and more, I see God's loving hand in my life ever working to redeem the large and small outcomes of my wrongdoing, striving to make them work together *for good* in spite of me. God is able to bring good out of evil, so I can trust that the plan of salvation is perfect.

As the plan of salvation unfolds—and our understanding of it grows greater and more wonderful day by day—we are learning how God has dealt with our guilt and our sin in Christ so that He can save us from both.

The Ordination Offering: Once we have put the messed-up life of sin behind us and worked our way through the pain and shame and the wretched outcomes of our sin that are summed up by the word *guilt,* then we are made new in Christ. We are made brand-new, I like to say, like Adam and Eve on their first day in the garden. We are restored to mint condition.

Now that all of that has been accomplished, we have to ask ourselves: "Now what? What are we to do?" Every morning when we wake up, what will be different? What is the right way, the better way, the good way to be—to conduct our lives—once we have achieved some success in discarding the dysfunctionality that a sinful world has fostered in us? What is our new life going to be like? What are we to become? What is God's special plan for each one of us? These are wonderful and exciting questions! Jeremiah 29:11 states, "For I know the plans I have for you," declares the LORD, "plans to prosper you and not to harm you, plans to give you hope and a future" (NIV).

The next offering after the sin and guilt offerings is the ordination offering. I think this suggests that the tradition of ordaining only priests, ministers, and elders may be too narrow in scope. They are not the only ones especially called by God. Romans 8:28 says that we are all the "called." Each one of us has a unique and marvelous purpose and calling in life that no one else in all of eternity can fulfill. Each one of us is important and precious to God. Each one has a vital contribution to make. Thus when we lay aside all that we should *not* be, we are able to learn from God what we *should* become.

I know that for each one of us, the plan that God has in His mind is the perfect plan to bless and fulfill us in every way. It will fit us perfectly and suit us so wonderfully that each one of us can believe that we have the most wonderful life in all of God's kingdom. Once we have committed our whole lives in obedience to His special plan and purpose for us, we are candidates to be "ordained" to that calling.

It is the shed blood of Jesus Christ that provides us with the power we need to live a new life, to meet the challenge of God's calling on our lives, and to be truly successful. Jesus' ability to live and work, freely doing the will of God, was perfect and complete all of His life ... until His arrest. His ability and freedom to do the will of God perfectly in ministry and to care for the people were both taken away by His arrest. Then all ministry was made completely impossible because He was literally "nailed down" in total helplessness on a cross. What a picture. Yet His complete disempowerment, taken for us, made the way for Him to empower us with His power.

Jesus became a perfect picture of helplessness and power-lessness because He was taking on our powerlessness and our helplessness in this world. What could be a more perfect picture of inadequacy than that? By coming to a place of complete powerlessness, hanging on a cross, Jesus took upon Himself all of my powerlessness in ministry and everywhere else. He became the powerless failure that I have so hated myself for being. That makes me a candidate to receive His limitless power and ability. That makes me a candidate to believe and receive the wonderful promise that says, "I can do all things through Christ who strengthens me" (Phil. 4:13 NKJV). Does that stir your heart with joy and hope? It certainly stirs mine.

Every Christian believer is ordained into his or her own special ministry in the kingdom of God as he or she is endued with power from on high when the Holy Spirit comes upon him or her (Acts 1:4–5; Luke 24:49; Phil. 4:13). With that power at work in us, each one of us can fulfill the calling on our lives, not in our own strength but in his.

Because of His suffering and death, we can walk in resurrection life and power and experience the joy of fulfilling God's individual and special plans for us. We can truly live a new life in Christ Jesus, the life God ordains us to live. Equally wondrous is the knowledge that He is such a great and mighty God that He is able to weave all of the good and bad events of our lives together for good. If it were not in the Bible, it would be hard to believe.

The Peace (Fellowship) Offering: Finally, all of us as believers can offer to God our own individual peace offering inside our own hearts. Jesus gave His life to be a peace offering for you. He loved you and wanted peace to fill your heart, so He emptied Himself of His own peace and filled His own heart with everything that troubles your heart. So the things that trouble our hearts are taken away by Jesus, and His own peace is put within us in place of everything that troubled us. It is such a wonder!

In his account of the night that Jesus was taken into custody by the temple guards and their mob of cronies, Matthew describes the beginnings of the process in which Jesus began to exchange our sin for His righteousness. It seems that He began at once to experience all of the things that trouble our hearts and make them afraid. Taking upon Himself our sorrow and our troubled hearts appears to be the very first of so many things that our Savior experienced on our behalf.

In the shadowy darkness of that night in Gethsemane, Jesus told Peter, James, and John, His closest friends, that the sorrow that was pouring through His life was overwhelming. The covenant He had just made with a dying world had laid upon Him all of the sorrow felt by every person who ever lived. It was so overwhelming that it was taking Him to the very point of death before the beatings and torture had even begun. Matthew 26:37–38 (NIV) says, "He took Peter and the two sons of Zebedee along with him, and he began to be sorrowful and troubled. Then he said to them, 'My soul is overwhelmed with sorrow to the point of death. Stay here and keep watch with me.'"

Jesus appealed to His friends for support that never came. Even that experience was an experience He took upon Himself for us because it made Him able to promise that anything we ever asked of Him would be given to us. He said in John 14:14, "If ye shall ask any thing in my name, I will do it." *Awesome* is an inadequate word to describe such an exchange!

Do take time soon to read the entire fourteenth chapter of the gospel of John to see this wonderful truth presented. When you do, you will see that the gift of Jesus' own peace is there to be had by every believer. But it is not automatic. It is ours through an act of the will. We have a role to play. We are told that Jesus gives us His own peace so we should not *let* our hearts be troubled. We go to the cross and go through exchanging everything that troubles our hearts and makes us afraid for Jesus' very own perfect peace. Jesus said, "Peace I leave with you, my peace I give unto you: not as the world giveth, give I unto you. Let not your heart be troubled, neither let it be afraid" (John 14:27).

Even though the peace we need has already been freely and completely given, we are still in charge of the situation. We are always in charge, because God has given each one of us the sovereign power to make the choices in our own lives. I can choose to accept by faith the peace of God day by day and situation by situation—and so can you.

Peace—A Fire That Never Goes Out

"And the fire upon the altar shall be burning in it; it shall not be put out; and the priest shall burn wood on it every morning, and lay the burnt offering in order upon it; and he shall burn thereon the fat of the peace offerings. The fire shall ever be burning upon the altar; it shall never go out" (Lev. 6:12–13). This offering is called the fellowship offering in the New International Version of the Bible. What a wonderful Hebrew word it must be that can be translated to mean both fellowship and peace. It represents the offering that is offered over and over, commemorating the wonderful peace we have with God through Jesus and His great goodness and blessing to us. It celebrates the "peace on earth and goodwill toward men" (Luke 2:14) that lies between us and God—a peace that can exist only because the work of salvation is complete and perfect. The fire under this offering rises continually to God. It never goes out.

God could not be at peace with us if sin (pain, sorrow, grief, guilt, shame, and all our offensive ways) still dominated our lives. Moreover, we cannot be at peace with God or anyone else if we are still tormented by endless shame, guilt, and neediness. It is the peace offering at work in our lives that underlies deep and satisfying fellowship and peace with God, with others and within ourselves. I believe we cannot have close fellowship with either God or man that is deep and satisfying without this sacrifice working in our lives. Why? Because we will continue to be like Adam and Eve when they sinned and couldn't face God.

Sinners have something to hide. Without the healing of God's peace and the restoration of fellowship with Him, we'll be hiding ourselves and needing to cover up who and what we are, the way Adam and Eve did when they crept off into the bushes and covered themselves with leaves to hide from God. In response to their shame, God slew animals and clothed them with those animal skins (Gen. 3:7, 21). Isn't God loving and kind? He could not undo what they had done, but He began at once to help them cope with its consequences. Meanwhile, we see that people then and now who are hiding are lonely and isolated. They are not having fellowship with anyone, certainly not with God.

In order to have peace, many things must be in place. Think for a minute. If you have a need, it presses you to act, and you cannot be at rest or be at peace until it is met. If you are angry, offended, frightened, overwhelmed by undone tasks, or experiencing fractured relationships, then peace is out of reach.

So when we celebrate an offering of peace, it presents a picture of beautiful abundance and provision in every area of life.

Over and over the Old Testament ritual of the peace offering is a picture of the celebration of our deep and abiding peace with God. It is the continual reaffirmation that our needs are met and our heavenly Father is not angry with us in any way—that His attitude toward us is one of goodwill and blessing. We know it is because God made a mighty move toward the earth to help us cover our sin forever with something much better than the skins of animals. Glorious peace and goodwill were the particular messages of the angels to all of us on the night when a baby named Jesus entered the world in a Bethlehem stable.

One of the richest sources of peace we can have in this world is the knowledge that, no matter what our age in life, we have a wonderful, loving Father who is taking care of us. He is a Father we can trust completely. We can know that God wants us to see Him as a Father, as a heavenly Father who loves us, because Jesus taught us to pray to Him by saying "our Father." Jesus specifically told us that the Father loves us (John 3:16; 16:27; 17:23). He cares for us as a loving and wise Father, so we can learn more and more to "cast our cares upon him" (Phil. 4:19; 1 Peter 5:7). That kind of assurance is a great source of peace and a cause for celebration and thanksgiving.

Endless Blessing

The following review of the sacrificial rituals that we are studying highlights for me six wonderful streams of living water that flow endlessly from the cross into my life. They flow like rivers from the place inside me … from my innermost being … where I have fellowship with God (John 7:38). It is the temple in my heart in which I worship Him and revere Him as my Lord. It is the secret place of the Most High who dwells in the tabernacle that is within each Christian's heart (Ps. 91:1). Here, again, is the list that describes benefits coming to you and me all of the time from the cross through the Word of God:

1. Jesus as the burnt offering consumes all past claims against me by God, others, and even myself (Luke 3:16–17; Heb. 8:12; 10:17).
2. Jesus as the grain offering gives me the truth about what is real (John 14:6; 1:14, 17; 1 John 2:27).
3. Jesus as the guilt offering takes the consequences or outcomes of my own and others' sin and works them together for good as I cooperate with Him (John 1:29; Heb. 10:6–12; Rom. 8:28).
4. Jesus as the sin offering gives me victory and power over sin that has previously had power over me (Phil. 1:6; 1 Cor. 15:57; 1 John 5:4).
5. Jesus as the ordination offering brings new life in the form of a special, individual calling that gives me meaning and purpose in life (1 Cor. 12:4–11; Ex. 19:6; Jer. 29:11).
6. Jesus as my peace offering quickens within me, as I choose it, the ability to trust God with everything that tries to trouble my heart or cause me to have fear and frees me to have wonderful, close fellowship with the Lord (Col. 3:15; Phil. 4:4–7; John 14:27).

Our current study verse from Isaiah particularly mentions one of the six kinds of sacrifices. It is the role of Jesus as our guilt offering. He laid down His life to take away the shame and guilt of our sins and to find a way to work together for good the grim outcomes of sin. By becoming a guilt offering for me and for you, He has removed the awful responsibility we each must assume for the pain and loss to ourselves and to others caused by our misdeeds and failures. The most terrible situation can be redeemed when it is put in His hands. It is good news indeed that Jesus takes away our guilt and gives us His innocence in its place.

Take a brief moment now to consider the second part of the passage from Isaiah that we are looking at in this study. Elsewhere in the Bible, we are told that "for the joy that was set before him," Jesus endured the cross (Heb. 12:2). There is a joy for Jesus in all that He endured. It is the outcome of what He suffered for you and me. The Bible says His suffering was worth it all to our loving Savior to be able to introduce endless blessing into your life and mine. Love like that is wondrous indeed.

Isaiah the prophet accurately describes here how Jesus was oppressed by the power structures in the land of His birth—those in the "church" (the high priests), those in the local government (Herod), and those who had conquered the land in which He lived (Pilate). Have you ever endured oppression? In America we experience less of it than people in other countries in the world have to deal with, but everyone encounters it in life. Jesus made provision to take upon Himself all that oppresses us and its power to bind us and hold us captive. In the place of oppression, He gives us a glorious liberty and freedom. Glory to His name!

Also in our current study verse, Isaiah correctly said that Jesus had no wife or child and that His life was "cut off" or cut short in His prime. But in the ages to come, He will see many ("his offspring") who had been added to the household of His Father through the cross that He endured. They are those to whom He has given life. For those who suffer the grief of having no husband or wife or children, Jesus also took for us the sorrow of what might have been. He bore that and all the rest of our sorrow and all our grief so that He could give us His peace and joy.

In all the ages to come, Jesus will see God's plan of salvation ("the Lord's will prospering in His hand") do its wonderful work in your life and mine and in the lives of multiple thousands of others. Day by day as we prosper in a new life, we praise Him, for we know that He has purchased that life for us by the loss of His own life on the cross.

Finally, we know that Jesus at last will see the bride that has been prepared for Him, with whom He shall enjoy the great marriage supper of the Lamb that will be celebrated in heaven. For you and me to be ready for that feast so we can appear there without spot or wrinkle, we have to complete our preparations (Eph. 5:25–27). Our goal is to have all spots and blemishes cleared up. The good news is that it really is possible to have them cleaned up and cleared up so we are ready for one of the greatest events of the ages.

Everything that is a part of who we are that is a blemish or distortion of what God intended for us to be can be taken away. The way it is taken away is through the very process that we are studying. We put our trust in Jesus to remove everything that blemishes our beauty and perfection by taking it to the cross. Once it is gone, He replaces it with His glorious perfection, thus restoring us to mint condition, like Adam, who was made in the image of God.

Another Quick Look at the Sacrifice

The daily reenactment of the sacrifice of the lamb was required of the priests right from the beginning, when the tabernacle was set up by Moses in the wilderness. Nothing else seems to have been as important or consistent in the lives of God's people. For example, there was no serious effort to develop an economic plan for the Hebrew children coming out of the land of Egypt. There was no educational plan developed, no cottage industry established, no universities or academies founded, no big transitional business plan formulated for life in a new land. No factories or industry or trade. Nothing like that was set in motion by God. It seems that the most important thing He built into the lives of His people when they came out of bondage and slavery and misery in Egypt was the daily ritual of the sacrifices. Indeed, descriptions of how it was to be done take up at least as much space in the Bible as any instructions that believers received about the establishment of worship or the organization of the church in the New Testament. The rituals of the sacrifices were very important.

For us as believers today, a daily reenactment of the sacrifice may be just as important. Reviewing what Jesus has done for us in the light of the daily happenings in our lives gives us a chance to transact the business of the exchange of His *perfect* everything for our *imperfect* everything. Remember, just *knowing about* this wonderful trade will not change our lives. We have to *do* it. We have to transact the business of exchanging our sin for His righteousness. His righteousness is everything that is right and good. Bringing specific things to Jesus from which we must be saved easily may need to be done as often as every day.

Daily reading of the Bible cleanses us by the washing of the water of the Word (Eph. 5:26–27). Through it, Jesus gives us perfect everything to prepare us for Himself. His goal is to make us perfect. Do you secretly believe that to be something even God cannot do? Do you really think that God, who knows everything, would undertake a job He could not do (Eph. 3:20–21)? Could there *be* a job He could not do? Of course not! It could not be. Nothing is impossible with God (Matt. 19:26). And one day we shall stand before Him in wonderful perfection because the plan of salvation is perfect and the Savior who implemented the plan here on earth is a perfect Savior (Heb. 13:20–21). What a day that will be!

> Now the God of peace, that brought again from the dead our Lord Jesus, that great shepherd of the sheep, through the blood of the everlasting covenant, Make you perfect in every good work to do

his will, working in you that which is wellpleasing in his sight, through Jesus Christ; to whom be glory for ever and ever. Amen. (Heb. 13:20–21)

Don't Miss This!

Let me ask you some things in all seriousness: Do you wish you had practiced the piano when you were a child and had the chance? Do you wish you had studied harder to achieve at a higher level academically? Do you wish you had trained harder to become the athlete you know in your heart you had the potential to become? Did you let drugs or laziness or something else in your youth keep you from reaching your potential?

Don't let that happen again. Engage now in this wonderful process of cleansing and renewing your life in Christ. It takes a little commitment of time and persistence to stay with the process until the work is done, but the rewards will be greater both now and in eternity than anything we foolishly threw away in youth.

Give the Holy Spirit your full cooperation for the rest of your life. The work is not heavy or hard. It is easy and light (Matt. 11:30). The Bible says that what God requires of us is an easy yoke and a light burden. Great are the rewards in heaven, and great are the immediate rewards right here on earth. This is the will of the Lord that Jesus died to see "prosper in his hand" (Isa. 42:10; Gen. 29:3).

A PRINCIPLE: Jesus became our burnt offering, and through it destroyed all claims against us. Jesus became our grain offering to show us the truth—what is real—in such a way that we can receive it and digest it. Jesus became our guilt offering by handling the outcomes and consequences of our sin for us, and He gives us His innocence, making innocence a fundamental part of who we are.

Jesus became sin for me, changing the fundamental patterns in me that make me miss the mark as a way of life, and in doing so He made me righteous—and you, too. Jesus became my ordination offering, taking away the things in me that have no meaning and purpose and giving me in their place the divine purpose and value as a person that Jesus has. Finally, Jesus took upon Himself everything that troubles my heart, making me able to trust God completely because He has become my peace offering.

Whatever God created Adam and Eve to be and to do in this world did not seem to work out as God wanted. And whatever He created me to be and to do didn't work out either. But with Jesus, all of that is turned around. In His strong and capable hands, the good and perfect will of the Lord is thriving and prospering in every way ... not in His life, which ended in the death that should have been mine, but in my life, which can now contain all of the blessings that Jesus earned and deserved.

AN AFFIRMATION OF FAITH: "God made Jesus Christ a perfect guilt offering. Jesus did the work perfectly when He took away my guilt and shame. None of it remains to trouble my heart. Jesus became guilt personified especially for me. He became guilty with my guilt so that I am pure and innocent with His goodness. By dying, Jesus gives me a new life. I enter the kingdom of God freely as a little child without a lifetime of sin and guilt to cover me with shame. I start today and every day with a fresh, new life under the watchful eye of my heavenly Father. My Father loves me and cares for me and helps me to grow. Day by day God's wonderful plan of salvation unfolds. He shows me His love and wisdom in the gifts and talents He has given me and in everything He helps me to do."

The Light of Life

A CHRISTIAN STUDY SERIES

The difference between darkness and light.

THE SCRIPTURE: "After the suffering of his soul he will see the light of life, and be satisfied; by his knowledge my righteous servant will justify many, and he will bear their iniquities." (Isa. 53:11 NIV)

A PROBLEM SITUATION: What does darkness mean to you? Does it mean ignorance? Does it carry the idea of depression? Does it suggest fear lurking in the unknown? Do you feel alone and isolated in the dark? Does it suggest groping about without the ability to see where you are or where you are going? I do not like darkness. All my life I have been reluctant to see the evening dusk that signals the coming of night. I seldom feel fear, but I love light and color and beauty. Darkness seems to be at war with all three.

Our current study verse tells us that Jesus would see the light of life after His suffering was over. Does that mean then that He did not see the light of life while He suffered? It does to me. He entered into the darkness that shrouds our sin and came to "know" it intimately, all the way to the darkest regions of hell. Because of that "knowledge," I can walk in light (1 John 1:5–7).

There is a surprising amount said in the Bible about darkness. The coming of Jesus into the world is described as the coming of a great light (Matt. 4:16; Isa. 9:2). It tells us that people living in darkness have need of a great light. That idea suggests that a whole world of people without Christ are living out their lives with darkness all around them (1 John 1:5).

Jesus' sermons about the future that awaits the folks who choose not to belong to Him are disturbing. He describes them as being "cast out into outer darkness" (Matt. 8:12; 22:13). I don't know quite what "inner" darkness may be like, but "outer" darkness has to be worse. It sounds dark indeed. Jesus gives us very firm and clear instructions that we are to "see to it, then, that the light within you is not darkness" (Luke 11:33–36). *I have learned to pay close attention to directions that are as clear and direct as those words are.* I know that I must see to it. I am the one who must do it. The matter is in my hands.

The first thing that we have to conclude from Jesus' commandment is unmistakable. There is a clear possibility that the light within us *could* be darkness. What could that mean? Jesus told us not to light a lamp and then put it under a bushel so that no light comes from it. His comments suggest that even when we have a lamp and even when the lamp is lit, we still may be in darkness. Even when we have the light of life, that light may be covered and hidden so that darkness surrounds us.

Jesus uses a vivid picture to show us that if our eyes are good—perceiving well what is real and true—then each person's whole body will be full of light (Matt. 6:22). I find that a delightful idea—to think that I may be a container for light and be absolutely full to maximum capacity with the glowing, radiant light of life. But Jesus said that when people's eyes are bad, "your whole body also is full of darkness"—not just containing dark corners here and there, but completely full (Matt. 6:23; Luke 11:34; Col. 1:12–13).

Without Jesus, it would appear that humankind lives in permanent darkness, now and in the life to come. Rather than seeing this as something frightening that looms in a threatening way, let's look at it as the natural state of our lives now "in the darkness of this world" until the plan of salvation does its wonderful work. The Bible tells us that we struggle with rulers of the darkness of this world (Eph. 6:12). We wrestle with them.

We are in a fight when we wrestle, a contest. Wrestling involves very close contact. The good news about the rulers of the darkness of this world is that they have to have darkness to be able to rule. They don't rule where light is. We have the answer for darkness. Let's get busy trimming and lighting and fueling the lamps that dispel it forever.

I am so glad that I do not have to figure out with some kind of technology what the light is and how to get it. The Bible explains that Jesus Himself is the Light of the world (John 8:12; John 9:5). So when I receive Him, I am receiving all the light I'll ever need. In Him, light and everything else I'll ever need has been lavishly provided. When my eye is good, my whole body is full of light. When my vision is of Jesus, I live in the light. When my eyes are on Him, then "whatsoever things are true, whatsoever things are honest, whatsoever things are just, whatsoever things are pure, whatsoever things are lovely, whatsoever thing is of good report" (Phil. 4:8) will dominate my thoughts; and everywhere there is virtue or praise, my life is dominated by His goodness and blessing.

Do you ever feel swallowed up by darkness? Is the darkness both inside and out? The good news is that God does not want you to be there and has made a way to transform you from a person of darkness to a person full of light (Col. 1:13; 1 Peter 2:9).

Lighten Up

For me, one of the greatest sources of darkness in the human heart is a feeling of shame. Operating under the old patterns that used to rule my life, I found that until I could manage to suppress a memory of something embarrassing, shame had the power to plunge me into a pit of darkness. An instant replay of whatever happened would go round and round in my head, creating real torment. Failures and mistakes were excruciating, so much so that I found myself reluctant at times to do new things for fear of experiencing those dark emotions again. Even now, I must be careful to choose to use what I know about Jesus when I feel stressed about or fearful of taking a risk. I shrink from doing things that might be painful. I avoid doing things that might make me feel guilty or stupid, things that could embarrass me, or overly ambitious things that could make me feel deeply ashamed. What can I achieve if I let this kind of darkness or the fear of darkness rule my life?

Perhaps overwhelming shame is the deepest suffering a human soul is capable of experiencing. Of all the terrible and painful things that Jesus experienced throughout His passion, we are told that it was the shame that He despised (Heb. 12:2). Everyone despises it.

Some things cause us such pain and shame that we cannot even bear to remember them. When that happens, psychologists tell us that a cloud of darkness comes over our thoughts and memories. Psychology describes that darkness in a variety of ways: denial, repression, suppression, delusion, dissociation, or the self-deception found in minimization or grandiosity. When you and I react in these ways, we are trying to cope with painful feelings of fear, guilt, or shame by shrouding them in darkness way down in our hearts. I sum it all up in the term *denial.*

Whatever form it takes, darkness grows out of pain and causes us loss and disability. It may be that darkness is caused by ignorance. There are things we ought to know and understand or things we need to know and understand. When we do not have that knowledge we are "in the dark." Yet another view of darkness would cover our hearts when we refuse to recognize suffering or injustice or neediness in the lives of other people. James tells us that those who know to do good and do not do it are in sin (James 4:17). What about those who do not know to do good? That ignorance is darkness indeed.

It is a glowing wonder to me that Jesus took away all of the darkness in our lives. The psalmist David wrote in Psalm 34:5, "those who look to him are radiant; their faces are never covered with shame." He took not only the punishment for our offenses but also the bitterness of memories we have and all of the guilt and shame that cast dark shadows over everything. God's perfect love covers my multitude of sins (1 Peter 4:8; John 3:16). Jesus knows the whole truth about me, and yet He has made a way to justify me. He defends me to God.

Think of that! Just imagine Jesus standing right up there in heaven and taking our side with God. He pleads our case today and seeks leniency and pardon for us (Heb. 7:25). God never says no to Jesus when He asks for mercy for any one of us. We know that is true because Jesus told us that "everyone who asks receives" (Matt. 7:7–8; John 15:7, 24). When we begin to read and study the Bible, patiently taking time to see what is really printed there, we find that it says the most amazing things.

Through His suffering and death, Jesus took away forever the iniquities and offenses that caused me to have shame and guilt in the first place. Though my face may have burned with shame in the past, all of that is gone forever because Jesus went to the cross for me. Why would someone so wonderful and loving as Jesus do such a thing for me? Well, for one thing, He knew He would see "the light of life" when it was over ... and so will we! The Bible tells us that this is a deep satisfaction to Him (Isa. 53:11).

Jesus loves me and loves you so much that He wants to take away the iniquities that have devastated our lives. By doing so, He makes it possible for me to see the light of life—abundant, precious, radiant life. And that is so satisfying for Him that He was willing to endure the cross to accomplish it for me and for you!

COMMENTS: We shall stand before God fully justified no matter what we have done, even though we have no basis in ourselves for that justification. Jesus took all of the suffering due to me so that He could satisfy every claim and complaint against me. On the cross, He made sure that justice was done so that, although I do not deserve it, I can enjoy the wonderful rewards due to a person whose life was perfect.

Our current study verse shows that the suffering of my soul is the part of life that plunges me into darkness and makes it impossible for me to live—really live—the way I feel in my heart that life was meant to be lived and the way the Bible seems to promise me that it should be lived. I believe that the Savior's love for me and for all people is so great that He will be profoundly satisfied by the success of the work He has done on the cross when He sees you and me justified, free of our iniquities, full of light, and living that kind of life.

No matter how vast and enormous the wickedness and wretchedness of humankind is, Jesus' salvation is bigger. He will see to it that salvation works in us and be deeply satisfied by its success, no matter how great the evil that surrounds us or is in us is. Because of His Passion and death, He is able to take the suffering of my soul away from me and take it upon Himself to the cross.

I am totally unable to justify my actions or my attitudes. Like everything else that stands in the way of the blessed life that God created me to have, my inability to justify myself went to the cross with Jesus. He took it away so that I—and many, many others with me—could be justified.

Sin Is One Thing, Iniquity Is Another

Jesus bore my iniquities. He took them away. In exchange for them, I take on board His goodness and all of His virtues. Way inside me, I want to be a good person. I am so grateful that He found a way for me to be good.

Sin is stupidity, carelessness, malfunctioning, inefficiency, and poor performance all the way around. It is missing the mark, failing to produce the way I should or in the way I was made to perform. It is falling short and messing up. I am a continual embarrassment to myself when I sin. Sin reveals that I am flawed and tend to fail constantly.

But iniquity is different. Iniquity is the part of who I am that covers me with shame and disgrace. Iniquity is ugly and abusive and offensive. It is perverse and contrary and twisted. When I really offend, it is iniquity showing itself again. Iniquity is the hardest thing for me to face in myself. The lengths to which I am willing to go to be in denial about my own iniquity are monumental. It would be too overwhelming ever to be able to be honest and real about the iniquity in my life if Jesus had not provided a way out of it for me and for every person who chooses to accept it.

A PRINCIPLE: Earlier in this study series, we talked about Adam and Eve eating the fruit of the tree of the knowledge of good and evil. We mentioned that God Himself pronounced that everything around these two—and everything about them—was good. Indeed God declared that it was very good. What Adam and Eve did not know *anything* about was evil. After the first bite of that fruit, they came to know evil very well.

To bring salvation to an evil world, Jesus also came to know and experience evil intimately as He had never known it before. The tree to which Jesus was nailed became for Him the tree of the fruit of the knowledge of evil as it had for Adam. It brought Him intimate knowledge of evil. It brought Him sin and death just as it had for Adam.

It was by His knowledge—by His intimate experience of the knowledge of evil as He hung on the tree—that Jesus, God's righteous servant, justified many and bore their iniquities exactly as the prophet proclaims for us in today's study verse. That tree became the tree of the knowledge of evil for Jesus. It has become the Tree of Life for us. The fruit of that tree brings the light of life to all who will believe. You and I may pick and eat forever of the fruit of the Tree of Life and blessing that grows in the paradise of God. It is there for you to pick now and always. God the Father sets before you, this day and every day, the freedom to choose life and blessing for your own life (Deut. 30:19).

AN AFFIRMATION OF FAITH: "I am fundamentally changed into a person radiant with life and God's goodness. There is a flawless beauty about my new self that reflects Jesus. I become capable of lightheartedness because light has filled my heart and darkness and heaviness are simply gone in its presence. I have entered God's kingdom freely and joyously like a little child who has not had a chance to do anything wrong. I go forward in my life today with a light heart, a clean slate, and a shining face. My life is full of light, and I love it!"

Study Twenty-One

—————⟶⟶◆◆⟵⟵—————

Winning in Life
A CHRISTIAN STUDY SERIES

Jesus gives us His own winner's prize.

THE SCRIPTURE: "Therefore I will give him a portion among the great, and he will divide the spoils with the strong, because he poured out his life unto death, and was numbered with the transgressors. For he bore the sin of many, and made intercession for the transgressors." (Isa. 53:12 NIV)

A PROBLEM SITUATION: Jesus is the greatest among those who are great on earth and in heaven. Every reward and all the blessings imaginable are due to Him. Yet these words from Isaiah tell us that Jesus stands ready to share those great blessings—all the spoils that go to the victor in battle—with His people (Rev. 2:7; 3:21). The infinite generosity of His heart surpasses all we mere mortals can understand. I would so like to be generous as He is lavish in His generosity, but I have had to struggle to learn to give with freedom and joy.

One of the more shaming memories of something that happened in my life occurred some years ago when I, as an adult who had so much, refused to share something with a

347

child. I had two identical paper weights. They were interesting, and a child who happened to be in our home wanted one very much. I did not give it to him. I refused to share one. I withheld them both. It was an eagle paper weight, and I had gotten two of them because I had two sons. I did not want to give one away because I wanted both of my sons to have one. Moreover, I did not want my comfort level disturbed even a little by having to decide which son would receive the remaining one if one were given away. Facing my own motives can be painful.

To this day, I still have both of those eagles. My now grown sons cared very little or nothing about them when I called attention to them. I have never gotten around to giving one to either of them. Yet I selfishly withheld them from a visiting child who had little of his own and wanted one very much. They have held no pleasure for me since that day. In the intervening years, I have become acutely sensitive to how often we are tempted to withhold what we have in our power to give and how painful that can be. Withholding what I had the power to give a child was a shameful, selfish thing to do.

COMMENTS: Jesus never withheld anything at all. He has given us everything there was to give. The rewards listed in the Bible as belonging to Jesus because of His obedience and His sacrifice are many and impressive (Rev. 3:21; John 17:22). Even those He has given to us. His generosity is so amazing that He is described in our study verse as sharing them long before He received them. He has given us everything He has.

There is nothing that Jesus has that has been withheld from us. Day by day as the Bible becomes more and more real to us, we are learning to understand His goodness and receive by faith everything Jesus has given us (Rom. 8:32). Would it not be tragic for Jesus to pay such a price to give us things that we do not receive and cherish? God's heavenly distribution center makes them all available to us when we believe the Bible's promises concerning them and accept them by faith (Mark 11:22–24). They come to us by faith the same way that the gift of salvation comes to us. It comes by asking and receiving, by simply believing the exceeding great and precious promises that are in the Bible and saying so right out loud to God (2 Peter 1:2–4).

Jesus gave everything He had to give down to His last breath, and then He gave His life for me and for every other person God created and loves. In return, God gave Him unmatched greatness in heaven and all the rewards of His great victory over sin and death. And even those rewards that were given to Him, He shares lavishly with us. He gives them to us freely as soon as we meet the conditions. The conditions are simple: (1) We grow strong enough in our understanding to grasp the meaning and scope of His redemption; (2) we overcome our fear that it is too good to be true; (3) we make His promises real in our lives by accepting them all in faith; (4) we proclaim our faith right out loud before all the hosts of heaven.

It's in the Blood

The Bible teaches that the life of every creature is in the blood (Lev. 17:11, 14; Deut. 12:23). It is interesting to have that perspective because Jesus did not merely shed His blood drop by drop. He poured it all out on the ground until He had no life left—until it was all gone and He was dead. He held nothing back. He was labeled a sinner, a heretic, and a blasphemer. He relinquished all claim to greatness, recognition, or righteousness in this life so that He could provide a way for me to receive all of that instead. There was never anyone like Jesus.

Jesus paid the full price for my sin and for everyone else's. After He did that, He became your representative and mine ... your attorney and mine ... at the very throne of God (Isa. 9:6; 1 John 2:1). Think of it. There is someone on your side who has

God's ear. He is always making intercession for you there—all the time (Heb. 7:25)!

You Are Well Represented

Just think of it, the best lawyer in heaven represents you with God, right now, today, even as you read these words. And more wonderful than that, He is your brother, who loves you. He is the brother who always stands up for you and always takes the blame for you no matter what you have done. He is the one who has done everything He could to get you out of trouble and keep you out of it.

God's Plan Fulfilled in Jesus

Now as we consider the final verse in Isaiah 53, it is important to take a moment to look at what Jesus said when He quoted a phrase from this verse that we are studying. In Luke 22:37 (NIV), you can read Jesus' words when He said, "It is written: 'And he was numbered with the transgressors'; and I tell you that this must be fulfilled in me. Yes, what is written about me is reaching its fulfillment."

The words of Jesus Himself are wonderful confirmation that all of this passage of Isaiah that we have been studying throughout this volume is indeed a description of what was to happen to our Savior during His Passion and death. It is an assurance that comes to us from His very own lips. How lovingly Jesus remembers to include every little detail of information and assurance that we might ever need. He is a Savior who has not overlooked a single tiny piece of what we need to be fully, completely, absolutely, and perfectly saved and restored to mint condition.

A PRINCIPLE: Jesus took away all of my sin. He took away everything about me that would disappoint God or make Him punish or reject me (Heb. 9:26). Jesus took away all of my sin and yours and provides perfect righteousness for us in its place. Let yourself really know that and feel it and enjoy the wonderful freedom it brings. Let it change the way you think, feel, behave, and view the whole world. Let it change the way you view your life and the potential you have. Even more, think about and consider the fact that Jesus speaks directly to God on your behalf right now (Heb. 7:25). Jesus intercedes before God on my behalf and yours all of the time.

Jesus shed His blood for me, and His whole life was poured out with it. As His life drained away, falling on the dusty earth beneath the cross, all of my shame and guilt was washed away. Generously giving to you and to me His perfection, Jesus felt and experienced all of the shame and guilt for our failures and every bad thing we ever have done.

Jesus is always welcome in God's presence, and even now He talks to God for us. He demonstrates again and again everything He has done for us to pave the way for God to bless us and to welcome us in heaven with wonderful surprises and blessings, including mansions and crowns, when we come into His presence (John 14:2; 2 Tim. 4:8; 1 Peter 5:4). Jesus divides the spoils of His victory with all of us who have been made strong with His strength, and He makes us victorious through His victory. Jesus gave up His status as the greatest "power player" in the world so that we could have a significant place among those who are great. In Him we have a position of status and success in life.

Jesus is glad when I am strong and blesses me for it instead of competing against me. He lavishly provides us with all of the resources we need for accomplishment and satisfaction. My Savior has made me a completely new person, one who is living a completely new life with everything I need for life and godliness (2 Peter 1:3–4). Our Savior has given you and me everything we'll ever need to be effective and productive in life (2 Peter 1:8 NIV).

Everyone on this earth is offered new life—resurrection life (Rom. 6:3–4). No matter who we are or what we have done or not done, the offer of a new life is lovingly given to us. Truly it is a life of joy. I am living the brand-new, wonderful life given to me from God, just the same way that life was given to Adam and Eve on the first day He created them in the world. In Christ, I am fully restored to mint condition. That is the gospel of salvation in Jesus Christ.

AN AFFIRMATION OF FAITH: "Jesus intercedes with God for me all of the time. My sins are all gone. It's just as though I'd never sinned. Jesus shed His blood for me, and His whole life was poured out upon me when it happened. So He makes me a completely new person who is living a completely new life with everything I need to be effective and productive. Jesus gave up being the greatest "power player" in the world so that I could have a place among those who are great—a place of status and success—a place that counts. I know that Jesus is glad when I am strong and blesses me for it instead of competing against me. He shares His rewards with me so that I am given all of the resources I need for achievement and satisfaction. Every day I experience resurrection life. It is truly a life of joy. I am living a brand-new, wonderful life given to me from God, the same way a brand-new life was given to Adam and Eve when the Garden of Eden was fresh and new. In Christ, I am fully restored to mint condition. That is a message of joy unspeakable and full of glory!"

Summary

J esus freely gives us all things! Everything that we could ever need to be whole, well, happy, productive, and successful was placed in humankind when God created us (2 Peter 1:2–8 NIV). We were made in the image and likeness of God Himself. We started out like Jesus, who is God's Son. He is the Son who resembles His Father in every way, so much so that He could say, "Anyone who has seen me has seen the Father" (John 14:9). We too were created in the image and likeness of God (Gen. 1:27). But when Satan, the thief, deceived us into giving him control, then he began at once to steal, kill, and destroy all that God had given us (John 10:10). In no time, he had brother murdering brother and everyone else plodding through a life of drudgery and struggle. He has been doing his nasty work ever since. But that is not the end of the story.

Without violating the autonomy He had given humankind or altering the normal consequences of our sovereign—albeit foolish—choices, God found a way to give back to us all that Satan has stolen. That way was the way of the cross. Jesus went to the cross to accomplish a great work for us.

Through His own suffering and loss, Jesus has given back our peace, our eternal welcome in God's family, our beauty, our grace and favor, our healing, our strength, our very life, and the provision of every resource we need. All of the experiences through which Jesus accomplished this great work occurred not just during the time after the nails were driven into the cross through His hands and feet. Rather, it all began at a very special moment during the Last Supper when all drank of the cup of a new covenant with God, and it continued right through to the resurrection and Jesus' ascension to heaven.

In a perfect moment in time, Jesus took a cup in His hand and pronounced it the new covenant in His blood. All of His life was in that blood. When everyone drank of that cup (that was symbolic of the blood He shed) on that wondrous occasion, humankind became linked in covenant with our Lord forever. All of the disciples who loved and followed Jesus drank of it then. All of us who love Him now drink of it in every Communion service.

Under His covenant, God's Son completely gives Himself to all of us who join with Him by giving ourselves to Him. It is a covenant made with you and me as surely as it was made with Peter and John and the others when Jesus took the cup and said, "This cup is the new testament [covenant] in my blood, which is shed for you" (Luke 22:20).

As soon as Jesus made His wonderful covenant with us, He began giving. And He gave and gave and gave until He had given all that He had and all that He was to all who would receive Him. He gave us His peace when He got under the burden of our sorrow, our grief, and everything else that troubles our hearts. He gave us His power when He became totally helpless with hands and feet nailed down to the cross. He gave us His righteousness when He took all of our sins. He gave us all the glory of heaven when He hung there covered by shame. He gave us all things in abundance because He hung there naked and stripped of absolutely everything. He gave us His position of favor and deep intimacy with the Father when He was forsaken and hung there on the cross, dying all alone. He gave us His very life and everything that went with it when He died. O Jesus, how we love You!

During the entire time of His Passion—from the moment of His arrest to the time of His resurrection, when He presented Himself and His finished work to the Father in heaven—Jesus absorbed every last bit of the "spilt milk" of human sin and folly. When it was all done and Jesus hung dead on that cross in filth and utter defeat, there was not a trace of His glory left. Why? Where was it? He gave it to you and me; He gave it to us all. As Jesus said in John 17:22a in His final prayer with His disciples, "And the glory which thou gavest me I have given them."

The wonder of the gift of God's glory, given through Jesus to us, is beyond description. Perhaps you know the old gospel song that contains these words:

> It's joy unspeakable and full of glory,
> Full of glory,
> Full of glory.
> Well, it's joy unspeakable and full of glory
> And the half has never yet been told!

The half has certainly not been told here on these pages, but much of the new material will be the subject of another book, soon to come, with studies from the gospel of Matthew. This volume looks ahead to the events of Jesus' Passion through the eyes of Isaiah the prophet. The gospel of Matthew recounts them in the words of one who lived them with Jesus. Meanwhile, there is one more item of exchange that seems to belong right here before we end our time together.

d.b.a. Jesus Christ

I love the gospel of John, especially the account of the Last Supper. The following verses are precious to me because they have been especially empowering. Why? It is because they underscore the fact that, along with everything else He has given us in the great exchange at the cross, Jesus has given us the power of His name.

You and I may have made a name for ourselves in this life, good or bad. But it is nothing like the name of Jesus. Our Savior, the Son of God, has exchanged whatever name we have made for ourselves for His name. In so doing, He has granted us power of attorney to act for Him, in His authority, in this life.

Have you ever gone to the courthouse and submitted an application to do business under the name of a company or organization. If you have, then thereafter you are "d.b.a." that name. Well, you and I are "doing business as" Jesus Christ on this earth. His name carries all the power and authority of the Prince of Heaven. He died to empower you with that kind of great power. Now we are privileged to go forth into the world and use it … to bring glory to the Father *in the name of Jesus*. Praise the Lord!

> Verily, verily, [truly, truly] I say unto you, He that believeth on me, the works that I do shall he do also; and greater works than these shall he do; because I go unto my Father. And whatsoever ye shall ask *in my name*, that will I do, that the Father may be glorified in the Son. If ye shall ask any thing *in my name*, I will do it. (John 14:12–14, emphasis mine)

> Ye have not chosen me, but I have chosen you, and ordained you, that ye should go and bring forth fruit, and that your fruit should remain: that whatsoever

ye shall ask of the Father *in my name*, he may give it you. (John 15:16, emphasis mine)

And in that day ye shall ask me nothing. Verily, verily, I say unto you, Whatsoever ye shall ask the Father *in my name*, he will give it you. Hitherto have ye asked nothing *in my name*: ask, and ye shall receive, that your joy may be full. (John 16:23–24, emphasis mine)

The following precious phrase from Jesus' last supper with His disciples reflects so accurately my thoughts and joy as I share these things with you that I cannot resist adding it here: "and these things I speak in the world, that they might have my joy fulfilled in themselves" (John 17:13b).

The information contained in this book is not just a message to be understood. *It is a tool to be used.* It is for you. Use it with joy and with power. Go to the cross every day! Maybe it would help you if you were actually to get down on your knees. Give Jesus everything you need to get rid of. As you kneel there, receive Him for Himself out of love because He is so wonderful a Savior. I love to do this in the sense of welcoming the Lord I love and who loves me into my new day. Then receive everything in Him that you need.

There is nothing we could ever want or need, indeed that we could ever imagine, that has not been given freely to us in Jesus (1 Cor. 2:9; 2 Cor. 10:8; Eph. 3:14–21; Phil. 4:19). Long ago, Jesus' gift of Himself was given to all. "Ho, every one that thirsteth, come ye to the waters, and he that hath no money; come ye, buy, and eat; yea, come buy wine and milk without money and without price" (Isa. 55:1). Like abundant waters that flow endlessly from a waterfall, the life of Jesus Christ is poured out freely for us to receive. A great outpouring of blessings is yours at the foot of the cross.

> Grace and peace be multiplied unto you through the knowledge of God, and of Jesus our Lord, according as his divine power hath given unto us *all things* that pertain unto life and godliness through the knowledge of him that has called us to glory and virtue; whereby are given unto us exceeding great and precious promises: that by these ye might be partakers of the divine nature. (2 Peter 1:2–4, emphasis added)

Do you see it there in those last words just above? Your new nature is to be like Jesus, who is divine. By claiming these great promises in faith, you may become like Jesus. We partake of Jesus' divine nature. By receiving the rich and constant flow of blessings that comes to us from the cross, we are receiving the qualities that transform us from battered and beleaguered sinners to the perfection that belonged to Adam and Eve in the first beautiful days of the world. It was the kind of perfection in which Adam reflected the image of God flawlessly. Our sin is gone. So we are made perfect day by day as every part of Jesus Himself is given to us to replace any part of us that is damaged in the slightest way by our struggles with sin. We are made complete. *We are made perfect!* We are restored to mint condition.

> Now the God of peace, that brought again from the dead our Lord Jesus, that great shepherd of the sheep, through the blood of the everlasting covenant, *make you perfect* in every good work to do his will, working in you that which is wellpleasing in his sight, through Jesus Christ; to whom be glory forever and ever. Amen. (Hebrews 13:20–21)

Conclusion

Well, beloved brothers and sisters in the Lord, we have come to the end of this time we have spent together seeking more of the new life that Jesus died to give us. Though we may not have met, the bond of love I feel toward you surprises me and touches me deeply. I know that there have been profound changes in your life, because God's Word is so powerful that new life and vitality simply emanate from it like light and heat from a flame. One day when we all gather together for times of good fellowship and sharing in heaven, I'll learn what has happened to you during these studies. I eagerly look forward to knowing you and sharing with you. Meanwhile, may God bless you richly and constantly.

As I have said, this is the end of this volume of studies about Jesus. It was originally intended to form a twenty-one-day study, but few people who read it were comfortable submitting to that discipline. Some read it straight through, and others digested it more slowly. In either case, the work was begun and divided into twenty-one separate studies with the idea that it takes twenty-one days to hatch an egg. I suggest that we ought to give God at least that long to enlarge our understanding of the new life He gives us in Christ.

Butterflies and birds and babies all come to us after a marked period of time that is devoted to quiet and steady development. When we learn to enjoy our walk with God as we enjoy the planting, sprouting, and growth of so much that is beautiful and good in life, we can be patient as our Christian lives unfold. We do not know now what we shall become, but "we shall be like him, for we shall see him as he is" (1 John 3:2). Won't that be glorious?

> Behold, what manner of love the Father hath bestowed upon us, that we should be called the sons of God: therefore the world knoweth us not, because it knew him not. Beloved, now are we the sons of God, and it doth not yet appear what we shall be: but we know that, when he shall appear, we shall be like him; for we shall see him as he is. (1 John 3:1–2)

May our Lord multiply His blessings on your life as you seek His kingdom and His righteousness. It is His righteousness that we seek at the foot of the cross day by day. We continually exchange it, by faith, for everything in our lives that is not right (righteous) or that is not working right. When we do that, "all these things"—everything that Jesus promised—will be added into our lives (Matt. 6:33).

If you have something that you would like to share about what Jesus has done for you during this series of Bible studies, it would be a blessing to know about it. Perhaps you'd like to drop me a note and tell about what has happened to you. In the future, I hope to share some of the testimonies that have been shared with me. Please mention whether or not you are willing for your story to be shared and whether or not your name may be mentioned. Write to: Connie Meisgeier, Southwest Center for Christian Studies, PO Box 723, Richmond, TX 77406.

> Now unto him that is able to keep you from falling, and to present you faultless before the presence of his glory with exceeding joy, to the only wise God our Savior, be glory and majesty, dominion and power, both now and ever. Amen. (Jude 24–25)

Endnotes

1. Catherine Marshall wrote *A Man Called Peter* (later a movie) about her husband, who served as chaplain of the United States Senate; many inspirational books such as *Something More*; and the novel *Christy*, which became a popular television series with the same name.
2. Name changed.
3. "Dysgraphia" is a learning disability that causes a child to have poor or illegible handwriting and/or difficulty expressing thoughts in writing and graphing. In the decades since Billy attended school, it has become much more widely recognized and accommodated.
4. According to biblical accounts of all that Jesus suffered, it was the shame that He despised (Heb. 12:2).
5. "The Steadfast Love of the Lord" by Edith McNeill Copyright 1974, 1975 Celebration. Reprinted by permission.
6. Dr. Jack Hayford (of Living Way Ministries), founding pastor of the Church On The Way in Van Nuys, California (1969–1999), is also founder and chancellor of The King's College and Seminary in Los Angeles.

7. *Strong's Concordance* translates the original Greek word used in all these references as either "testament" or "covenant." J. Strong, *Strong's Exhaustive Concordance of the Bible: Updated Edition,* (Peabody, MA: Hendrickson Publishers), 1150 (G1242).

8. See directions for recording affirmations included in the 21/21 Program beginning on page 129.

Additional copies of MINT CONDITION may be ordered at the address below. Discounts are available for ministries and study groups.

If you have something to share about what Jesus has done in your life through this series of Bible studies, it would be a blessing to know about it. In the future, the author hopes to share some testimonies, so please mention whether you are willing for your story to be shared or your name mentioned. E-mail or write to: connie.mintcondition@comcast.net or Connie Meisgeier at SW Center for Christian Studies, P. O Box 723, Richmond, TX 77406, or contact Connie by phone at 281-342-3539.

Contribute to the free distribution of *Mint Condition* or production of subsequent volumes in this series by contacting:

mintconditionbook.org

or

Southwest Center for Christian Studies
P. O. Box 723, Richmond, TX 77406

WinePressPublishing
Great Books, Defined.

To order additional copies of this book call:
1-877-421-READ (7323)
or please visit our website at
www.WinePressbooks.com

If you enjoyed this quality custom-published book,
drop by our website for more books and information.

www.winepresspublishing.com
"Your partner in custom publishing."